पथिक पिता के पथ पर पुत्र के पांव

Son's Feet on the Wanderer Father's Trail

Dr. P.N. Sharma

walnutpublication.com

INDIA • UK • USA

Paperback ISBN: 978-93-48945-28-0

eBook ISBN: 978-93-48945-47-1

First Published in November, 2025

Published by Walnut Publication
(an imprint of Vyusta Platforms Private Limited)

www.walnutpublication.com

India

Unit# 909, 9th Floor, Wave Silver Tower, Sector-18, Noida - 201301

UK

71-75 Shelton Street, Covent Garden, London, WC2H 9JQ, UK

Distributed by

ZopioTail

From This Book

"बूझा ख़ुशगवार थी ज़िंदगी"

आगे रहस्यमय तिमिर पसरा,
आगत कैसा है, भान ही नहीं।
गत धूमिल, और छटा मद्धम है;
चलो, चहल-क़दमी करें वहाँ।

चाहें तो आप भी साथ चलें;
आप अपनी देखें, मैं अपनी।
करें बखान अपने क़िस्सों का;
चाहें तो कुछ पे पर्दा-दारी रखें।

खोले तस्मे, गर्द को साफ़ करा,
देखने लगी मुझे मेरी ही ज़िंदगी।
कितने क़िस्से बँधे हैं इस गठरी में!
यह पता नहीं था मुझे ता-ज़िंदगी।

कितना कुछ हसीन हुआ था;
कुछ दर्द से लबरेज़ लम्हे थे।
कुछ तो हैरत-अंगेज़ भी हुए;
कितने रंग देखे मैंने, ऐ ज़िंदगी!

जो भी हुआ था इस ज़िंदगी में,
सब मेरा ही था, मेरी ज़िंदगी।
कितने अपने, कितने यार मिले;
भरपूर सम्मान, तुष्टि, प्यार मिला।

हाँ, कुछ अय्यार ज़रूर मिले थे;
सबक़ लिया, दर-किनार किया।
रंगों पर जमी हुई गर्द की परत,
साफ़ हुई, बाक़ी रंग चमक उठे।

कुछ हैं, तो कुछ चले गए;
पोथी में कितने नाम मिले!
लेखा-जोखा करने बैठा जब,
"बूझा, ख़ुशगवार थी ज़िंदगी।"

कुल-मिला के, ख़ुशगवार थी ज़िंदगी।

From This Book

"The Splendour and the Story of Autumn"

The AUTUMN is now finally here,
heralding the oncoming winter.
The leaves rustle in the breeze,
withered & now no more green.

Shortly will they part from the twigs,
through air, take a short fall, free.
From the perch, to the foot of tree,
a swinging, Swaying, Spiralling flight.

The tree branches, now stark naked,
ghostly, yet Beautiful in a way.
Hitherto, colorful sky concealed,
is Visible again, in jungles dense.

The trails on ground, are hidden,
under millions of fallen blades.
These crumble under our toes,
create the weird crackling tone.

A strange Godly phenomenon,
the old, have to pave the ways,
so, the fresh, energetic & young,
take up their duties from there.

The Spring would be ushered in,
in only a few months from now.
Trees would get laden up again,
with Foliage, Blossoms & Berries.

Dedication

The Section I Is

Dedicated To My Revered Father
Late Mr. G. N. Sharma

The Section II Is

"Dedicated To My
Braveheart Brethren in Uniform"

The Section III Is

Dedicated To My Family, My Hope.

Son Walks the Same Trail as His Father

मेरे बारे में: चिकित्सा स्नातक होने के बाद, मैंने लगभग 40 वर्षों तक विभिन्न क्षमताओं में काम किया है, जिसमें से 20 वर्षों तक दुर्ग भिलाई (छत्तीसगढ़) भारत के विभिन्न आई.सी.यू. में एक गहन चिकित्सा चिकित्सक (क्रिटिकल केयर मेडिसिन) के रूप में काम किया है। इस दौरान अधिकांश स्पेशलिटीऔर सुपर स्पेशलिटी के गंभीर रोगियों की देखभाल की। जिससे अच्छा अनुभव और प्रतिष्ठित डॉक्टरों से परिचय, मार्गदर्शन, प्रोत्साहन और स्वीकृति मिली।

मेडिकल कालेज में 1-2 अधकचरी कविताएं लिखी थीं। अब एक लाइन भी याद नहीं। एक पुनर्जन्म पर थी, जिसका कि केवल सार याद है। यह कि पुनर्जन्म, मनुष्य का एक मानसिक आविष्कार है। जो मनुष्य ने केवल इसलिए किया है कि मरते समय भरोसा रहे कि हम वापस आने वाले हैं और तसल्ली कर सकें कि कुछ भी छूटने वाला नहीं है। ऐसा इसलिए, ताकि अलगाव का दुख और पीड़ा सह्य हो सके।

एक साल पहले 15-16th/June/2020, की वह काली दुखद रात थी, जिसका खुलासा 16th/June की सुबह टी वी कर रहा था। गलवान में चीन से झड़प हुई है और 3 जवान वीरगति को प्राप्त हुए। जैसे कि इतना दुख काफी न था, शाम होते होते आंकड़ा 20 जा पहुंचा। पूरे देश में इतनी जांबाज फौज और सरकार पर अविश्वास फैल रहा था। पीड़ा तले सिर झुके हुए थे, शंकाओं से दिल बेहिसाब और बेतरतीब धड़क रहे थे। जब वीरता के किस्से और चीनियों की मौतों के अपुष्ट आंकड़े आए, तब गर्व और विश्वास वापस लौटा, अलबत्ता दर्द बरकरार था।

इसी पीड़ा और गर्व की मिली जुली मनःस्थिति में कुछ विचार उपजे, जो उंगलियों के पोरों से होते हुए फ़ोन के की बोर्ड पर उतरते चले गए। कुछ गद्य था, कुछ पद्य, और एक कविता “गलवान के बलवान” व एक कवि का जन्म हो गया। हालांकि यह तय नहीं था कि सिलसिला चल पड़ा है और सफर जारी रहेगा।

इसी बीच राफेल विमानों के भारत पहुंचने की चर्चाएं जोर पकड़ने लगी थीं। नवजात कविमन में फिर कुछ घुमड़ने लगा। उद्गार शब्दों में तब्दील हो रहे थे, काफी रिसर्च भी करनी पड़ी। अब मेरी दूसरी कविता

"लो आ गए रफाल" तैयार थी। अब इंतजार था 28th/July/2020 का, जिस दिन रफाल आने वाले थे।

इस दिन और समय को कविता का, जिसे रिलीज़ या début (डेब्यू) कहते हैं, करने के लिए चुना था।

यह दिन बड़े सुकून और विश्वास से भरा होने वाला था। पर फिलहाल समय सब्र और उसके इम्तेहान का था। 28th/July/2020 मैं टीवी से चिपक कर बेसब्र बैठा था। पांचवे रफाल को पारंपरिक "वाटर सेल्यूट" मिलने की सूचना प्रसारित होने के तत्काल बाद (यह रियल टाइम सूचना नहीं थी), मैंने अपनी कविता 50 से अधिक व्हाट्सऐप ग्रुप और व्यक्तिगत एकाउंट्स पर प्रसारित कर दी।

"लोग अक्सर पूछते हैं, मुझ से,"
तुम इस उम्र में कवि कैसे बने?
ऐसा क्या था जो उत्प्रेरक बना,
तुम्हारी मूक जिह्वा को शब्द मिले?

वह दिन था, जब गलवान घटा—
देश की असीम पीड़ा व आक्रोश;
शहीद परिवारों का दूरस्थ क्रंदन—
निर्झर-झरना बन, मन फूट पड़ा।

सफ़र तो परवाज़ भर चुका है,
कितनी बुलंदगी हासिल होगी?
सब समय के गर्भ में छिपा है,
समय ही तोलेगा, वही बोलेगा।

About Me

After graduation in medicine, I worked in various capacities for nearly 40 years, of which in 20 years in ICU (Critical Care Medicine) of Bhilai (CG) INDIA. During this time, I tackled critical cases of most of the Specialties & many Super specialties. I received good experience, exposure & interaction, encouragement & acceptance from the eminent doctors of these cities.

I had written 1-2 half cooked immature poetries in medical college. I don't even remember a single line now. First one was on **"Reincarnation"**, of which only the essence is what I remember. That the concept which man has created solely for the reason that while dying we have an assurance that we are going to come back and can be reassured that nothing is going to be amiss. We do this so that pain & suffering of separation becomes tolerable.

It was that dark tragic night of 15-16/June/2020, which was being telecasted the next morning. There had been a clash with China in Galwan & 3 of our soldiers got martyred. As if this suffering wasn't enough, by evening the figure reached 20. Distrust in such a brave army & government was spreading throughout the country. Heads were bowed in pain & shame; hearts were beating uncontrollably due to clouds of uncertainty. When stories of heroism & unconfirmed figures of enemy deaths arrived, pride & confidence returned, although the pain remained. In this mixed state of pain & pride, some thoughts arose, which passed through the tips of my fingers to the keyboard. It took some time to organize it into verse & a poem **"The heroes of Galwan" (Galwan Ke Balwan" originally in Hindi)** & a poet was born. However, it was not certain that the process that had started & the journey would continue for long.

Meanwhile the news of "Rafael fighter jets" reaching India had gained momentum. Something again started taking shape, in the mind of the newborn poet. The feelings were being converted into words, this time a lot of research had to be done. Then I & my 2nd poem **"Lo Aaa Gaye Rafael"** (Behold **"Rafael jets have arrived"**) was ready. I waited for 28th/July/2020, the day "Rafael" were to arrive. This day & time, I had chosen for what is called the release or début of the poem. This day was going to be full of great comfort and faith. But right now, the time was a test of patience. On 28th/July/2020, I sat glued impatiently to the TV. Immediately after the news of the fifth "Rafael" receiving the traditional "water salute" was broadcast (not a real time information, though), I circulated my poem on more than 50 WhatsApp groups & personal accounts. I consider these 2 poetries my best & will always consider them so. Readers applauded without any reservations & perhaps more than what was probably appropriate. Even without these reactions, I am not only proud but also arrogantly so, about these poetries. This is & will be my first & last boast.

"People often ask me,"
how I became a poet at this age.
What was the catalyst
that gave words to a silent tongue?

It was the day Galwan happened—
the country's immense anguish and anger,
the distant cries of martyrs' families—
my heart burst like a spring and spilled into words.

The journey has already taken its flight;
How high will it soar?
It is all hidden in the womb of time;
only time will weigh it, and only time will tell.

My Father Late Mr. G. N. Sharma

My father had a deprived childhood. He studied initially in Hindi medium Government schools, which were pretty much basic. He had to support himself partially by acting as a street vendor, selling toys & small stationary items, to cover his expenses on books & other small needs. He was an avid reader from the very beginning, always aiming for excellence & his subjects of interest were wide. He taught himself English & developed as a young man excellent in both languages, Science & Mathematics.

As a result, he secured admission in Thompson College of Civil engineering, Roorkee (Established 1847). It is now known as IIT Roorkee. It was one of the most prestigious colleges in India. The expenses were too high & he thought that clearing the entrance examination was the ceiling for his aspirations. By that time his elder brother had established himself in Ayurvedic medicine. He decided to help his younger brother, to enhance family reputation, though it meant paying through his teeth.

My father almost a street boy, suddenly found himself in an absolutely alien atmosphere of English aristocracy. He adopted quickly & passed out as the brightest student 4 years later. Apart from academics, He also earned the post of an NCC senior under officer (a Govt. sponsored semi military training). So, to say, he always excelled at whatever he tried his hands at.

Soon after graduation he joined UP state Public Works Department (PWD). In the meantime, the foundation stones of "Bhilai Steel Plant" had been laid down in late 1956. He opted for that Job & got it. He headed the Civil engineering Department from the very beginning. He perhaps, rather surely was the person to utilize the plant library facility to the maximum. He always tried & indulged in scientific innovations & research. The family never came to know about his achievements in the plant, as he was a very non-assuming, unboastful & a quiet person.

He rose through the ranks & upon reaching management positions, was handed over the reins of "Bhilai Township" as the Chief Town Administrator. Bhilai township had purposefully been developed on barren, uncultivable "Bhata" land, so named in local jargon. During this period, his love for ecology gained wings. He & his horticulture team, using the Govt. scheme of "Urban afforestation" worked tirelessly to plant Millions of trees & nurture them till they gained strong roots. He also developed many parks within the township. The results were astounding. Bhilai, is perhaps one of the greenest cities of the country. He is long gone but as I travel around the town, I notice soothing greenery all around & a significant drop in atmospheric temperature & pollution. I feel my father is whispering in my ear, "Dear son, I did this for you, your family & your entire generation".

Post retirement, he indulged in writing verses, which I present to the world.

Love You, Papa...

This book is published with the hope and intention of becoming a family chronicle, continuing under the same title in future volumes such as Volume 2, 3, and beyond by later generations, should they choose to write.

Contents

SECTION-I
MY FATHER

हिंदी/उर्दू में स्वरचित, "पथिक" स्वर्गीय जी. एन. शर्मा (मेरे पिता)

Composer "Wanderer", My Father, Late Mr. G. N. Sharma
Translated into English by "Loquacious Doctor", Dr. P. N. Sharma

इंसाँ

मूल लेखक: "पथिक" (स्वर्गीय जी. एन. शर्मा)

ये 'इंसाँ' तुझे ही छू ले
उसको ये शफ़ा दी है।
अपनी जान कुर्बां कर दे,
कुछ ऐसी ही वफ़ा दी है।

फिर वो कौन सी तल्ख़ी रही,
ऐ मौला, दिल-ए-पाक में?
वो हैवाँ भी बन सकता है,
उसको ये सज़ा दी है।

Humans

Translated by: "Loquacious Doctor" Dr. P. N. Sharma

"Humans" may reach you, may touch you,
they have been granted this grace.
To sacrifice their lives for you,
they've been gifted such loyalty.

Then what bitterness prevailed,
O' God, within your heart fair?
They can turn into, even a devil,
they've been given such a fate.

गिरते अश्क

मूल लेखक: "पथिक" (स्वर्गीय जी. एन. शर्मा)

समझा नहीं तह ज़िंदगी,
मैं इस ज़िंदगी के मायने।
बनते और टूटते रहे,
मेरे ख़्वाबों के आईने।

चुपके से मेरी क़ब्र पर,
किसी ने आँसू गिरा दिए।
एक लम्हे को मैं जी गया,
अपनी ज़िंदगी के मायने।

ता उम्र मैं चलता रहा,
उन निगाहों से बेख़बर,
जो छुपाती रहीं हर दम,
"गिरते अश्कों" के मायने।

Unconfined Tears

Translated by: "Loquacious Doctor" Dr. P. N. Sharma

Couldn't appreciate all my life,
the explication of this life.
My dreams kept forming,
then falling apart,
like mirrors reflecting what was mine.

Upon my grave, in secrecy,
someone shed a tear unseen.
For a fleeting moment, I lived again,
the meaning of my life.

I kept on treading all my life,
oblivious of those wet eyes,
that kept hiding all the time,
the secret of their "Unconfined
Tears".

ख़लिश

मूल लेखक: "पथिक" (स्वर्गीय जी. एन. शर्मा)

फूल भी खिलते तो हैं,
पर कांटों की ख़लिश लिए हुए।
वो वफ़ा दिखाते तो हैं,
पर बेवफ़ाई की नीयत लिए हुए।

यह क्या तासीर है ऐ ख़ुदा,
दुनिया में तेरे निज़ाम की?
तेरी इबादत होती तो है,
पर ख़ौफ़-ए-क़यामत लिए हुए।

तुझसे तो यह उम्मीद थी,
कि हर रात पूनम होगी,
पर यह चाँद बनाया कैसा,
जो अमावस की स्याही लिए हुए।

ज़मीं पर जब होती इबादत,
अक्सर मंज़ूर नहीं होती,
मंदिर मस्जिद हैं बहुत यहाँ,
बहिश्त को इन्हें बख़्शिश कर दे।

गर है बहिश्त दिल का चैन,
तो ज़मीं भी तेरी दर्द-ए-दिल है,
भले ही फ़रिश्ते ना आएँ यहाँ,
फ़र्ज़-ए-इंसानी से ज़मीं रौशन कर दे।

क्यों छूट है मुजरिमों को यहाँ,
न दें अपने गुनाहों का जवाब?
क्यों छूट है लुटेरों को यहाँ,
लूटने फूलों का शबाब?

Sling of Thorns

Translated by: "Loquacious Doctor"
Dr. P. N. Sharma

Flowers do bloom,
but carry the sting of thorns.
They do project loyalty,
yet harbour betrayal in form.

O' God, what kind of
disposition is this,
of your order in the world?
Though you are
worshipped with devotion,
there still exists, the fear of doom.

We hoped from you, O' divine,
that every night would be
lit by a full moon.
But why this moon have you created,
that bears the black of the new moon?

When prayers rise from the earth,
they're often not accepted.
Temples and mosques abound here,
may you award heavens to them.

If heaven is peace of heart,
then earth is your aching soul.
Even if the angels won't descend, dear
almighty,
at least illuminate
the earth with humanity.

Why do a free hand here,
have the criminals,
why aren't they
accountable for their crimes?
Why are robbers free here,
to loot the splendour of flowers?

अश्क

मूल लेखक: "पथिक" (स्वर्गीय जी. एन. शर्मा)

हम तो निकले थे ढूंढने,
कि वफ़ा-ए-दिल कहीं मिलें।
हर चौराहे पर मिले फ़रोशी,
सजाए हुस्न के वही क़िले।

क्या यह दिल का शौक़ था,
या थीं उनकी मजबूरियाँ?
माँ के दूध से खींचें शराब,
उसके अश्कों से शमा जले।

Tears

Translated by: "Loquacious Doctor" Dr. P. N. Sharma

I had set out in search,
hoping to find a loyal heart.
I found merchants thronging every crossroad,
with the same forts of decorated charm.

Was it a passion of their hearts,
or were their overpowering compulsions?
To draw wine from a mother's milk,
and light the lamp with her tears.

"हिदायत"

मूल लेखक: "पथिक" (स्वर्गीय जी. एन. शर्मा)

इक बार तो ऐ ख़ुदा,
इंसान को बहिश्त में पैदा कर दे।
लाज़िम हो तो कुछ फ़रिश्ते,
इस ज़मीं को भी अता कर दे।

माना कि यह होगी उदूली,
क़ुदरत के अहम उसूलों की,
तेरे लिए नहीं यह मुश्किल,
एक बार यह इनायत कर दे।

दूध की नदी बहे ज़मीं पर,
जन्नत में भी अज़ा होगी।
गुनाह ज़मीं से मिटा दें,
यह फ़रिश्तों को "हिदायत" कर दे।

"The Directive"

Translated by: "Loquacious doctor"
Dr. P. N. Sharma

O' God, just for once,
create humans in the heavens.
If essential, then some angels,
award to this Earth also.

Maybe it will be a violation,
of the important dictates of nature.
But this is not difficult for you,
please award this kindness once.

Let rivers of milk flow on the Earth,
there will be envy in heaven also.
Let them eradicate sins from the Earth,
may you pass this "directive" to the angels.

"प्यासा"

मूल लेखक: "पथिक" (स्वर्गीय जी. एन. शर्मा)

कोई बेक़सूर क्यों मरे,
तेरी ही अदालत के सामने?
सच की क्यों होली जले,
झूठी वकालत के सामने?

तेरे इंसाफ़ पर शक करना,
लगता तो है वाजिब नहीं,
पर कोई "प्यासा" क्यों मरे,
शाही हमामों के सामने?

"Thirsty"

Translated by: "Loquacious doctor" Dr. P. N. Sharma

Why should the chaste die,
in front of your court?
Why should truth suffer.
from crooked advocacy?

Though it seems disobliging,
to doubt your justice,
why should one die "thirsty",
before the royal bathing pools?

"इंसानों में इंसान"

मूल लेखक: "पथिक" (स्वर्गीय जी. एन. शर्मा)

तुझे कमी क्या फ़रिश्तों की,
जो यह अजूबा-ए-आदम पैदा किया?
क्या अहद-ए-वफ़ा से दिल भर गया,
जो यह शैतान-ए-जिगर पैदा किया?

फिर भी यह कैसे हुआ,
कि बुद्ध वो ईसा जन्मे यहाँ?
सलाम तुम्हारी क़ुदरत को,
जो "इंसां में इंसां" को पैदा किया।

"Humans, Within a Human"

Translated by: "Loquacious doctor"
Dr. P. N. Sharma

You have no dearth of angels,
so why did you create this wonder, "Adam"?
Did you get fed up with their loyalty,
that you created this devil of a man?

Still, how did it happen,
that Buddha and Jesus were also born here?
Salute to your created cosmos,
that you created "Humans within a Human".

"तृषित"

मूल लेखक: "पथिक" (स्वर्गीय जी. एन. शर्मा)

गहरे तूफ़ानों से घिरा हूँ,
और साहिल से दूर हूँ।
क़िस्मत की कश्ती में फँसा,
एक इंसान-ए-मजबूर हूँ।

पर अब डूब भी जाऊँ,
तो कोई ग़म नहीं मुझको।
लम्हे भर को बना इंसान,
बस इसका मशकूर हूँ।

मुझे नहीं यह चाहत,
कि तूफ़ाँ से निकल जाऊँ।
आब-ए-समंदर से नहीं शिकवा,
चाहे "तृषित" ही मर जाऊँ।

बस इंतज़ार है तो इतना,
कह दे कि तेरा नूर हूँ।
उठा दे क़ुदरत का ये पर्दा,
बता दे तुझ से, कितना दूर हूँ।

"Thirstful"

Translated by: "Loquacious doctor" Dr. P. N. Sharma

I am caught in a treacherous storm,
and far from the shore.
Stuck in the boat of fate,
I am a helpless human being.

But now, even if I drown,
I will have no qualms.
I am simply grateful,
that I became a human for a
moment.

I have no desire,
to escape this storm.
I have no grievance with the ocean,
even if I die "thirstful".

All that I wait for is just this:
that you proclaim I am dear to you.
Lift this veil of nature,
and tell me how far I am from you.

"ज़हाँ"

मूल लेखक: "पथिक" (स्वर्गीय जी. एन. शर्मा)

क़ुदरत के ये सितम,
हैं सबक़ किसके लिए?
जो बह गए सैलाब में,
या तरसते हैं बूँदों के लिए।

या जो दब गए भूचाल में,
या मिली नहीं मिट्टी जिन्हें,
जब इंसाँ ही मरता रहा,
तो ये "ज़हाँ" किसके लिए?

"The World"

Translated by: "Loquacious doctor" Dr. P. N. Sharma

These atrocities of nature,
are lessons, but for whom?
For those swept away in the floods,
or those who yearn for drops.

Or those buried in the earthquake,
or those who did not get a grave.
When humanity kept on dying,
to whom does "The World" belong?

"वहशत"

मूल लेखक: "पथिक" (स्वर्गीय जी. एन. शर्मा)

जब इंसाफ़ की बात इंसाँ करे,
उसके मक़सद की कोई बीमा नहीं।
इंसानियत ही जब करे क़त्ल,
उस कुफ्र की कोई सीमा नहीं।

मंदिर-मस्जिद बने हैं इंतिहा,
क्या नज़र में बदल आया कोई?
कुफ्र और इंसाफ़ में जब फ़र्क़ न हो,
इंसान की "वहशत" का कोई ज़िम्मा नहीं।

"Savagery"

Translated by: "Loquacious doctor" Dr. P. N. Sharma

When men talk of justice,
there is no guarantee of their motive.
When humanity itself becomes murderous,
there is no limit to its savagery.

Temples and mosques are in abundance,
Have they changed anyone's vision?
When blasphemy and
justice lose distinction,
there are no limits to man's "savagery".

"बंधन"

मूल लेखक: "पथिक" (स्वर्गीय जी. एन. शर्मा)

अमीरी के झरने बहे,
पर ग़रीबी का दामन न छोड़ पाया।
वही तो साख थी इंसाँ होने की,
एक अटूट रिश्ता न तोड़ पाया।

प्यार की मंज़िल में बना फ़रिश्ता,
पर मैं इंसाँ के क़ाबिल न हो पाया।
रिश्ते तो बहुत देखे मगर,
साथ चला न कोई श्मशान तक।

दामन में मेरे जो गिरे आँसू,
उनका "बंधन" न तोड़ पाया।

"The Bond"

Translated by: "Loquacious Doctor" Dr. P. N. Sharma

The springs of wealth spilled freely,
but I could not let go of my poverty.
That was the integrity of being
human;
I could not break that devout
relation.

I became an angel in the arena of
love,
but could not be worthy of
being a human soul.
I have had many relationships,
but none walked with me to the
crematorium.

The tears that fell into my lap,
I could not break their "bond".

"द्वंद्व"

मूल लेखक: "पथिक" (स्वर्गीय जी. एन. शर्मा)

दीपावली की सुखद बेला में,
मैं कैसा गीत सुनाऊँ?
चिरकाल से क्षुब्ध कंठ में,
मैं कैसा रस टपकाऊँ?

क्या कुछ नहीं मिला मुझे,
संस्कारों की झोली से?
नहीं तकरार विधि से कोई,
इस होनी या अनहोनी से।

पर मन में उठे "द्वंद्व" का,
यह क्रंदन किसे सुनाऊँ?
दीपावली की सुखद बेला में,
मैं कैसा गीत सुनाऊँ?

अट्टालिकाओं की परिधि में,
उत्सव सदा ही होते हैं।
पर उनमें आमंत्रण पाने वाले,
कदाचित भाग्यवान ही होते हैं।

लगता मैं वासी खंडहर का,
तृण कुटियों में सोता हूँ।
उनमें पलते कृश शिशुओं को,
देख-देख मैं रोता हूँ।

अंदर टिमटिमाते दीपक में,
मेरा मन उलझा रहता है।
इस अंधकार और प्रकाश की,
छाया किसे दिखाऊँ?

दीपावली की सुखद बेला में,
मैं कैसा गीत सुनाऊँ?

"Conflict"

Translated by: "Loquacious Doctor"
Dr. P. N. Sharma

During the festivities of Deepawali[1],
what song should I sing?
What nectar do I pour,
in my eternally parched throat?

What all have I not received,
from the bag of values?
I have no dispute with destiny,
with these events or non-events.

But the anguish of this inner "conflict",
to whom should I voice this cry?
During the festivities of Deepawali,
what song should I sing?

Festivals are always held,
in the confines of mansions.
But only the fortunate, it seems,
receive an invitation to them.

I look like a resident of ruins,
who sleeps in huts of straw.
Seeing the frail babies fostered there.
again and again, I weep.

In the flickering lamp inside,
my mind remains entangled.
The shadow of this darkness and light,
to whom should I reveal it?

During the festivities of Deepawali,
what song should I sing?

[1] Deepawali, a Hindu festival of light and splendour.

"क्यूँ"

मूल लेखक: "पथिक" (स्वर्गीय जी. एन. शर्मा)

कहा कुछ और किया कुछ,
यह सिफ़त आदम में है।
रुख़ किया मस्जिद की तरफ़,
और मिला मयकदे में है।

उसे अब तक न आई,
क्या राह-ए-मंज़िल की समझ?
जब चला मशरिक़ की जानिब,
और मिला मग़रिब में है।

सदा करे या करे गुनाह,
है कौन जो समझाए उसे?
यह फ़िक्र आदम "क्यूँ" करे,
सज़ा-ए-गुनाह तो दोज़ख़ में है।

"Why"

Translated by: "Loquacious doctor" Dr. P. N. Sharma

He says one thing and does the opposite;
this attribute lies within "Adam".
He turned towards the mosque,
but was found in a tavern.

Has he not yet been able to discern,
the path to his destination?
He went towards the East,
but was found in the West.

Should he do charity or commit sins?
Who is there to explain it to him?
"Why" should "Adam" bother with this?
The punishment for sin lies only in Hell.

"व्यथा"

मूल लेखक: "पथिक" (स्वर्गीय जी. एन. शर्मा)

ज़िन्दगी-भर चलते-चलते,
जब थक गया मैं एक दिन।
एक फ़रिश्ते से इंसाँ ने,
मुहब्बत से सहलाया मुझको।

मंज़िल तो वहीं थी तेरी,
जहाँ से चले थे एक दिन।
वह तो इंतज़ार में था,
बस तुमने न पुकारा उसको।

"Agony"

Translated by: "Loquacious doctor" Dr. P. N. Sharma

Walking my whole life,
I grew weary one day.
An angel in the form of a human,
caressed me with love.

"Your destination was right there"
said he,
"where you had started from one
day.
He had been waiting for you;
it is just that you did not call him."

"मक़सद"

"Purpose"

मूल लेखक: "पथिक" (स्वर्गीय जी. एन. शर्मा)

Translated by: "Loquacious doctor" Dr. P. N. Sharma

फूल पीले हों या लाल,
मक़सद ख़ुदा की बंदगी से है।
हम वफ़ा करें या दें ज़कात,
मक़सद ख़ुशहाल-ए-ज़िंदगी से है।

किसी के दर्द में गिरे आँसू,
मक़सद तो फ़र्ज़-ए-इंसानी से है।
क्या हक़ ज़िंदगी छीन ले उससे,
जो क़ाबा तक न चल पाए?

दो फूल न हों जिन्हें मयस्सर,
वो इबादत ही न कर पाएँ।
उठाते रहो जो गिर जाए,
यही मक़सद इंसान-ए-ज़िंदगी से है।

जब संगदिल ही बनाना था,
तो इंसान ही क्यों बनाए?
ऐ मौला तेरी फ़ितरत,
तो है रहम-ओ-करम की।

जो तुझसे दुआ माँगें,
क्यों उन पर ही क़हर गिराए?
वाजिब तो नहीं है मुझको,
तेरे इंसाफ़ पर उज़्र करना।

नफ़रत-ओ-रहम के ये जज़्बे,
इक ही दिल में क्यों बनाए?

Whether the flowers are yellow or red,
the "purpose" is to worship the Lord.
Whether we show loyalty or give charity,
the "purpose" is to have a fulfilled life.

If tears are shed for another's pain,
the "purpose" is the duty of humanity.
What right has one to snatch a life,
from someone who cannot walk to the shrine?

Those who do not have even
two flowers to offer,
they cannot even pray?
Keep lifting those, who waver or fall,
this is the "purpose" of human life.

If you had to create a stone-hearted creature,
then why did you create human beings?
O Lord, your nature
is one of mercy and kindness.

Why then unleash your wrath,
upon the very people who pray to you?
It is not proper for me,
to object to your justice.

But why did you create these conflicting traits,
of hate and mercy in the same heart?

"निगह-ए-पाक"

मूल लेखक: "पथिक" (स्वर्गीय जी. एन. शर्मा)

तुम रहम करते रहे,
जब हम ख़ता करते रहे।
तुमने पिलाया आब-ए-हयात,
जब हम गुनाह करते रहे।

फिर इन "निगह-ए-पाक" में,
फ़र्क़ आने की वजह क्या?
संगदिल बने तुम इंतिहा,
जब हम दुआ करते रहे।

क़ुदरत के उसूल तो साफ़ हैं,
मुरव्वत की गुंजाइश नहीं।
क्यों क़त्ल के फ़तवे दिए,
जब हम गिला करते रहे?

"The Pious Gaze"

Translated by: "Loquacious doctor" Dr. P. N. Sharma

You kept showering mercy,
while we kept committing wrongs.
You gave us the coveted "water of life",
while we kept on sinning.

Then what caused the switch,
in your "pious gaze"?
You became stone-hearted
to the extreme,
while we kept on praying.

Nature's statutes are resolute;
there is no scope for leniency.
Why did you issue decrees of death,
when we were only complaining?

“सदा”

मूल लेखक: “पथिक” (स्वर्गीय जी. एन. शर्मा)

यह कोई बंदिश नहीं,
कि तुम “सदा” करते रहो।
तन ढँकना जब है ज़रूरत,
गर न हो, ख़ता करते रहो।

गर आराम है इतना मयस्सर,
कि काम करना न हो मुफ़ीद,
कुछ और भी तन ढँकने को,
जो कुछ बने, करते रहो।

“Charity”

Translated by: “Loquacious doctor” Dr. P. N. Sharma

There is no compulsion,
that you should keep doing “charity”.
When you need to cover your body,
if you cannot, then keep committing wrongs.

If you have so much comfort available,
that working is no longer useful,
Then to clothe your body,
keep doing whatever it takes.

"ऐतबार"

मूल लेखक: "पथिक" (स्वर्गीय जी. एन. शर्मा)

बहुत परखे हैं हमने,
इंसानी फ़रिश्ते क़रीब से।
पर वक़्त पर वो काम आया,
जिस पे हमें "ऐतबार" न था।

जान तो ली शैतानों ने,
अच्छी दोस्ती की हामी भर कर।
हमने सज़ा दी एक मयकश को,
जो हमारा क़सूरवार न था।

ज़िंदगी तो बिताई हमने,
मज़हब के उसूल पढ़ते-पढ़ते।
पर दिल में अँधेरा ऐसा था,
जो और भी बढ़ता ही गया।

इक लौ जली और खिली,
पर नशा था जो चढ़ता ही गया।

"Faith"

Translated by: "Loquacious doctor" Dr. P. N. Sharma

We have tested many,
human angels from up close.
But the one who helped
in our time of need,
was the one in whom we had no
"faith" at all.

Our lives were taken by devils,
under the pretext of good
friendship.
We punished an inebriate
boozer instead,
who was not our culprit.

I spent my life,
reading the doctrines of religion.
But the darkness in my heart was such,
that it only kept on growing.

A flame lit up and flashed,
but it was an intoxication
that kept on rising.

"अनजाने पथ"

मूल लेखक: "पथिक" (स्वर्गीय जी. एन. शर्मा)

यह अनदेखा "अनजाना पथ" है,
मुझे इसी राह पर जाने दो।
अपने अंतस की गहराई में,
मुझे चेतन दीप जलाने दो।

जीवन में क्या पाया मैंने?
लगता बस खोया ही खोया है।
चहुँ ओर बिखरे दुखों को मैंने,
बस अपने में सँजोया है।

यह अनदेखा "अनजाना पथ" है,
मुझे इसी राह पर जाने दो।
जलती आँखों में आँसू भर दे,
मुझे उसी राग को गाने दो।

विश्राम नहीं है इस पथ में,
क्षुधित कंठ को न जल-कण हैं।
जल कर अंतस शीतल हो जाए,
मुझे ऐसा स्नेह जगाने दो।

यह अनदेखा "अनजाना पथ" है,
मुझे इसी राह पर जाने दो।
मेघ घने गहराए मन में,
पर शीतल वर्षा का नाम नहीं।

हिमकणों के लगे अंबार,
पर शीतलता का आभास नहीं।
ऐसे जीवन की नैया को,
बस तूफ़ानों में खो जाने दो।

यह अनदेखा "अनजाना पथ" है,
मुझे इसी राह पर जाने दो।
अनंत काल से बहता झरना,
उसका जल मैं बन जाऊँ।

सागर से पर्वत तक उठकर,
उस पर हिमकण बरसाऊँ।
ऐसे स्वप्निल जीवन का सुख,
कुछ क्षण मुझे भी पाने दो।

यह अनदेखा "अनजाना पथ" है,
मुझे इसी राह पर जाने दो।
पर क्यों मरुस्थल की ओर,
मैं अनायास ही बढ़ता जाता हूँ?

मृदंग-सितार की झंकारों में,
क्यों मैं आर्तनाद ही सुनता हूँ?
फूल-भरी बगियों में चलता,
मैं क्यों काँटे ही चुनता हूँ?

इन भँवरों से ऊपर आ कर,
मुझे अपनी राह बनाने दो।
यह अनदेखा "अनजाना पथ" है,
मुझे इसी राह पर जाने दो।

The "Unventured Trail"

Translated by: "Loquacious doctor" Dr. P. N. Sharma

This is an unseen, "unventured trail";
let me go down this very path.
In the depths of my soul,
let me light the lamp of conscience.

What have I achieved in life?
It seems I have only ever lost.
I have only cherished within myself,
the sorrows scattered all around.

This is an unseen, "unventured trail";
let me go down this very path.
The one that fills my
burning eyes with tears,
let me sing that very song.

There is no rest on this trail,
no drop of water for a thirsty throat.
Let me awaken such a love,
that my soul, by burning,
becomes cool.

This is an unseen, "unventured trail";
let me go down this very path.
Dark clouds have gathered in my
heart,
but there is no sign of cooling rain.

Heaps of snowflakes have formed,
but there is no feeling of cold.
Let the boat of such a life,
just be lost within the storms.

This is an unseen, "unventured trail";
let me go down this very path.
The eternally flowing waterfall,
let me become its water.

Rising from the sea to the mountains,
let me shower snowflakes upon them.
The joy of such a dream-like life,
let me also have it for a few moments.

This is an unseen, "unventured trail";
let me go down this very path.
But why, towards the desert,
do I inexplicably keep walking?

In the resonance of the
Mridangam[2] and *Sitar*[3],
why do I hear only a cry of pain?
Walking in gardens full of flowers,
why do I pick only the thorns?

Rising above these whirlpools,
let me make a path of my own.
This is an unseen, "unventured trail";
let me go down this very path.

[2] Mridangam: A double-headed drum, barrel-shaped, played with both hands

[3] Sitar: Indian stringed musical instrument.

"मज़लूम"

मूल लेखक: "पथिक" (स्वर्गीय जी. एन. शर्मा)

समंदर में ये तूफ़ान उठाए किसलिए?
हवाओं से साये उड़ाए किसलिए?
माना कि बेमुरव्वत हैं क़ुदरत के उसूल,
पर बेक़सूरों को सज़ा दी किसलिए?

गर "मज़लूम" के अश्कों का कोई मोल नहीं,
तो इस बदबख़्त को आँसू दिए ही किसलिए?

"The Oppressed"

Translated by: "Loquacious doctor" Dr. P. N. Sharma

Why did you raise these storms in the ocean?
Why blow away the sails with the winds?
I agree that the principles of nature are harsh,
but why did you punish the innocent?

If the tears of the "oppressed" are of no value,
then why did you give tears,
to this hapless soul at all?

"पैग़ाम"

मूल लेखक: "पथिक" (स्वर्गीय जी. एन. शर्मा)

ज़िंदगी का "पैग़ाम" क्या है,
यह बहस कब तक चले?
जले हर शाम महफ़िल में शमा,
या ज़िंदगी ख़ुद ही चले?

दौर-ए-सुकूँ कुछ यूँ चले,
कि क़यामत रोक ले अपने क़दम।
गिरे आँसू नहीं एक भी,
यह ज़िंदगी कुछ यूँ चले।

ग़म-ओ-ख़ुशी का दौर माना,
पड़ते भुगतने हैं ज़रूर।
इक तरफ़ बस ग़म ही ग़म हों,
इक तरफ़ जीवन के सुरूर।

तक़दीर अब ये बताए,
यह सिलसिला कब तक चले?

"The Message"

Translated by: "Loquacious doctor"
Dr. P. N. Sharma

What is the "message" of life?
How long will this debate continue?
Should a candle burn in every evening's gathering,
or should life proceed on its own?

May an era of peace proceed in such a way,
that Doomsday itself stops in its tracks.
May not a single tear be ever shed;
this is how life should get led.

This cycle of sorrow and joy, I accept,
we have to endure them for sure.
But why on one side there be sorrows only,
while on the other, the ecstasies of life?

Now let fate tell,
how long should this continue?

"राह"

मूल लेखक: "पथिक" (स्वर्गीय जी. एन. शर्मा)

क्या-क्या न किया होगा,
ज़मीं पे इंसाँ को लाने के लिए?
मज़हबी उसूल-ओ-फ़र्ज़ बनाए,
इसे "राह" दिखाने के लिए।

फिर भी क्या कमी रही,
इसकी तक़दीर लिखने में?
जो न करना था वही किया,
वह भी तुझे पाने के लिए।

अभी भी कुछ नहीं बिगड़ा,
इसमें कुछ तो सुधार कर दे।
न हो, इक अवतार ही ले ले,
अपनी ज़मीं बचाने के लिए।

The "Righteous Path"

Translated by: "Loquacious doctor" Dr. P. N. Sharma

What would you not have done,
to bring man to the Earth?
You drafted religious principles and duties,
to show him the "righteous path".

And yet, what was lacking,
in the writing of his fate?
He did what he should never have done,
and that too, only to beget you.

Nothing is lost as yet;
at least make some amends.
Or perhaps, take incarnation once more,
to save your own Earth.

"फ़रिश्ता"

मूल लेखक: "पथिक" (स्वर्गीय जी. एन. शर्मा)

मुहब्बत की तारीफ़ बहुत सुनी थी।

पर मिली तो वही,
जो माँ के आँचल से बही थी।

अपनों से रिश्ते पाए थे लाखों,
पर बहन की राखी की सानी नहीं थी।

जब महफ़िल में गाने आया,
तो ख़ुशियाँ बिखरी थीं बेहद।
पर दिल में उतरीं तो बस,
वे आँखें जो गीली रही थीं।

दोस्तों के प्यार ने तो,
दोज़ख़ से भी उबारा मुझको।
करिश्मा-ए-दिल-ए-इंसानी तब देखा,
जब दुश्मन के आँगन में पनाह मिली थी।

"The Angel"

Translated by: "Loquacious doctor" Dr. P. N. Sharma

I had heard much praise for love.

But the only one I found,
was that which flowed from my mother's Bosom.

I had a million bonds with my kin,
but nothing could compare to my sister's *Rakhi*[4].

When I came to the gathering to sing,
immense happiness was scattered all around.
But the only thing that touched my heart,
were those eyes that were wet with tears.

The love of my friends,
rescued me even from the Hell.
But I saw the true miracle of the human heart,
when I found shelter in the courtyard of an enemy.

---

[4] Rakhi: A decorative thread, tied by a sister on her brother's wrist in a Hindu ceremony to request his protection.

"दिल के तूफ़ान"

मूल लेखक: "पथिक" (स्वर्गीय जी. एन. शर्मा)

"दिल के तूफ़ानों" को
प्यार नहीं कहते,
प्यार होता है जब
हवस का नशा टूट जाता है।

प्यार की बहुत कोशिश की हमने,
पर ना-मालूम था मुझको,
प्यार किया नहीं जाता,
प्यार तो अनजाने हो जाता है।

दिल की गहराइयों में,
जब एक कशिश तड़पती है,
वो प्यार बन जाती है,
जब दिल टूट जाता है।

"Storms in the Heart"

Translated by: "Loquacious doctor" Dr. P. N. Sharma

"Storms in the heart"
are not love;
love happens only when,
the intoxication of lust is broken.

I tried very hard to find love,
but I did not know,
love cannot be planned or done;
it just happens Unwittingly.

In the depths of the heart,
when an attraction yearns,
it becomes love,
only when the heart breaks.

"कवि"

मूल लेखक: "पथिक" (स्वर्गीय जी. एन. शर्मा)

"कवि" सदा अधूरा होता है,
लिखता जाता, लिखता जाता।
फिर भी नहीं पूरा होता है,
विधवा का संसार हो जैसा।

ऐसा उसका परिहास होता है,
क्यों उसका जीवन अनर्थक प्रयास होता है?
क्यों उसकी व्यथा का अंत नहीं होता?
क्यों वही केवल समाज का क़र्ज़ ढोता है?

क्यों वही जागता,
जब संसार सोता है?

The "Poet"

Translated by: "Loquacious doctor" Dr. P. N. Sharma

The "poet" is always unfulfilled;
he keeps writing, and writing.
Still, he is never complete,
just like the world of a widow.

Why is he mocked in this way?
Why is his life a futile effort?
Why does his suffering never end?
Why is he the only one to bear
society's debt?

Why is he the one who remains
awake,
when the whole world sleeps?

"शायरी"

मूल लेखक: "पथिक" (स्वर्गीय जी. एन. शर्मा)

कालिदास की मूढ़ मति में,
मेघदूत का काव्य छुपा था।

सूरदास के अंध-जगत में,
गोपियों का प्यार छुपा था।

तुलसीदास की रागनियों में,
रामायण का सार छिपा था।

कबीर दास की तंगहाली में,
आदर्शों का भंडार छिपा था।

ग़ालिब की मदहोश नज़र में,
"शायरी" का संसार छिपा था।

"Poetry"

Translated by: "Loquacious doctor" Dr. P. N. Sharma

In the simple mind of Kalidas[5],
the poetry of the Meghdoot[6] was hidden.

In the blind world of Surdas[7],
the love of the Gopis was hidden.
(Maidens)

In the verses of Tulsidas[8],
the essence of the Ramayana[9] was hidden.

In the poverty of Kabir Das[10],
a treasure trove of ideals was hidden.

In the intoxicated eyes of Ghalib[11],
the world of "poetry" was hidden.

---

[5] Kalidas – Renowned classical Sanskrit poet and playwright of ancient India.
[6] *Meghdoot – A celebrated Sanskrit lyrical poem by Kalidas.*
[7] *Surdas – Famous devotional poet known for his compositions on Lord Krishna and the Gopis.*
[8] *Tulsidas – Author of the epic Ramcharitmanas, based on the Ramayana.*
[9] *Ramayana – One of the two great epics of ancient India, narrating the life of Lord Rama.*
[10] *Kabir Das – Mystic poet and saint, known for his dohas and spiritual philosophy.*
[11] *Ghalib – Iconic Urdu and Persian poet of the Mughal era, celebrated for his ghazals.*

"छवि"

मूल लेखक: "पथिक" (स्वर्गीय जी. एन. शर्मा)

मुझ-सा कवि, उसकी ऐसी "छवि",
सुबह अंडा-टोस्ट खाता है,
दिन-भर आइसक्रीम खाता है,
बस रात को रागिनी सुनाता है।

ख़ादी का कपड़ा पहनने से,
उसे एलर्जी रोग हो जाता है।
एयर-कंडीशनर न मिला तो,
ग़रीबी पर कविता लिखने का,
मूड ख़राब हो जाता है।

The "Image"

Translated by: "Loquacious doctor" Dr. P. N. Sharma

A poet like me, his "image" is so strange:
he eats egg and toast for breakfast,
savours ice cream all day long,
and only at night does he sing his songs.

From wearing Khadi[12] cloth,
he gets an allergic disease.
If he does not get an air-conditioner,
his mood for writing poetry on poverty,
is completely spoiled.

[12] Khadi: Hand-woven cotton fabric, a symbol of Indian self-reliance and, by extension, social equality.

"दामन"

मूल लेखक: "पथिक" (स्वर्गीय जी. एन. शर्मा)

i)

शीशा उड़ेल कर जब,
पैमाना न भरा बराबर।
तो साक़ी ने मेरी ख़ातिर,
आँसू से भरा उसको।

ii)

सिफ़त-ए-हुस्न गर यही है,
कि दीवाना बना दे।
तो क्या उज़्र कि परवाना,
शमा में न जल मरे?

iii)

आसाँ बहुत है दूसरे का,
नुक़्स पढ़ना।
अपने ही गरेबाँ में झाँके,
ऐसा इंसान न मिला मुझको।

iv)

हुजूम खोज में था देखने,
कि एक वारदात हो गई।
कुछ इंतज़ार के बाद,
शायर का जनाज़ा निकला।

v)

चलने को मजबूर था,
तो मस्जिद में दुआ माँगी।
पाँवों में जान आई,
तो मयख़ाने की राह ली।

vi)

अफ़सोस नहीं मुझको,
ज़िंदगी-भर इबादत नहीं की।
पर शहर की हर मैय्यत को,
कंधा तो दिया था।

vii)

ख़ुदा का नूर बरपा है,
ज़र्रे-ज़र्रे में।
तो ज़रूरत क्या हमें,
अपनी ही इबादत करने की?

viii)

ज़माना बड़ा ख़राब है,
पर हमें क्या ग़रज़?
"दामन" में पैबंद इतने,
कि सिलने की जगह नहीं।

ix)

सुना था कि शायर की,
तबीयत ख़राब है।
मालूम हुआ बहुत दिन से,
बज़्म का बुलावा नहीं मिला।

"The Hem"

Translated by: "Loquacious doctor"
Dr. P. N. Sharma

---

i)
When, after pouring from the bottle,
the goblet did not fill.
The barmaid, for my sake,
filled it with her tears.

ii)
If this is the quality of beauty,
that it drives one to madness,
then what complaint can the moth have,
if it burns to death in the flame?

iii)
It is very easy,
to read the faults of others.
But one who looks into his own soul,
I have not found such a person.

iv)
The crowd was thronging to see,
what incident had occurred.
After some waiting,
the poet's funeral procession appeared.

v)
When I was unable to walk,
I prayed in the mosque.
When strength returned to my feet,
I took the path to the tavern.

vi)
I have no regret that,
I did not pray my whole life.
But shoulder the bier, didn't I
of every corpse in the city?

vii)
God's divine radiance shines,
in every single atom, across the universe, atomically.
So what need do we have,
to worship our own kind?

viii)
The times are terrible,
but why should I care?
There are so many patches on my "hem",
that there is no space left for sewing.

ix)
I heard that the poet,
was not keeping well.
It turns out that for a long time,
he had not received an invitation to a gathering.

"मुसाफ़िर"

मूल लेखक: "पथिक" (स्वर्गीय श्री जी. एन. शर्मा)

एक भटका हुआ "मुसाफ़िर",
खोजता था अपनी राह।
आरज़ू थी इक हमसफ़र की,
या मिले थोड़ी पनाह।

संगदिलों के क़ाफ़िले से,
मैंने उसे देखा मगर,
दूर जाना था मुझको बहुत,
मैं चला अपनी ही राह।

क़ाफ़िला टूटा भँवर में,
जिस्म पर बिखरे थे घाव।
मैंने देखा वही मुसाफ़िर,
खे रहा था मेरी नाव।

"The Traveller"

Translated by: "Loquacious doctor" Dr. P. N. Sharma

A lost "traveller",
I was searching for my path.
I longed for a companion,
or to find a little shelter.

From the caravan of the heartless people,
I saw him from afar,
but I had very far to go,
so regardless, I went my own way.

The caravan got wrecked up in a whirlwind,
wounds were scattered across my body.
I saw that same traveller,
rowing my boat for me.

"फ़र्ज़"

मूल लेखक: "पथिक" (स्वर्गीय जी. एन. शर्मा)

नहीं जाता मैं घंटी बजाने,
या अपना शीश नवाने मंदिर में।
महसूस तो होता है कि,
यह फ़र्ज़ भी निभाया होता।

क्या पूरा न होता "फ़र्ज़" अपना,
गर इक बंदे को उठाया होता?
मैं कौन हूँ जो करे शिकवा,
इन ख़ून के बने रिश्तों से?

हर ख़ून का रंग है एक ही,
यह तो मुझे सिखाया होता।
ख़ून बहा के कौन अमर हुआ,
तारीख़ ने यह तो बताया होता।

"Obligations"

Translated by: "Loquacious doctor" Dr. P. N. Sharma

I do not go to the temple
to ring the bell,
or to bow my head before the idol.
And yet, I do feel at times,
that I should have fulfilled
this duty too.

But would my "obligations"
not have been fulfilled,
if I had lifted up one fallen soul?
Who am I to complain,
about these relationships
made of blood?

Every blood is the same colour;
you should have at least
taught me this.
Who ever became immortal by
shedding blood?
History should have at least
told me that.

SECTION – II

CHAPTER – 1

"Dedicated to My Braveheart Brethren in Uniform"

स्वरचित मूल लेख (हिन्दी) "वाचाल चिकित्सक"

Self-Composed (Hindi) and Translated into English by "Loquacious Doctor", Dr. P. N. Sharma

"गलवान के बलवान"

जून 2020 (मेरी प्रथम कविता)
स्वरचित: "वाचाल चिकित्सक" (डॉ. पी. एन. शर्मा)

उत्तर का प्रखर प्रहरी, हिमालय वृहद् विराट,
उत्तुंग शिखरों पर, केवल धवल हिम का वास।
सर्द, शुष्क, तीक्ष्ण समीर, जो तन-मन गला दे,
नीरवता ऐसी, जो कठोर हौसला भी हिला दे।

न तृण, न पशु-पक्षी, न किसी मानव का वास,
न शब्द, न शोर, न रस, न स्वाद, न स्पर्श, न संग,
न प्रकाश, निशा तिमिर घनघोर, सिवा श्वेत न रंग।
समर हर श्वास, हर पग, सर्द जकड़े अंग-प्रत्यंग।

श्वेत यूँ शांति-प्रतीक, पर पसरा वहाँ स्याह गरल,
देख लो, जान लो, रिपु निष्ठुर, चालबाज़, कुटिल।
लालची, कपटी, दुस्साहसी, चलता निकृष्ट चाल,
धोखा, वादा-ख़िलाफ़ी, यही उसकी चाल-ढाल।

लपटें लपलपाता अजगर, रक्त-पिपासु अधम,
फन उठाए फुफकारें, राग मिलाएँ साथी भुजंग।
नव-धनाढ्य का गर्व पालता, चलता अढ़ाई चाल,
स्वप्न विश्व-विजय, सोच उसकी विकृत, विकराल।

पर माँ भारती के लाल डटे, तन पर वर्दी धवल,
हाथ थामे अस्त्र-शस्त्र, चित्त अधीर, दावानल।
बिसार कुटुंब समूचा, पितु, माता, भार्या, संतान,
मन में बसा मात्र हिंद, और प्रबल उसका मान।

प्रवृत्ति अनुसार किया था उसने, धोखे से घात,
शहीद हुए वीर सी.ओ., साथ ही वे बीस जवान।
बाक़ी टूट पड़े दुश्मन पर, किया हत और वध,
लेने के देने पड़े, हुआ वह हक्का-बक्का, स्तब्ध।

हुई बर्फ़ ख़ून से लाल, तोड़ी गर्दन, फोड़े कपाल,
तांडव भयंकर, तिलक लगा माँ काली के भाल।
था ये गलवान के बलवानों का शानदार कमाल,
फिर तिरंगे में लिपटे आए, सारी माँओं के लाल।

जनता विचलित, सँभली, दी विदाई वीरोचित,
ली शपथ हमने, कि रहेगी अनवरत हिस्सेदारी।
थामेंगे डोर, शहीदों के परिवारों की ज़िम्मेदारी,
रुके, पोंछे आँसू, फिर चलाए प्रतिशोध के बाण।

उठ खड़े हुए हम सब, समस्त नर, नारी, नरेंद्र,
देने साथ सेनानियों का, मिल कर हुए प्रतिबद्ध।
न देंगे एक इंच, अपितु वापस लेंगे शत-प्रतिशत,
लिया यह प्रण, चाहे जितना भी भीषण हो रण।

वहीं उसके मृत सैनिक रखे गए गुमनाम,
न बाक़ायदा अंतिम संस्कार, न ही कोई सम्मान।
है गूँगी, ग़ुलाम, उसकी जनता और परिवार,
आलोचना से डर, सत्य छुपाती, कायर सरकार।

साथ देने धर्म का, आ डटे सच्चे मित्र अनेक,
फूँके गए शंख, गूँजा गगन, महागर्जना घनघोर।
साथ देते दैव, केवल धर्मवीरों और कर्मवीरों का,
गीता की शाश्वत यह सीख, रखना सदा स्मरण।

"The Bravehearts of Galwan"

June 2020 (My first poem)
Composed and translated by: "Loquacious doctor" Dr. P. N. Sharma

---

A fierce sentinel of the north, the Himalayas vast and huge,
upon whose lofty peaks, only white snow finds refuge.
A cold, dry, sharp breeze that freezes body and mind,
a silence so intense, it daunts the dauntless.

No blade of grass, no bird or beast, nor any human dwelling,
no sound or smell, noise, no taste or touch, no fellowship or feeling.
No light, the night's darkness is absolute, no colour but for white,
each breath a battle, each step a struggle, the cold grips every limb.

Though white symbolises peace, a black poison is also lounging,
see and discern, the enemy is cruel, vile and cunning.
Greedy, deceitful, and audacious, he moves with wicked design,
betrayal and broken promises are his only sign.

A dragon flicking its tongue of flame, a bloodthirsty and evil,
hoods raised, hissing, its cohort reptiles join the chorus.
Nurturing the pride of the newly rich, it walks a crooked way,
dreaming of world conquest, its intent monstrous and depraved.

But the sons of Mother India stand firm, clad in white uniforms,
weapons in hand, their hearts impatient, like a wildfire
Forgetting their entire families: father, mother, wife, and child,
only India resides in their hearts, and the pride in her is strong.

True to its nature, the enemy attacked with deceit;
the brave C.O. was martyred, along with twenty of his men.
The rest fell upon the foe, they slaughtered and they slew;
the tables were turned, leaving the enemy stunned and struck dumb.

The snow turned red with blood, necks and the skulls were broken,
Mother Kali[13] danced her tandava[14] with black Tilak, adorning her brow.
This was the splendid feat of the brave hearts of Galwan,
who then returned, wrapped in the Tricolour, sons of all moms.

The nation, though in mourning, composed itself and gave a hero's farewell;
we all took an oath, that our support would be everlasting.
We will take up the reins, the responsibility for the martyrs' families;
we paused, wiped our tears, then fired the arrows of revenge.

We all stood up as one: every woman, man, and leader Narendra,
committed to standing with our soldiers, united together.
We will not cede an inch; indeed, we will take back every part.
This vow we have taken, no matter how fierce the battle becomes.

Meanwhile, their dead soldiers were kept anonymous;
no proper last rites were performed, nor was any respect shown.
Their people and their families are but mute slaves;
afraid of criticism, the cowardly regime hides the truth.

To stand for righteousness, many true friends came and stood with us;
conches were blown, the sky resonated with a great and mighty roar.
The gods give their support only to the conscientious and the diligent;
this is the eternal lesson of the Gita, which we must always remember.

---

[13]Kali: A Hindu goddess associated with death and destruction, often depicted on the battlefield.
[14]Tandava: The vigorous, destructive dance of the Hindu god Shiva.

"किस माटी के बने हो तुम?"

स्वरचित: "वाचाल चिकित्सक" (डॉ. पी. एन. शर्मा)

यूँ तो हम-तुम एक माटी से ही बने हैं,
तो ये फ़र्क़ कब, कैसे और कहाँ से उपजा?
वर्दी पहन, मिट्टी भाल लगा, जब निकलते हो,
कैसे तुम परिवार की चिंता छोड़ देते हो?

किस माटी के बने हो तुम?

वर्दी पहनते ही सेना, यूनिट और साथी,
कैसे तुम्हारा प्रथम परिवार हो जाता है?
माता-पिता, भार्या और बच्चों का मोह,
कैसे देश-प्रेम के सामने गौण हो जाता है?

किस माटी के बने हो तुम?

देश की आन, बान और शान के पीछे,
सुविधाओं और प्राण को तुच्छ मान लेते हो?
क्या तुम सच ही, वास्तव में, डर से परे हो,
या प्रभु ने ही तुममें ये बीज डाला है?

किस माटी के बने हो तुम?

कैसे तुम प्राण क़ुर्बान करने को तैयार रहते हो,
वर्दी के आदेश की उदूली नहीं करते हो?
सेवा-निवृत्त होने के बाद भी,
तुम ता-ज़िंदगी सैनिक बने रहते हो?

किस माटी के बने हो तुम?

दुर्भाग्य से यदि बीच रण तुम होते धराशायी,
तो बहते लहू के साथ, दो बूंदें अश्क की,
आँखों की कोरों से ढलकती तो होंगी?
फिर भी बिना पछताए परिवार तज देते हो।

किस माटी के बने हो तुम?

"Of Which Clay are You Molded From?"

Composed and translated by: "Loquacious doctor" Dr. P. N. Sharma

Though you and I are made of the same clay,
from where, when, and how did this difference arise?
When you venture out in uniform, and smear soil on your brow,
how do you leave behind all worry for your family back home?

"Of Which clay are you molded from?"

The moment you don your uniform, the army, unit, and comrades;
how do they become your first family?
The love and duties towards mother, father, wife and children;
how does it become trivial before your patriotic fervor?

"Of Which clay are you molded from?"

For the honour, pride, and glory of the nation,
you consider comfort and even life itself to be trivial?
Tell me truthfully, are you really beyond fear?
or is it God himself who has planted this seed in you dear?

"Of Which clay are you molded from?"

How are you always ready to sacrifice your life?
How do you never disobey the orders of the uniform?
Even after retiring from service,
how do you remain a soldier for your life entire?

"Of Which clay are you molded from?"

If, by misfortune, you should ever fall in the midst of battle,
then along with the flowing blood, two drops of tears;
don't they roll out from the corners of your eyes?
And yet, without regret, you bid your family goodbye.

"Of Which clay are you molded from?"

"वीरों तुम सबको शत-शत नमन"

स्वरचित: "वाचाल चिकित्सक" (डॉ. पी. एन. शर्मा)
कर्नल मनोज कुमार सिन्हा की आपबीती पर लिखित उनकी स्वयं की रचना, "एक लड़ाई ख़त्म हुई," से प्रेरित।

पहली लड़ाई शत्रु, दूजी मौत से,
तुम में से कइयों ने दोनों ही लड़ीं।
कोई दोनों जीता, कोई केवल एक,
वीरों तुम सबको, शत-शत नमन।

अदृश्य, पर लड़ाई तीजी भी थी,
जो घरों पर परिजनों ने लड़ी थी।
सामान्य-सी ही दिखती दिनचर्या,
पर सूने एहसास, आशंकित मन।

वीर योद्धा का जितना था पराक्रम,
उतनी ही प्रेरक व हृदय-आंदोलक,
उनकी रचित एक मार्मिक कविता,
आभार प्रभु, उनको अवसर दिया।

कर्नल मनोज की कही, मेरी सुनी,
बात एक, अंतर कितना उल्लेख्य!
उन्होंने साथियों संग, जी भी थी,
वहीं हमने तो बस सुनी-भरी थी।

धराशायी थे वे, मुँदती हुई आँखों से,
माटी में मिलता अपना रक्त देखा।
देखा पल-पल छीजता निज जीवन,
देखे, धुँधले होते अक्स में परिजन।

देखे चिंतित, संतप्त, उद्विग्न साथी,
सुनी उनकी, ढाढ़स बँधाती वाणी।
साथ ही सुना, उद्घोष विजय का,
व देखी, फहराती जयश्री-पताका।

यह कैसा, अनोखा-सा एक पल था,
पीड़ा-युक्त विश्राम, दुःख-रंजित सुख।
जीत-मिश्रित हार, संतोष-भरी अकुलाहट,
उस एक ही पल में, कैसे साथ-साथ?

प्रभु, आपका धन्यवाद, आपकी माया,
मृत्यु के द्वार से वीर वापस लौट आया।
जननी-जनक को मिला, आँखों का नूर,
संतानों को पिता और भार्या को सिंदूर।

कितने वीर रहे होंगे, इतने सारे सालों में,
सब लड़े होंगे यहाँ और वहाँ, साथ-साथ।
कई हुए शहीद, कुटुंबी रह गए रीते हाथ,
उन सबको मेरा नमन, सबका आभार।

वीरों तुम सबको, शत-शत नमन।

"A Hundred Salutes to You, O' Heroes"

Composed and translated by: "Loquacious doctor" Dr. P. N. Sharma
Inspired by the personal experience of Colonel Manoj Kumar Sinha, as written in his poem, "One Battle is Over."

The first battle is with the enemy, the second with death;
many of you fought both.
Some won both, some only one;
to all of you heroes, a hundred salutes.

Invisible, but a 3rd fight was also fought,
by the families waiting back at home.
Their daily routine looked deceptively normal,
but their feelings were numb, their minds full of fear.

As great as the valour of the warrior,
was the poignant poem he himself composed;
inspiring and heart-rending.
Thank you, 'O' Lord, for giving him this second chance.

What Colonel Manoj narrated, and what I heard,
were the same story, yet how vast the difference was!
He, along with his comrades, had truly lived it;
we, in our safe havens, had merely heard it.

Fallen to the ground, with his eyes in near death stare,
he watched his own blood mix with the soil.
He watched his own life seeping away, moment by moment;
he saw his family, as if in a gradually fading reflection.

He saw his worried, distressed, and anxious comrades;
he heard their strained but comforting voices.
And at the same very moment, he heard the victory chant,
and saw the Tricolour, the flag of triumph, fluttering high.

What a strange and unique moment that was:
rest filled with pain, joy tinged with sorrow;
a victory mixed with defeat, a satisfaction full of unease.
In that very one moment, how could so many opposites coexist?

O Lord, thank you for your grace, your wondrous ways;
the brave warrior returned from the death's gates.
The mother and father got back the light of their eyes;
the children got their father, and the wife her sindoor[15].

How many brave souls must there have been, over so many years?
All of them would have fought, here and there, side by side.
Many were martyred, leaving their families empty-handed;
my salutes to them, my gratitude to them all.

"A hundred salutes to all of you, O Heroes."

[15] Sindoor or Vermilion, a red pigment, applied on scalp hair parting, as a symbol of being a married woman

"लो आ गए रफ़ाल, एक तूफ़ान"

स्वरचित: "वाचाल चिकित्सक" (डॉ. पी. एन. शर्मा)
(जब पहले ५ रफ़ाल विमान आए)

लो आ गए रफ़ाल, तूफ़ान नाम दूजा, साक्षात काल,
हिंदुस्तानी दिलों का सुकून, उन्नत हुआ हिंद-भाल।
वीर सेनानियों के तूणीर में, एक और तीर लाजवाब,
थी लंबी प्रतीक्षा, ये पाँच पांडव हैं बैरियों को जवाब।

दुश्मन से ओझल, बाज़-नेत्र इसके, देखें दूर का हाल,
रफ़्तार है बेपनाह, नापता गगन की बुलंदियाँ तत्काल।
चलाता ब्रह्म-बाण, भेदता एक ही साथ लक्ष्य अनेक,
भेद सके न कोई अस्त्र, ऐसा है समर्थ इसका कवच।

समय चलता तेज़, सदा परिवर्तनशील, गतिमान,
क़दम मिलाना, मिला के चलना, मनीषियों का काम।
निज क्षमता बढ़ाने, बैरी-दिल दहलाने, रुलाने, दफ़नाने,
लो आ गए रफ़ाल, तूफ़ान नाम दूजा, साक्षात काल।

भान था नरेंद्र को, अपरिहार्यता और इसके बल का,
लिया निर्णय, अड़ा-लड़ा, न डिगा, आक्षेप झेले अनेक।
पान किया गरल, रहा सरल, हटाए अवरोध, प्रतिरोध,
बल देते, दृढ़-निश्चय, पाक-दामन, माँ, राष्ट्र, प्रभु-आशीष।

"Behold, the Rafale Has Come: A Storm"

Composed and translated by: "Loquacious doctor" Dr. P. N. Sharma
(On the arrival of the first five Rafale aircraft)

Behold, the Rafale has come: its other name is Storm, the whispering death
A comfort to Indian hearts, the brow of India is held high.
Another peerless arrow in the quiver of our brave warriors;
the wait was long, but these five Pandavas[16] are the answer to our foes.

Invisible to the enemy, its hawk-eyes see things from afar;
its speed is boundless, it scales the heights of the sky in an instant.
It fires the Brahma-missile[17], to pierce simultaneously targets multiple,
its armour is so strong that no weapon can penetrate.

Time moves swiftly; it is ever-changing and dynamic.
To keep in step with it, to walk in time with it, is the work of the wise.
To enhance our capacity, to make the enemy tremble and to bury them;
Behold, the Rafale has come: its other name is Storm, the whispering death.

Narendra[18] was aware of its necessity and its power;
he took the firm decision, did not waver, endured all accusations.
Drank the poison, stayed serene, removed all obstacles and opposition
His strength is firm resolve, clean conscience, blessings of Mother, Nation and God

[16]Pandavas: The five heroic brothers who are the protagonists of the Hindu epic, the Mahabharata.
[17]Brahma-missile (Brahmastra): A divine, supernatural weapon mentioned in Hindu texts.
[18]Narendra: Refers to Narendra Modi, the Prime Minister of India who oversaw the acquisition of the Rafale jets.

"जनरल रावत"

स्वरचित: मर्माहत "वाचाल चिकित्सक" (डॉ. पी. एन. शर्मा)

"जनरल रावत", हिंद-सेनापति,
रिपु-मर्दक, विलक्षण महारथी।
सदा संगिनी और वीर साथी,
अचानक यूँ ही कैसे चले गए?

वह नर-नाहर जो कभी डरा नहीं,
उत्तरदायित्व निभाने में रुका नहीं।
अपेक्षाओं के बोझ-तले दबा नहीं,
नूतन राही, पुरानी राह चला नहीं।

बैरी को बारंबार धूल चटाई थी,
चाहे "डोकलाम" हो या "गलवान"।
या जाना हो "म्यांमार" सीमा-पार,
सर्जिकल-स्ट्राइक या "बालाकोट"।

ये दारुण दुःख क्यों दिया तुमने?
छीना भारत का अवलंब तुमने।
इस रहस्य पर पड़े ये पर्दे खोलो,
हे राम, तुम अब तो कुछ बोलो!

क्या कोई नियोजित षड्यंत्र था?
या पराभूत का छिपाया ख़ंजर था?
जिसने राष्ट्र का सीना चीरा था,
हे राम, तुम अब तो राज़ खोलो!

विदीर्ण हमारा तन और मन है,
राष्ट्र शोकमग्न और हत-भग्न है।
संतप्त परिवारों को संबल दो,
हमें आश्वस्त करो, पथ-प्रदर्शन करो।

"General Rawat"

Composed and translated by: "Loquacious doctor" Dr. P. N. Sharma

"General Rawat," Commander of India,
a vanquisher of foes, an exceptional warrior.
With his ever-present wife and brave companions,
how could they all leave us, so suddenly?

A lion among men who was never afraid,
who never hesitated in fulfilling his duty.
He was never crushed by the weight of expectations;
a new traveller, he never walked the old paths.

Again and again, he made the enemy bite the dust,
whether it was in "Doklam" or in "Galwan."
Whether it was crossing the border into "Myanmar,"
for a surgical strike, or the air strike on "Balakot."

God, why did you give us this excruciating pain?
Why did you snatch away India's greatest support?
Unveil the curtains that hang over this mystery;
O Ram*, you must break your silence and speak.

Was it a planned conspiracy?
Or was it a hidden dagger of the defeated?
A dagger that pierced the very heart of the nation;
O Ram, you must now reveal the sinister secret!

Our bodies and souls are torn to pieces;
the nation is grief-stricken and broken-hearted.
Give strength to the grieving families;
reassure us, and show us the path forward.

*Ram: A principal deity in Hinduism, often invoked in times of distress.

To Param Vir Chakra recipient, 2nd Lt. Arun Khetrapal

Martyred 16th December 1971,
The very last day of the war.

On the Golden Jubilee of his sacrifice

16th December 2021

"एक परमवीर की शहादत (अरुण खेत्रपाल)"

स्वरचित: "वाचाल चिकित्सक" (डॉ. पी. एन. शर्मा)
जन्म से योद्धा
सबसे कम उम्र के, सर्वोच्च वीरता पुरस्कार
"परम वीर" चक्र, से सम्मानित

सैनिक पिता, माता महेश्वरी का लाल,
प्यारा-सा नाम उनका, अरुण खेत्रपाल।
नाम के अनुरूप ही थी आभा सूरज की,
हसरत छोटी-सी, बस आकाश छूने की।

माता-पिता की आशा, आँखों का तारा,
लंबा-चौड़ा, आदर्शवादी तरुण अरुण।
अपने ख़ुद के सपने, अपना पूरा जीवन,
सब कुछ उसने कैसे दाँव पर लगा दिया?

इक्कीस साल का ऐसा नौजवान था,
बचपन गया, न पूरा यौवन आया था।
अभी सैनिक-जीवन जिया ही न था,
कि वो सैनिक की वीरगति पा गया।

अभी यंग-ऑफ़िसर ट्रेनिंग पूरी न थी,
कि '71 के युद्ध का बुलावा आ गया।
घर से विदा ले कर, चला वो मतवाला,
मुस्कुराता, हिम्मत बँधाता, नौनिहाल।

मन में थी अभिलाषा, परमवीर-चक्र की,
बच गया तो लाहौर में गोल्फ़ खेलने की।
विजयी साथियों संग जीत के जश्न की,
पर होनी तो अभी आनी, और होनी थी।

1971 में शकरगढ़-सेक्टर, बसंतर-युद्ध,
आगे बढ़ चुकी थी इन्फ़ेंट्री-बटालियन।
पाकी अमरीकी पैटन-टैंकों से घिरी थी,
17 पूना-हॉर्स सेंचुरियन, उनके रक्षक थे।

अनुभवहीन अरुण को आगे भेजने को,
कमांडर "हंटी" हनूत सिंह तैयार नहीं थे।
अरुण ज़िद पर अड़ गए, उनसे लड़ गए,
अरुण सपनों से दूर कैसे रह सकते थे?

"फ़ामागुस्ता" उनके टैंक का नाम था,
नायाब नाम, नायाब काम करना था।
राह में सक्रिय "बारूदी-सुरंग-क्षेत्र" था,
रात के अंधकार में ही पार करना था।

अपनी इन्फ़ेंट्री को अकेले कैसे छोड़ दें?
सबने जोखिम लिया, फ़ील्ड पार किया।
दुश्मन के आधुनिक टैंकों से सामना था,
पर कोई डरा नहीं और कोई हटा नहीं।

रण भीषण हुआ, और अंत तक ही हुआ,
अरुण ने ख़ुद चार दुश्मन टैंक भेद दिए।
लहूलुहान तन, किंतु हौसला अदम्य था,
टूटा "फ़ामागुस्ता", पर तोप में अभी दम था।

कमांडर उन्हें वापस बुलाता ही रह गया,
अरुण ने रेडियो-संपर्क ही काट दिया।
नज़रें पाँचवें पैटन-टैंक पर टिकी हुई थीं,
दोनों ने ही, एक-दूजे पर गोले दाग़ दिए।

दोनों के निशाने सटीक, लक्ष्य भेद गए,
पाकिस्तानी कमांडर भाग्यवश बच गए।
अरुण के भाग्य में शहादत लिखी थी,
पाकी जान गया, शेर से पाला पड़ा था।

नभ में अरुण उदित, धरा पर अरुण अस्त हुए,
विधि की विडंबना, कुछ घंटों के अंतराल में,
पस्त बैरी ने अपने हथियार डाल दिए।
"बांग्लादेश तो आला, पण अरुण गेला।"*

पाकी के मन में अरुण का सम्मान था,
तब उसे पता न था, अरुण 21 का था।
पश्चाताप हुआ, पर वो भी तो मजबूर था,
सालों बाद वीर के पिता-समक्ष रोया था।

"The Martyrdom of a Paramvir (Arun Khetrapal)"

Composed and translated by: "Loquacious doctor" Dr. P. N. Sharma
Born to battle
The youngest recipient of India's Highest Gallantry Award
The "Param Vir" Chakra

Son of a soldier father and mother Maheshwari,
a dear name he was given: Arun Khetrapal.
Like his namesake, the sun, his aura shone bright;
his only small wish was just to touch the sky.

The hope of his parents, the apple of their eyes,
a tall, strong, and idealistic young Arun.
His own dreams, his entire life;
how did he put everything on line?

He was just twenty-one years old, a young man still;
childhood had passed, but youth had not yet fully arrived.
He had barely begun the life of a soldier,
when he embraced a soldier's heroic death.

His Young Officer's training was not yet complete,
when the call to duty came: the war of '71 had begun.
Taking leave of his family, the brave one departed,
a smiling, reassuring, and cherished young son.

In his heart was the desire for the Param Vir Chakra,
and, if he survived, to play golf in Lahore.
To celebrate with his victorious comrades;
but destiny had other plans in store.

In 1971, in the Shakargarh Sector, the Battle of Basantar;
the infantry battalion had already advanced.
It was surrounded by Pakistani-American Patton tanks;
the 17 Poona Horse Centurions were their protectors.

Commander "Hunty" Hanut Singh,
was not ready to risk the inexperienced Arun.
But Arun was adamant, he argued his case;
how could Arun be kept away from his dreams?

"Famagusta" was the name of his tank;
a unique name, for a destined task.
An active minefield lay in their path;
they had to cross it under the darkness of the night.

"How can we leave our infantry all alone?"
Everyone took the risk; they crossed the field.
They were facing the enemy's modern tanks,
but no one was scared, and no one retreated.

The battle was fierce and raged until the very end;
Arun himself destroyed four enemy tanks.
His body was bloodied, but his courage was indomitable.
"Famagusta" was broken, but its cannon still had fire.

The commander kept ordering him to retreat,
but Arun, unwilling, broke off the radio link.
His eyes were fixed on the fifth Patton tank;
both of them fired their shells at the same time.

Both shots were true, both targets were hit;
the Pakistani commander, by a stroke of luck, survived.
But martyrdom was written in Arun's fate;
the Pakistani knew he had faced a lion.

The sun (Arun) rose in the sky, while the son (Arun) set on the earth.
And the irony of fate: within a few hours,
the defeated enemy laid down their arms.
"Bangladesh was gained, but Arun was lost."[19]

The Pakistani commander held great respect for Arun;
at the time, he did not know that Arun was only twenty-one.
He was filled with remorse, but he too had been helpless;
years later, he wept before the hero's father.

[19]A Marathi phrase expressing the bittersweet nature of the victory.

"सबसे कम उम्र के परमवीर चक्र प्राप्तकर्ता"

लंबे-तगड़े सेकेंड-लेफ़्टिनेंट अरुण खेत्रपाल का जन्म एक सैनिक परिवार में हुआ था। उन्हें सर्वोच्च बलिदान व समर्पण के लिए भारत सरकार द्वारा 1972 में मरणोपरांत परमवीर चक्र से सम्मानित किया गया था। उनके दादा प्रथम विश्व युद्ध में, तथा पिता, ब्रिगेडियर खेत्रपाल, द्वितीय विश्व युद्ध और 1965 की लड़ाई में लड़ चुके थे। वीर की माताश्री का नाम माहेश्वरी था।

जन्म:14 अक्टूबर 1950। **सैन्य-जीवन का आरंभ:**13 जून 1971। **बलिदान:**16 दिसंबर 1971 (केवल सात माह के सैन्य-जीवन के पश्चात्)।

1971 में युद्ध के बादल मंडराते ही, ट्रेनिंग कर रहे युवा सैनिक-अफ़सरों को कोर्स के बीच से ही बुला कर रेजिमेंट में भेजने का फ़ैसला लिया गया। अरुण खेत्रपाल भी उनमें से एक थे। वो और उनके साथी ट्रेन से दिल्ली आए थे, जहाँ से अरुण ने अपनी मोटरसाइकिल उतरवाई और घर पहुँच गए।

अगले दिन परिवार ने देखा कि अरुण अपना सामान बाँध रहे हैं, जिसमें उन्होंने एक सूट और गोल्फ़-किट भी रखा था। पूछने पर, अरुण ने कहा, "जीतने के बाद मैं लाहौर में गोल्फ़ खेलूँगा; पार्टी भी तो होगी ही। ये उसी की तैयारी कर रहा हूँ।" उसी शाम वे फ्रंट के लिए रवाना हो गए।

1971 के भारत-पाक युद्ध के पश्चिमी मोर्चे पर, शकरगढ़-सेक्टर में बसंतर का युद्ध हुआ। पाकिस्तान के पास 5 बटालियन और आधुनिक पैटन-टैंक थे, जबकि भारत के पास केवल 3 बटालियन और और 17 पूना-हार्स के पुराने सेंचुरियन-टैंक थे। पाकिस्तान का पलड़ा काफ़ी भारी था।

अरुण के कमांडर, कर्नल हनूत सिंह (महावीर चक्र), उन्हें आगे भेजने से हिचक रहे थे क्योंकि वे अभी पूरी ट्रेनिंग के बिना और अनुभवहीन थे। पर अरुण ने उन्हें यह कह कर मना लिया कि अगर वो इस युद्ध में भाग नहीं ले पाए, तो शायद ही उन्हें अपने जीवन में युद्ध

का तजुर्बा फिर कभी मिल पाए। उनकी ज़िद से विवश हो कर ही कर्नल हनूत सिंह उन्हें युद्ध में आगे भेजने के लिए माने।

तीन सेंचुरियन-टैंकों के साथ, 17 पूना-हॉर्स के सेकेंड-लेफ़्टिनेंट अरुण खेत्रपाल को पाकिस्तानी 13-लांसर्स के पैटन-टैंकों को रोकने की महती ज़िम्मेदारी दी गई। अरुण के सेंचुरियन-टैंक, "फ़ामागुस्ता" का नाम साइप्रस के एक बंदरगाह के नाम पर रखा गया था।

उनके साथ एक अनुभवी वरिष्ठ सूबेदार थे, लेकिन एक्शन शुरू होने के मात्र एक घंटे के अंदर ही वे वीरगति को प्राप्त हुए। उनके दूसरे साथी, रिसालदार-मेजर नत्थू सिंह, बचे रहे, जिन्होंने बाद में इस घटना का पूरा विवरण दिया।

16 दिसंबर की अँधेरी रात में, पूना-हॉर्स के तीनों टैंक एक कतार में आगे बढ़े। हर टैंक, अगले टैंक के पीछे जल रही एक छोटी-सी लाल बत्ती के सहारे चल रहा था। वो बत्ती ज़मीन की तरफ़ केवल हल्की-सी रोशनी दे रही थी, ताकि दुश्मन को वे नज़र न आएँ। उनको बारूदी-सुरंगों से बिछे डेढ़ किलोमीटर के रास्ते को पार करना था, और इतना समय नहीं था कि सैपर-टुकड़ी उन सुरंगों को निष्क्रिय कर पाती। एक बड़े हमले के लिए पाकिस्तानी टैंक जमा हो रहे थे, और अगर भारतीय टैंक समय पर नहीं पहुँचते, तो उन्हें रोकना कठिन हो जाता। समय की कमी को देखते हुए, ख़तरा उठा कर कैप्टन मल्होत्रा, लेफ़्टिनेंट अहलावत और सेकेंड-लेफ़्टिनेंट अरुण खेत्रपाल को 'बी' स्क्वाड्रन की मदद के लिए भेजा गया। भारतीय टैंकों ने कुछ ही समय में सात दुश्मन-टैंक ध्वस्त कर दिए, पर इसी बीच लेफ़्टिनेंट अहलावत का टैंक ख़ुद भी निशाना बन गया।

उसके तुरंत बाद ही अरुण के टैंक पर गोला लगा और उसमें आग लग गई। टैंक में आग तो लग गई थी, पर उसकी तोप अभी भी काम कर रही थी। कैप्टन मल्होत्रा ने अरुण को टैंक छोड़ने का हुक्म दिया, लेकिन इसके बावजूद अरुण पीछे हट रहे एक पाकिस्तानी टैंक को बरबाद करने में सफल हो गए। अब तक अरुण के खाते में छह टैंकों को बरबाद करने का श्रेय आ चुका था। कैप्टन मल्होत्रा बार-बार उनसे अपने टैंक को छोड़ने के लिए कह रहे थे। अरुण ने जवाब दिया, "मेरी गन अभी भी काम कर रही है... आई विल गेट दोज़।" इसके बाद, अरुण ने जान-बूझकर रेडियो-सेट बंद कर दिया। तब तक कैप्टन मल्होत्रा का टैंक भी बरबाद हो चुका था, तो अरुण को लगा कि अब सारी ज़िम्मेदारी केवल उन पर ही है।

इसके बाद, अरुण ने अपने अचल हो चुके टैंक से पाकिस्तान के कमांडर के टैंक पर निशाना साधा। उस टैंक ने भी अरुण के टैंक पर फ़ायर किया। दोनों टैंक एक-साथ ध्वस्त हो गए। पाकिस्तानी कमांडर तो कूद कर बच निकले, पर बुरी तरह से घायल अरुण अपने टैंक से बाहर नहीं निकल पाए और उन्होंने दम तोड़ दिया।

अरुण को इस वीरता के लिए भारत का सर्वोच्च वीरता पुरस्कार, परमवीर चक्र, दिया गया।

उसी दिन, मात्र कुछ ही घंटों के भीतर, दुश्मन ने हथियार डाल दिए। पूरे देश की तरह खेत्रपाल परिवार भी ख़ुश हो रहा था। वे जानते थे कि 16 दिसंबर को बसंतर में भयंकर टैंक-युद्ध हुआ है और वहाँ पर अरुण की रेजिमेंट ही लड़ रही है। वे सब अब अरुण का बेसब्री से इंतज़ार कर रहे थे। तभी घर की घंटी बजी। अरुण की माताजी ने दरवाज़ा खोला; वहाँ एक पोस्टमैन खड़ा था। उसके हाथों में एक टेलिग्राम था, जिसमें लिखा था, "डीपली रिग्रेट टु इनफ़ॉर्म यू, दैट योर सन सेकेंड लेफ़्टिनेंट अरुण खेत्रपाल रिपोर्टेडली किल्ड इन एक्शन ऑन 16 दिसंबर। प्लीज़ एक्सेप्ट सिंसियर कंडोलेंसेज़।" अरुण की माता वहीं बेहोश हो गईं और सारा परिवार सदमे में चला गया।

इस घटना के सालों बाद, अरुण के पिता, ब्रिगेडियर खेत्रपाल, की इच्छा हुई कि वे अपनी जन्म-भूमि सरगोधा देखने पाकिस्तान जाएँ। जब वे लाहौर पहुँचे, तो एक पाकिस्तानी ब्रिगेडियर ने उनका स्वागत किया। वे पाक-सेना की 13-लांसर्स के ब्रिगेडियर नासिर थे।

एक दिन, रात के खाने के बाद, ब्रिगेडियर नासिर उनके पास आकर बोले, "सर, मैं एक बात आपसे कहना चाहता हूँ। 16 दिसंबर 1971 की सुबह, आपका बेटा और मैं लड़ाई में आमने-सामने थे। मुझे अत्यंत दुःख है कि आपका बेटा मेरे हाथों ही मारा गया था। लड़ाई में अरुण की हिम्मत बेमिसाल थी। उसने जान की परवाह किए बिना, बहादुरी से हमारा मुक़ाबला किया। हम दोनों ने एक-साथ ही एक-दूसरे पर निशाना लगाया। भाग्य से मैं बच गया और अरुण शहीद हो गया। मैं आपके बेटे की बहादुरी और आपको भी सेल्यूट करता हूँ।"

पूरी घटना सुनने के बाद ब्रिगेडियर खेत्रपाल काफ़ी देर तक ख़ामोश रहे। फिर उन्होंने सिर्फ़ इतना कहा, "तुम अपनी ड्यूटी कर रहे थे और वह अपनी।"

The Youngest Recipient of the Param Vir Chakra

A tall and robust young man, Second Lieutenant Arun Khetrapal was born into a family of soldiers. For his supreme sacrifice and dedication, he was posthumously awarded the Param Vir Chakra by the Government of India in 1972. His grandfather had fought in the First World War, and his father, Brigadier M. L. Khetrapal, had fought in the Second World War and the 1965 war. The hero's mother's name was Maheshwari.

Born: 14 October 1950.
Military service began: 13 June 1971.
Sacrificed his life: 16 December 1971 (after only seven months of military service).

In 1971, as the clouds of war gathered, a decision was made to recall young military officers from their training courses and send them to their regiments. Arun Khetrapal was one of them. He and his fellow officers arrived in Delhi by train, from where Arun collected his motorcycle and went home.

The next day, his family saw him packing his bags, in which he had also placed a suit and his golf kit. When asked, Arun replied, "After we win, I am going to play golf in Lahore; there will be a party too. This is the preparation for that." That same evening, he left for the front.

On the western front of the 1971 Indo-Pak war, the Battle of Basantar took place in the Shakargarh Sector. Pakistan had five battalions and modern Patton tanks, while India had only three battalions and older Centurion tanks. The Pakistani forces had a considerable advantage.

Arun's commander, Colonel Hanut Singh (Maha Vir Chakra), was hesitant to send him to the front, as he was still an inexperienced officer who had not completed his training. But Arun convinced him, arguing that if he did not participate in this war, he might never get the experience of battle again in his life. Compelled by his insistence, Colonel Hanut Singh agreed to send him forward.

Along with two other Centurion tanks, Second Lieutenant Arun Khetrapal of the 17 Poona Horse was given the crucial responsibility of stopping the Patton tanks of the Pakistani 13th Lancers. Arun's Centurion tank, "Famagusta," was named after a port in Cyprus.

He was accompanied by an experienced senior subedar, but within an hour of the action starting, the subedar was killed. His other companion, Risaldar Major Nathu Singh, survived and later recounted the full details of the incident.

On the dark night of 16 December, the three tanks of the Poona Horse advanced in a line. Each tank followed the small red light burning on the back of the tank in front of it. The light cast only a faint glow towards the ground so that they would not be visible to the enemy. They had to cross a one-and-a-half-kilometre stretch of land riddled with mines, and there was not enough time for the sapper unit to deactivate them. Pakistani tanks were amassing for a major attack, and if the Indian tanks did not arrive in time, it would be difficult to stop them. Due to the lack of time, Captain Malhotra, Lieutenant Ahlawat, and Second Lieutenant Arun Khetrapal took the risk and were sent to help 'B' Squadron. In a short time, the Indian tanks destroyed seven enemy tanks, but in the process, Lieutenant Ahlawat's tank was itself hit.

Immediately afterwards, Arun's tank was hit by a shell and caught fire. Although the tank was on fire, its gun was still operational. Captain Malhotra ordered Arun to abandon the tank, but despite this, Arun succeeded in destroying a retreating Pakistani tank. By now, Arun was credited with destroying six tanks. Captain Malhotra repeatedly ordered him to abandon his tank. Arun replied, "My gun is still working... I will get those bastards." After this, Arun deliberately switched off his radio set. By then, Captain Malhotra's tank had also been destroyed, so Arun felt that the entire responsibility now rested on him alone.

After this, from his now immobile tank, Arun took aim at the Pakistani commander's tank. That tank also fired at Arun's. Both tanks were destroyed simultaneously. The Pakistani commander managed to jump out and save himself, but the badly wounded Arun could not get out of his tank and succumbed to his injuries.

For this act of bravery, Arun was awarded India's highest gallantry award, the Param Vir Chakra.

That very day, within a matter of hours, the enemy laid down their arms. Like the rest of the country, the Khetrapal family was also celebrating. They knew that a fierce tank battle had taken place at Basantar on 16 December, and that Arun's regiment was fighting there. They were all eagerly awaiting Arun's return. Just then, the doorbell rang. Arun's mother opened the door; a postman was standing there. In his hands was a telegram that read, "Deeply regret to inform you that your son, Second Lieutenant Arun Khetrapal, was reportedly killed in action on 16 December. Please accept sincere condolences." Arun's mother fainted on the spot, and the entire family went into shock.

Years after this incident, Arun's father, Brigadier Khetrapal, expressed a wish to visit his birthplace, Sargodha, in Pakistan. When he arrived in Lahore, a Pakistani brigadier welcomed him. He was Brigadier Naser of the Pakistani army's 13th Lancers.

One day, after dinner, Brigadier Naser came to him and said, "Sir, I want to tell you something. On the morning of 16 December 1971, your son and I were facing each other in battle. I am extremely sorry that your son was killed by my hands. In the fight, Arun's courage was unmatched. Without any thought for his own life, he fought us bravely. We both fired at each other at the same time. By a stroke of luck, I survived, and Arun was martyred. I salute your son's bravery, and I salute you."

After hearing the full story, Brigadier Khetrapal remained silent for a long time. Then he said only this: "You were doing your duty, and he was doing his."

परमवीरों की पराक्रम गाथा

स्वरचित मूल लेख (हिन्दी), "वाचाल चिकित्सक" — डॉ. पी. एन. शर्मा
28 जुलाई 2020

1947 में दुश्मन ने जब घेरा हिंद का ताज "काश्मीर",
लूटा, मारा, जन-जन को, किए जघन्य अत्याचार।
जब कांपे राजा हरिसिंह, लड़े नेहरू, पटेल, सोमनाथ[1],
करमसिंह[1], राणे[1], पीरू[1], उस्मान[2], वायुवीर व जदूनाथ[1]।

1962 में मिली हार, मां भारती हुई निढाल और बेरंग,
वीर थापा[1], शैतान सिंह[1], जोगिन्दर[1], जसवंत[2] संग,
खोए लाल अनेक, दंश गहरा था, पीड़ा अकल्पनीय,
सीख ली, बदलेंगे, बदला लेंगे, लिया संकल्प सराहनीय।

1965 में लाल बहादुर के नन्हे नेट्स ने, गिराए सेबर यान,
वृद्ध मिस्टियर, वैम्पायर, कैनबरा ने भी पाया नवयौवन।
नाथ[2], गुडमैन[2], गौतम[2], प्रेम[2], कीलर बंधु[3], नेब[3], राठौर[3],
ग्रीन[3], गांधी[3], पठानिया[3], संधू[3] ने तोड़ा शत्रु का अहंकार।

चाविंडा में परमवीर तारापोर[1] व साथियों का टूटा सब्र,
पूना हॉर्स सेंचुरियन टैंकों ने खोदी थी, पैटनों की कब्र।
हवलदार अब्दुल हमीद[1] ने खेमकरण में तोड़ा शत्रु तंत्र,
महत्वपूर्ण होते युक्ति, साहस और योद्धा, न होता यंत्र।

1971 में इंदिरा, मानेक शॉ, घुटनों आया पाक, हुआ दो फांक,
जब एडमिरल नंदा, एयर मार्शल लाल ने लगाई हांक।
सागर तल के हवाले हुई गाज़ी, आग में झोंकी कराची,
सेखों[1], मंगत[2], वायु वीरों ने नेट विमानों से रिपु कलाई तोड़ी।

अल्बर्ट एक्का[1], अरुण खेत्रपाल[1], होशियार सिंह[1],
साथियों संग पूरब व पश्चिम की जीती जमीनी जंग।
चांदपुरी[2] व साथियों ने, लोंगेवाल पैटन कब्रगाह बनाया,
ज्यादतियों का बदला लिया, बांग्लादेश भू पर आया।

1961 में गुरबचन सिंह[1] ने कांगो में शांति हेतु दिया बलिदान,
1987 श्रीलंका में उसी राह चले रामास्वामी परमेश्वरन[1]।
1987 में बाना सिंह[1] ने सियाचिन में इतिहास रच दिया,
"कायद चोटी" बनी "बाना चोटी", राजीव[3] का बदलालिया।

1999 में गरजा था सरल कवि वाजपेई का आहत दिल,
धोखा दे पहाड़ों पर चढ़ा बैरी, जख्मी किया कारगिल।
दहाड़ी बोफोर्स, गुर्राए मिराज, फहराई विजय पताका,
मनोज[1], संजय[1], योगेन्द्र[1], विक्रम बत्रा[1] बने परमवीर।

2016 में उरी कैंप पर आतंकी हमला, उन्नीस हुए शहीद,
कृद्ध मोदी, डोवाल और सोहाग ने ऐसे दांव लगाए।
10 दिन बाद भारतीय जांबाज़ पीओके में घुस गए,
सर्जिकल स्ट्राइक में 40 आतंकी व फौजी मार दिए।

2019 में पुलवामा अटैक, शहीद जवानों का बदला,
वायुसेना ने बालाकोट उड़ाया,300 आतंकी मार दिए।
डोवाल, जनरल रावत, एयर चीफ धनोआ का प्लान था,
दुश्मन घाव छिपाता, लीपापोती ही करता रह गया।

अगले दिन शत्रु ने हिमाकत की, हवाई हमला करा,
उनकी शान F-16, अभिनंदन वर्धमान[3] ने मार गिराया।
अभिनंदन पकड़े गए, पर साठ घंटे के भीतर रिहा हुए,
हिंद की भृकुटी यों तनी देख, दुश्मन घुटनों पर आ गए।

The Valor of Our Bravehearts

Written in Hindi and translated by "Loquacious Doctor" Dr. P. N. Sharma

---

In 1947, the enemy invaded Hind's crown, "Kashmir",
Looted, killed, committed heinous atrocities.
King Hari Singh trembled, Nehru, Patel stood firm,
Rose Somnath[1], Karam Singh[1], Rane[1], Piru[1], Jadunath[1], Usman[2],

In 1962, defeat struck, Mother India turned pale,
Thapa[1], Shaitan Singh[1], Joginder[1], Jaswant[2] stood tall.
Many sons lost, the wound ran deep, the pain was immense.
Lessons learned, resolve to change, to avenge, was intense.

In 1965, Lal Bahadur's Gnats downed Saber jets,
Old Mystere, Vampire, Canberra regained their zest.
Nath[2], Goodman[2], Gautam[2], Prem[2], Keeler Bandhu[3], Neb[3], Rathore[3],
Green[3], Gandhi[3], Pathania[3], Sandhu, shattered the enemy's sheen.

In Chawinda, Tarapore[1] and troops lost patience,
Poona Horse Centurions dug Patton's grave with defiance.
Abdul Hamid[1] broke the enemy's spine at Khemkaran,
It's courage and strategy, not machines, that win wars.

In 1971, Indira and Manek Shaw split Pakistan in two,
Admiral Nanda, Air Marshal Lal led the breakthrough.
Submarine Ghazi was sunk, Karachi burned in flames,
Sekhon[1], Mangat's[2] Gnats broke enemy's game.

Albert Ekka[1], Arun Khetarpal[1], Hoshiar Singh[1],
won ground battles on both Eastern and Western wings.
Chandpuri[2] turned Longewal into Patton's tomb,
avenged the atrocities, Bangladesh was born.

In 1961, Gurbachan Singh[1] gave his life for Congo peace,
In 1987, R. Parameswaran[1] followed that noble lease.
Bana Singh[1] rewrote history at Siachen's height,
"Quaid Hill" renamed "Bana Hill", avenged Rajeev[3].

In 1999, poet PM Vajpayee's heart roared in pain,
Foe climbed the peaks, Kargil bled again.
Bofors thundered, Mirages growled, Tricolour soared,
Manoj[1], Sanjay[1], Yogendra[1], Batra[1], Paramveers restored.

In 2016, terrorists struck Uri camp, 19 martyred,
Furious Modi, Doval, Sohag, tactics chartered.
Within 10 days, Indian braves entered POK,
Surgical strike, 40 terrorists and soldiers slain.

In 2019, Pulwama attack, revenge was swift,
Air Force bombed Balakot, 300 terrorists adrift.
Doval, General Rawat, Air Chief Dhanoa's plan,
Foe tried to hide wounds, but failed to withstand.

Next day, enemy dared an air attack,
Their pride, F-16, Abhinandan Varthaman[3] shot it down.
Captured, but freed within 60 hours,
India's fierce gaze, made the enemy cower.

[1] Param Vir Chakra Winner

[2] Maha Vir Chakra Winner

[3] Vir Chakra Winner

All 21 "Param Vir Chakra" Awardees

Of these 21 heroes, 17 were awarded the medal posthumously. As of today, three of the living recipients are still with us.

Indo-Pakistani War (1947–48)

Major Somnath Sharma (Posthumous), 1947

Naik Jadunath Singh (Posthumous), 1948

Second Lieutenant Rama Raghoba Rane, 1948 (Died 1994)

Company Havildar Major Piru Singh Shekhawat (Posthumous), 1948

Lance Naik Karam Singh, 1948 (Died 1993)

Congo - UN Peacekeeping Mission (1961)

6. Captain Gurbachan Singh Salaria (Posthumous), 1961

Sino-Indian War (1962)

7. Major Dhan Singh Thapa, 1962 (Died 2005)
8. Subedar Joginder Singh (Posthumous), 1962
9. Major Shaitan Singh Bhati (Posthumous), 1962

Indo-Pakistani War (1965)

10. Company Quartermaster Havildar Abdul Hamid (Posthumous), 1965
11. Lieutenant Colonel Ardeshir Burzorji Tarapore (Posthumous), 1965

Bangladesh Liberation War (1971)

12. Lance Naik Albert Ekka (Posthumous), 1971
13. Flying Officer Nirmal Jit Singh Sekhon (Posthumous), 1971
14. Second Lieutenant Arun Khetrapal (Posthumous), 1971
15. Major Hoshiar Singh Dahiya, 1971 (Died 1998)

Siachen Conflict (1987)

16. Naib Subedar Bana Singh (Living), 1987

Sri Lanka - Indian Peace Keeping Force (1987)

17. Major Ramaswamy Parameswaran (Posthumous), 1987

Kargil War (1999)

18. Captain Manoj Kumar Pandey (Posthumous), 1999
19. Captain Vikram Batra (Posthumous), 1999
20. Rifleman Sanjay Kumar (Living), 1999
21. Grenadier Yogender Singh Yadav (Living), 1999

"Valor of the Rat Miners"

"श्रमवीरों की पराक्रम-कथा"

"उत्तराखंड टनल-परीक्षा 2023"

स्वरचित: "वाचाल चिकित्सक" (डॉ. पी. एन. शर्मा)

वहाँ 41 साँसें पल-पल घुट रही थीं,
यहाँ उद्विग्न हम, लाचारी से देख रहे थे।
करने वाले जो बन पड़ा, सो कर रहे थे,
फिर भी साँसें हमारी, थमी जा रही थीं।

हठात् बड़ा देश, छोटा परिवार बन गया,
सारे मतभेद, धर्म और जाति भूल गया।
प्रतिदिन सुबह-सवेरे, पालते थे आशा,
दिन ढलता, हाथ आती केवल निराशा।

वे 41 भी प्राण-प्रण से डटे हुए थे,
संकट, भय, निराशा को झटक रहे थे।
गब्बर नेगी ने भीतर कमान सँभाली,
अनुशासन में ढाला, आस भर डाली।

आशा और हौसला अंदर से बाहर,
और बाहर से अंदर, आ-जा रहा था।
परिजन निश्चित ही भयभीत थे, पर,
यही लेन-देन निराशा पर भारी था।

प्रधान, सामान्य, विशेषज्ञ, सेना, विदेशी जुटे थे,
आधुनिकतम मशीनें और जतन लगे थे।
सफलता निकट थी, पर फिसल रही थी,
धैर्य, कौशल-परीक्षा की विकट घड़ी थी।

17 दिन रीत गए, यत्न अधूरे रह गए,
तब विकल्प बन, 12 अनजाने आ गए।
अजब "रैट-माइनर" नाम से जाने गए,
डूबते को तिनके का सहारा माने गए।

जटिलताओं का उन्हें पूरा भान था,
निज पर मँडराते ख़तरों का ज्ञान था।
उन्हें स्व-क्षमता पर पूर्ण विश्वास था,
मन भाईचारे, जोश से आंदोलित था।

ख़तरे ताक पर रख, बीड़ा उठा लिया,
फिर दुर्गम में, सबल क़दम बढ़ा दिया।
ख़ुद की साँसों में धूल घुल रही थी,
पर अनजानी साँसों की फ़िक्र थी।

अंततः जय मिली, आत्म-विश्वास, शौर्य से,
लगन और अथक सम्मिलित प्रयास से।
यह प्रकरण हमें आशा, विश्वास दे गया,
राष्ट्र-चरित्र, सामर्थ्य का परिचय दे गया।

"Uttarakhand Tunnel Ordeal, 2023"

Composed and translated by: "Loquacious doctor" Dr. P. N. Sharma

---

Forty-one souls were suffocating, moment by moment;
here, we watched on in helpless anxiety.
The rescuers were doing everything they possibly could,
and still, our own breath was catching in our throats.

Suddenly, a large country became a small family,
forgetting all differences of religion, caste, and class.
Every morning, we would awaken nurturing a new hope;
but as each day ended, only despair came to hand.

Those forty-one men also stood firm, with all their life's will;
they were shaking off crisis, fear, and despair.
Inside, Gabbar Singh Negi[20] took command;
he moulded them into a disciplined force and filled them with hope.

Hope and courage travelled from the inside out,
and from the outside in.
Their family members were certainly facing scare,
but this exchange of hope was overpowering their despair.

The Prime Minister, common people, experts,
the army and foreigners had all assembled;
the most modern machines and all possible efforts were employed.
Success was near, yet it kept slipping away;
it was a terrible moment, a test of patience and skill.

---

[20]Gabbar Singh Negi: One of the trapped workers who, as the foreman, helped maintain morale and discipline inside the tunnel.

Seventeen days passed, and all efforts had failed;
then, as a new option, twelve unknown men arrived.
They were known by the strange name of "rat-miners,[21]"
and they were seen as a drowning man's last straw.

They were fully aware of the complexities of the task,
and of the dangers that loomed over their own heads.
But they had complete faith in their own abilities;
their hearts were stirred with brotherhood and zeal.

Putting the dangers aside, they took up the challenge;
they advanced their strong steps into that impassable place.
Dust was choking their own breaths,
but their only concern was for those unknown souls.

In the end, victory was achieved, through self-confidence and valour,
through dedication and tireless, joint effort.
This episode gave us all new hope and faith;
it was a testament to the nation's character and its strength.

[21]Rat-miners: A term for miners who use a traditional, narrow-tunnel digging technique, which ultimately proved successful in reaching the trapped men.

"एक अकविता"

स्वरचितः "वाचाल चिकित्सक" (डॉ. पी. एन. शर्मा)

इस बुढ़ापे में सनक की बानगी देखें,
एक ज़रूरी, बड़ी मशीन, पसंदीदा,
न ख़रीद, दूजी महँगी ख़रीद, ख़ुश हूँ,
फिर भी, आज मैं बहुत-बहुत ख़ुश हूँ।

दुश्मन-अर्थव्यवस्था को चोट दी, पर,
दुःख ये कि मशीन और महँगी होती,
तो ख़ुशी कितनी अधिक गहरी होती!
फिर भी, आज मैं बहुत-बहुत ख़ुश हूँ।

अब दीपावली का है बेसब्र इंतज़ार,
कुछ और तगड़ी चोट देने की तमन्ना।
दिवाली चाहे न मनाऊँ, या कम मनाऊँ,
इस इंतज़ार में ही, बहुत-बहुत ख़ुश हूँ।

आगंतुक एक सौम्यतम विदेशी चेहरा,
कहे कि हम एक और एक ग्यारह बनें।
पर मैं उसकी मक्कारी पहचान गया हूँ,
सच में, आज मैं बहुत-बहुत ख़ुश हूँ।

मैं ऐसा तो कभी भी, बिल्कुल न था,
पर अब तो ऐसा हो गया हूँ, इसलिए,
न पहचाना ख़ुद का अक्स आईने में।
फिर भी, आज मैं बहुत-बहुत ख़ुश हूँ।

देखो, कैसे भरे बुढ़ापे में बच्चा बन कर,
ऐसे ही, आज मैं बहुत-बहुत ख़ुश हूँ।
इस बुढ़ापे में सनक की बानगी देखें,
क्योंकि आज मैं बहुत-बहुत ख़ुश हूँ।

"An Un-Poem"

Composed and translated by: "Loquacious doctor" Dr. P. N. Sharma

See an instance of my obsession in this old age:
I did not buy a necessary, large, favourite machine;
instead, in vengeance, I bought a more expensive one happily.
And still, today, I am very, very happy.

I hurt the enemy's economy a dime, but,
my only regret is that if the machine had been even more expensive,
my happiness would have been that much deeper.
And still, today, I am very, very happy.

Now, I am impatiently awaiting Deepawali[22],
with a desire to land a few more heavy blows.
Even if I do not celebrate Deepawali, or celebrate it with less pomp,
just in this anticipation, I am very, very happy.

A visitor comes, with the gentlest of foreign faces,
and says that we should become like one and one making eleven.
But I have recognised his cunning;
truly, today, I am very, very happy.

I was never revengeful at all like this before,
but now I have become one, and that is why,
I could not recognise my own reflection in the mirror.
And still, today, I am very, very happy.

See how, in my ripe old age, I have acted like a child;
just for that avengement, today, I am very, very happy.
See the madness in me, at this old age;
because of that, today, I am very, very happy.

[22]Deepawali: A major Hindu festival of lights, often associated with significant purchases.

"मैं हूँ सीमा का प्रहरी"

स्वरचित: "वाचाल चिकित्सक" (डॉ. पी. एन. शर्मा)

कानों में गूँजती बच्चे की मासूम किलकारियाँ,
नज़रों में तैरते, प्रियतमा से विदाई के पल।
याद आते हैं, माता का कँपकँपाते हाथ,
उनका आशीर्वाद देना, भाल पर टीका करना
उनकी दर्दीली आँखों में झिलमिलाते अश्रु।
पिता के चेहरे पर सप्रयास गुम, अबोला दर्द,
दोस्तों की चुहल की आड़ में उनका ख़ौफ़,
जब चला था मैं, माँ भारती की पुकार पर।
ट्रेन से देखता रहा, अपना सब पीछे छूटता,
मन में दर्द, भविष्य के प्रति अनिश्चितता थी।

अपनापन लिए हमारा छोटा-सा कच्चा घर,
बूढ़े हो चली अम्मा और मितभाषी बाऊजी,
भीगती मूँछों लिए अल्हड़ छोटा भाई,
जवानी की दहलीज़ पर खड़ी बहना,
पर्दे की ओट खड़ी प्रियतमा, गोद में हमारा बेटा।
बचपन से जुड़ी ये गलियाँ, चौबारे और पेड़,
पुराने मित्र, खेल के मैदान, वो पुराना स्कूल,
ये चाचा-चाची, काका-काकी, वो बूढ़े ताऊ,
ये जीवन-भर की यादें, परिचित परिवेश,
क्या अपनों से, फिर कभी मिल पाऊँगा?

"मैं हूँ सीमा का प्रहरी"

पलटन में पहुँचा, तो मिला अब का परिवार,
हर चेहरा मुझसे बेहद जुदा, अलग रंग-रूप,
अलग प्रांत, अलग भाषा, अलग मिज़ाज,
अलग प्रकार के भोजन, अलग भगवान।
फिर भी हम, कैसे इतने एक हो चुके थे?
भरोसा ऐसा, कि एक-दूजे पर मर-मिटने को तैयार थे।
मुझे देखा तो सब दौड़े आए, लिपट गए,
क्षण में सारी थकान और रंज-ओ-ग़म हर ले गए।
काँधे पर उठा, नाचते-कूदते टेंट तक ले गए,
मेरे कोने में मेरा बिस्तर तैयार कर रखा था।

निहायत अपनेपन से, मेरा सामान खोल के,
माँ और भार्या की बाँधी गई मिठाई-नमकीन,
पूरे अधिकार से, बराबर बाँट के डकार गए।
फिर शुरू हो गया रोज़ाना का फ़ौजी रूटीन,
सरहद पर प्रकृति की आपदाओं के बीच,
रिपु के अनैतिक इरादों से संघर्ष का इरादा।
कहीं गहन वन, कहीं बियाबान रेतीले पथ,
हिमाच्छादित शिखरों पर घुटती साँसों बीच,
काँधे पर पिट्ठू में लदी यायावर ज़िंदगी,
नींद से दूर, हर वक़्त थकी पर चौकस निगाहें।

"मैं हूँ सीमा का प्रहरी"

माता के अप्रतिम सौंदर्य से अभिभूत,
उन वादियों पर न्योछावर मन लिए मैं,
माता की सीमाओं की पहरेदारी का ज़िम्मा,
देशवासियों के प्रेम, आदर, भरोसे का मान,
मैं सालों अपनी ज़िम्मेदारी निभाता रहा।
आज मेरे सीने में अकस्मात् धँसी गोली ने,
आख़िर मुझे पूर्ण-विश्राम का तोहफ़ा दे दिया।
और अब मैं अपने घर की यात्रा पर चला,
तन पर तिरंगा, तिरंगे पर फूल और मालाएँ,
मेरी आगवानी में चारों ओर जुटा जन-सैलाब।

द्वार पर पिता, मेरे दो दोस्तों के सहारे खड़े थे,
मैं चौंक गया, शायद कुछ बीमार हो गए होंगे।
बिलखती माँ देख, मैंने उसके कान में कहा,
"माई, रोती क्यों है? अब तो मैं वापस आ गया हूँ।"
पर वह कुछ सुन और समझ ही नहीं पाई,
भारी भीड़ थी और शोर जो इतना हो रहा था।
ख़ैर, मैंने सोचा, अभी कुछ नींद ले लेता हूँ,
बुरी तरह थके शरीर को विश्राम ज़रूरी है।
यह कोलाहल जब भी थमेगा,
तब मैं सबको मामला समझा दूँगा।

"मैं हूँ सीमा का प्रहरी"

"I am the Guardian Vanguard"

Composed and translated by: "Loquacious doctor" Dr. P. N. Sharma

The innocent cries of my child echo in my ears;
the moments of farewell with my beloved float before my eyes.
I remember my mother's trembling hands,
giving her blessing with placing the tilak on my forehead,
the unshed tears shimmering in her pained eyes.
My father's face, struggling to hide his unspoken grief;
the fear of my friends, concealed behind their playful banter,
as I left, answering Mother India's call.
From the train, I watched every thing mine recede behind;
my heart was in pain, the future uncertain.

My small, simple house, so full of belonging;
my aging mother and my reticent father;
my carefree younger brother, his moustache just beginning to show;
my sister, standing on the threshold of her own youth;
my beloved, standing behind the curtain, our son in her arms.
These streets, courtyards, and trees, tied to my childhood;
old friends, playing fields, that old school;
these uncles and aunts, those elders;
a lifetime of memories, this familiar world.
Will I ever be able to meet my loved ones again?

"I am the Guardian Vanguard."

When I reached the platoon, and joind my new family.
Every face was so different from mine, in colour and in form;
a different province, a different language, a different temperament,
a different kind of food, a different God.
And yet, how had we all become so one and so united?
Such was our trust that we were ready to die for one another.
When they saw me, they all ran to me, embraced me;
in a moment, they took away all my weariness and sorrow.
They lifted me onto their shoulders,
dancing and jumping all the way to the tent;
in my corner, my bed had been made ready for me.

With the utmost sense of belonging, they unpacked my luggage,
and the sweets and snacks packed by my mother and my wife,
they devoured with full authority, dividing them equally amongst themselves.
Then began the daily military routine:
on the border, amidst the calamities of nature,
the resolve to struggle against the immoral intentions of the enemy.
Sometimes a dense forest, sometimes a desolate, sandy path;
amidst the suffocating air on snow-covered peaks,
a wanderer's life, loaded in a pack on my shoulders;
far from sleep, my eyes were always tired, but always alert.

"I am the Guardian Vanguard."

Overwhelmed by the unparalleled beauty of the Motherland,
with my heart sacrificed to those valleys,
I took on the duty of guarding the Mother's borders,
honouring the love, respect, and trust of my countrymen;
for years, I fulfilled my responsibility.
Today, a bullet that suddenly lodged in my chest,
has finally given me the gift of complete rest.
And now, I have set out on the journey towards my home,
the Tricolour draped on my body, flowers and garlands on the Tricolour,
and a sea of people gathered all around to welcome me.

At the door stood my father, supported by two of my friends.
I was startled; perhaps he had fallen ill.
Seeing my wailing mother, I whispered in her ear,
"Mother, why are you crying? I have come back now."
But it seems, she could not hear or understand a thing;
there was such a huge crowd, and so much noise.
"Never mind," I thought, "I will take some sleep now".
Rest is essential for this terribly tired body.
Whenever this commotion subsides,
I will explain the matter to everyone."

"I am the Guardian Vanguard."

"वाचाल भारतीय" पर लोग मुझे इंडियन कहते हैं।

स्वरचित: "वाचाल चिकित्सक" (डॉ. पी. एन. शर्मा)

मैं हूँ एक "वाचाल" भारतीय,
आप जैसा "होमो-सेपियन"।
हो सकता हूँ अनजाना शायद,
बता दूँ, लोग मुझे इंडियन कहते हैं।

आप लोगों के जैसे सारे सपने,
वैसे ही बुनता, पालता हूँ मैं भी।
फ़र्क़ नहीं मुझमें और आपमें,
पर शायद कुछ फ़र्क़ है ज़रूर।

मैं इस फ़र्क़ को तवज्जो नहीं देता,
आप देते हों, तो मुबारक आपको।
हम अपने ईश्वर को, अलहदा मानें,
पर वो एक ही परम है, यह जानें।

मैं कुदाल, फावड़े आदि ले कर,
इस खाई को पाटने निकला हूँ।
आप चाहें तो मेरा हाथ बटाएँ,
काम यक़ीनन आसान होगा।

"I am a Vocal Bharatiya" But people call me Indian.

Composed and translated by: "Loquacious doctor" Dr. P. N. Sharma

---

I am a "Vocal Bharatiya[23],"
a "Homo sapien" just like you.
I may be a stranger to you, perhaps,
but let me tell you, people call me Indian.

Like all your own desires and dreams,
I too weave them, I too nurture them.
There is no great chasm between you and me,
but maybe there is some difference, after all.

I do not give this difference any importance;
if you do, then congratulations to you.
We may give our God different names,
but let us keep it in mind that the Supreme Being is one.

I have set out with my spade and my shovel,
to fill this gaping chasm between us.
If you wish, you can lend me a hand;
the task will certainly be easier.

---

[23]Bhartiya: A person from Bharat, the Hindi name for India. The term is often used to invoke a deeper, more indigenous sense of national identity.

CHAPTER – 2

प्रकृति, वनस्पति, पशुपक्षी, पर्यावरण

"सरिता सागर द्वार"

कवि और दार्शनिक ख़लील जिब्रान से प्रेरित।
स्वरचित: "वाचाल चिकित्सक" (डॉ. पी. एन. शर्मा)

मुहाने पे ठिठकी सरिता,
लख रौद्र सागर विशाल।
पर मिलना विवशता थी,
वापसी भी संभव न थी।

सागर ने पसार बाँहें अपनी,
पुकारा अपनी बिटिया को।
"तू अकारण क्यों कर डरती है?
मैं पिता, ये मायका है तेरा।"

जीवन-धात्री, माता धरती है,
धरती मेरी माँ, तेरी दादी है।
तुझ पर भी उनका क़र्ज़ है,
उसे चुकाना तेरा ही फ़र्ज़ है।

जीव के जीवन का सवाल है,
सर्वोत्तम अन्न-जल का दान है।
तेरे बिना, जीवन संभव नहीं,
अतः मैंने तुझे भेजा था वहीं।

जब तू जन्मी, थी अणु-अणु,
फिर बादलों का आकार पाया।
तेरा भ्राता समीर, छोड़ आया,
तुझे काका हिमालय के द्वार।

वहाँ हिम-रूप तूने पाया था,
पितामह सूर्य की आज्ञा मान।
हरियाली बिखेरती चहुँ ओर,
तू बह निकली, घर की ओर।

जब तू इस कठिन डगर चली थी,
झरनों में गिरी, पाषाणों में उलझी,
मानव-निर्मित प्रदूषण भी सहा,
तब चोट तो अवश्य पहुँची होगी।

देख कटे जंगल और लुटती रेत,
राह में बनाए गए नाना अवरोध,
तुम ग़ुस्से से उफन भी पड़ी थीं,
तटों की मर्यादा तुमने तोड़ी थी।

पर शांत हो, सच बताना मुझको,
हँसते-गाते, आह्लादित जन-जन,
हरे-भरे खेत, खलिहान, कानन,
चारों ओर क्या न दिखे तुझको?

हम जल के ही विभिन्न स्वरूप हैं,
जीवन हम पर ही निर्भर होता है।
विधाता ने यह काम हमें सौंपा है,
तूने ये महत्त्वपूर्ण कार्य निभाया है।

अब तुझे विश्राम-काल मिला है,
मेरी बाँहों में खेल, कूद या मचल।
अगले वर्ष पुनः ये चक्र आएगा,
तब तक तू, मैं बन, जीवन जी ले मन का।

"The River at the Ocean's Door (Fear)"

Inspired by the poet and philosopher Kahlil Gibran[24]
Composed and translated by: "Loquacious doctor" Dr. P. N. Sharma

---

The river hesitated at the estuary,
seeing the ocean's fierce, vast expanse.
But to merge was her destiny;
turning back was no longer an option.

The ocean, spreading its arms wide,
called out to its daughter.
"Why are you so afraid, for no reason?
I am your father, and this is your home."

"Mother Earth is the giver of all life;
she is my mother, and your grandmother.
You too owe a debt to her;
it is your duty to repay it.

It is a matter of life for all creatures,
and the greatest gift is that of food and water.
Without you, life is not possible;
that is why I sent you there.

When you were born, you were but an atom,
then you took the shape of the clouds.
Your brother, the Breeze, took you,
and left you at the door of your uncle, the Himalayas.

---

[24]Kahlil Gibran (1883-1931) was a Lebanese-American writer, poet, and philosopher, most famous for his book The Prophet.

There you took the form of snow,
and obeying the command of your grandfather, the Sun,
spreading greenery in all directions,
you flowed back towards your home.

When you walked that difficult path,
falling in cascades, entangled in rocks,
enduring man-made pollution,
you must surely have been hurt.

Seeing the felled forests and the plundered sand,
and the many barriers built in your way,
you seethed with rage,
and broke the boundaries of your banks.

But be calm now, and tell me the truth:
the laughing, singing, joyful people,
the green fields, the barns, the forests;
did you not see them all around you?

We are but different forms of water;
the elixir of life and all depend on us.
The Creator has entrusted this work to us,
and you have fulfilled this important task.

Now you have a time of rest;
play in my arms, leap and frolic.
Next year, the cycle will repeat itself;
until then, become me, and live the life of your heart."

"पता नहीं मौसम क्यों बौरा रहा"

स्वरचित: "वाचाल चिकित्सक" (डॉ. पी. एन. शर्मा)

पता नहीं मौसम क्यों ऐसे बौरा रहा,
वर्षा न आई, तो कब तक न आई।
और जब आई, तो जाना भूल गई,
उत्तर से दक्षिण, केरल तक डूब गया।

समंदर धरती पर चढ़ता जा रहा है,
पढ़े-लिखे मौसम-विज्ञानी कहते हैं।
यह ग्लोबल-वार्मिंग का ही असर है,
पर हमें लगा, इस बेर ठंड कड़क है।

"I Don't Know Why the Weather Has Gone Mad"

Composed and translated by: "Loquacious doctor" Dr. P. N. Sharma

---

I don't know why the weather has gone so crazy;
the rains did not come, and for so long, they did not come.
But when they did come, they forgot when to wane;
from north to south, even Kerala was drowned.

The seas are rising over the lands,
or so the educated meteorologists say.
They say it is the effect of global warming,
but all I felt was that this year, the cold was unusually harsh.

"पतझड़ की छटा और कथा"

स्वरचित: "वाचाल चिकित्सक" (डॉ. पी. एन. शर्मा)

वसंत-काल में नव-पल्लव-स्फुटन हेतु,
प्रौढ़ पात, खोते रंगत व कुम्हला जाते।
आए पतझड़, स्वयं झर-झर विदा लेते,
बहार माँगते तरु, फैला विपर्ण भुजाएँ।

नयनों से ओझल था जो नभ-आनन,
मध्य गहनतम आच्छादित कानन।
शाख़ से विलग, जब पर्ण गिरे भुवि पर,
सहसा हुआ उठ खड़ा, नज़रों के आँगन।

स्वयं धूल-धूसरित, विस्मृत, बिसरित,
निहारें नव-पर्ण-आच्छादित तरु-शीर्ष।
जन-मन आह्लादित, ख़ुशियाँ मनाते,
पर वे तो पग-तले, तार-तार हो जाते।

प्रकृति का यही है प्राकृतिक विधान,
उम्रदराज़ की जगह लेते नौजवान।
पनपते नव-पर्ण, पुष्प और पुष्पज,
नई ऊर्जा से ओत-प्रोत हो मधुमास।

लघु जीवन-काल, कर निष्काम-कर्म,
प्रकृति-नियत आचरण, वे मानते धर्म।
प्रकृति-प्रदत्त, प्रकृति को ही लौटाते,
निस्वार्थ-प्रीत-कथा, तब सुनाते पर्ण।

बसंत-ॠतु का आगमन,
कुछ ही महीनों में हो जाएगा।
पेड़ फिर से पत्तियों, फूलों,
और फलों से लद जाएँगे।

"The Splendour and the Story of Autumn"

Composed and translated by: "Loquacious doctor" Dr. P. N. Sharma
It is my independent composition & not a translation.

The AUTUMN is now finally here,
heralding the oncoming winter.
The leaves rustle in the breeze,
withered & now no more green.

Shortly will they part from the twigs,
through air, take a short fall, free.
From the perch, to the foot of tree,
a swinging, Swaying, Spiralling flight.

The tree branches, now stark naked,
ghostly, yet Beautiful in a way.
Hitherto, colorful sky concealed,
is Visible again, in jungles dense.

The trails on ground, are hidden,
under millions of fallen blades.
These crumble under our toes,
create the weird crackling tone.

A strange Godly phenomenon,
the old, have to pave the ways,
so, the fresh, energetic & young,
take up their duties from there.

The Spring would be ushered in,
in only a few months from now.
Trees would get laden up again,
with Foliage, Blossoms & Berries.

"ऋतुराज वसंत"

स्वरचित मूल लेख अंग्रेज़ी, और हिंदी अनुवाद: "वाचाल चिकित्सक" (डॉ. पी. एन. शर्मा)

सभी ऋतुओं में से,
वसंत राजा है।
यह हमें राहत देता है,
भले ही थोड़े समय के लिए।

जीवन में आशा जाग उठती है,
एक और सौर-चक्र जीने की।
यह उन कठिनाइयों से मुक्ति देता है,
जो अन्य ऋतुएँ हम पर ढाती हैं।

यह मुर्झाएपन को दूर कर,
ताज़गी और नूतनता बिखेर देता है।

सूरज पूरी चमक से दमकता है,
फिर भी हल्का और सुकून-भरा।
हवाएँ ख़ुशबुओं से संपृक्त होती हैं,
स्वच्छ और प्रदूषण-मुक्त होती हैं।

पत्तियाँ ताज़ी और चटख हरीतिमा लिए हुए,
शाखाएँ फूलों से लदी और अवनत होती हैं।
कीट नाचते-गाते पराग फैलाते हैं,
फल और बीज पैदा करने हेतु।

"Soothing Spring"

Composed originally in English by: "Loquacious doctor" Dr. P. N. Sharma

---

Of all the seasons,
Spring is the King.
It gives us relief,
even though brief.

The hope to survive rekindles,
to live another solar cycle.
It relieves us of the hardships,
that other seasons place upon us.

It clears away all that is withered,
and brings forth all that is fresh and new.

The sun shines brighter,
yet is milder and cosier.
The winds bear a fragrance,
and are clean and free of pollution.

The leaves are fresh and dark green,
the branches laden with flowers.
Insects sing their songs and spread the pollen,
to produce fruits and seeds.

"बरखा का मौसम"

स्वरचित: "वाचाल चिकित्सक" (डॉ. पी. एन. शर्मा)

हर मौसम अलग, अनूठी कहानी,
बसंत है ऋतुराज, तो बरखा रानी।

बसंत में मदमाती, महकती समीर,
बरखा में बूँदों, झरनों का संगीत।
एक-दूजे के पूरक, पूरे बरस का खेल,
अपना-अपना रूप, अपना महात्म्य।

समर बिखेरता झुलसाती, तीक्ष्ण उष्णता,
प्रशस्त करता वर्षा-ऋतु का आगमन।
सागर से उठ, इत-उत धरा पर बरसते,
मॉनसून का अमृत देता, सबको जीवन।

इंद्र-राज में, उमड़ते-घुमड़ते बदरा कारे,
कड़कता-चमकता वज्र, हृदय दहलाए।
इंद्रधनुष सुरम्य छटा, इतराए, भरमाए,
भरते नाले-नद, झर-झर झरते झरने।

बरखा की फुहारें, मिट्टी की सोंधी गंध,
चहुँ ओर छाती हरियाली, लुभाती मन।
हर्षित किसान, हरे खेत, भरे खलिहान,
उपज हो भरपूर, बगियों में छाएँ फूल।

झूम-झमाझम बरसे, निर्मल, शीतल जल,
तर-ब-तर तरुण मन, खिलें प्रणय-कमल।
काग़ज़ की छोटी नाव, छतरी की छाँव,
छप-छप करते भागें, छोटे-छोटे से पाँव।

चातक राग सुनाए, मोर का नाच सुहाए,
शोर मचाएँ सारे कीट-पतंग और मंडूक।
सावन के मेले, कितने ही तीज-त्योहार,
गीत गाते हर मन, हो उमंग से सराबोर।

"The Monsoon"

Composed in Hindi and translated by: "Loquacious doctor" Dr. P. N. Sharma

---

Every season has a different story to tell;
if Spring is the king of seasons, then the Monsoon is the queen.

In spring, an intoxicating, fragrant breeze blows;
in the monsoon, there is the music of raindrops and waterfalls.
They complement each other in a year-long game;
each has its own form, its own magnificence.

Summer spreads its scorching, sharp heat,
heralding the arrival of the rainy season, which soothes.
Rising from the ocean, raining here and there upon the land,
the nectar of the monsoon gives life to all.

In the reign of the Rain God, dark clouds swell and swirl,
the thunderbolt cracks and flashes, making the heart tremble.
The beautiful rainbow shows off its enchanting splendour;
streams and rivers overflow, and waterfalls cascade down.

The showers of rain, the sweet, earthy smell of the soil;
the greenery spreading all around, tempting the heart.
The farmers are joyous, the fields green, the barns are full;
the harvest is plentiful, and the gardens with flowers, are abloom.

Let the heavens pour down, cool and pure water;
young hearts are soaked, and the cupid plays its ploys.
Small paper boats, the shade of an umbrella;
a host of tiny feet run, with a pitter-patter sound.

The cuckoo sings its melody, the peacock's dance is pleasing;
all the insects, moths, and frogs make their own clamour.
The rainy season is full of many festivals and fairs;
every heart sings a song, drenched in hope and flair.

"बारिश का इंतज़ार था, मैं (कमल) खिल गया"

स्वरचित: "वाचाल चिकित्सक" (डॉ. पी. एन. शर्मा)

कमल उवाच

बारिश का इंतज़ार था, मैं खिल गया,
देवलोक का दरवाज़ा मानो खुल गया।
आ गए हैं भ्रमर-भँवरे, अपना राग सुनाने,
तितलियाँ बिखेरने, शोख़ पंखों की छटा।

कारी कोयल, कुहुक-कुहुक, कूकने लगी,
प्रसन्न-वदन परिंदे, आकाश चीरने लगे।
खेत, खलिहान, मैदान सब हरिताभ हो गए,
पर्वतों का सीना फाड़, झरने बह निकले।

तर-ब-तर तन में जैसे, बिजली दौड़ गई,
शिथिलता भागी, चपलता भर गई।
चेहरे पर टपकती ये बरसात की बूँदें,
जमा हुआ सारा अवसाद, पखार गईं।

यूँ वीरान-से पड़े, ये सारे ताल-सरोवर,
बरखा-फुहारों से, जैसे जीवंत हो उठे।
हो उठा "वाचाल", मेरा मुरझाया मन,
कहने लगा क़िस्से और गीत, नए-नए।

"The Awaited Rains Arrived, and I Blossomed (lotus)"

Composed and translated by: "Loquacious doctor" Dr. P. N. Sharma

"The Lotus Sang"

The awaited rains poured down, and I blossomed;
it seemed as if the doors to heaven had opened.
The bees and bumblebees have come, to sing their tunes;
the butterflies are also here, to show off the splendour of their bright wings.

The black cuckoo began to coo, to sing its song;
happy-faced birds began to tear across the sky.
The fields, the barns, the meadows all turned a verdant green;
bursting from the chests of the mountains, waterfalls gushed forth.

It was as if lightning ran through my drenched body;
languor fled, and liveliness filled me.
These raindrops, dripping on my face,
washed away all my accumulated gloom.

All the ponds and lakes, which had lain so desolate,
seemed to come alive with the monsoon showers.
My withered mind and soul became "Loquacious[25],"
and began to tell stories and sing songs, fresh and new.

[25]Loquacious: The author's pen name, meaning "talkative" or "chatty."

"छोटी सी जान, ऊँचे काम"

स्वरचित: "वाचाल चिकित्सक" (डॉ. पी. एन. शर्मा)

प्रकृति के नाना हैं चमत्कार,
हर कृति अनुपम व होनहार।
छोटे-से पखेरू भी लाँघ लेते,
सागर वृहद्, अति विकराल।

गोल्डन-प्लोवर, पक्षी नन्हे-से,
शीत से रक्षा, उनका अभिप्राय।
अलास्का से, सामूहिक उड़ान,
गंतव्य हवाई-द्वीप, है बहुत दूर।

सवा सहस्र कोस, सागर पार,
यात्रा भी अनवरत, लगातार।
घनघोर रात, मौसम की मार,
न नक़्शा, दाना-पानी, न विश्राम।

शरीर में है सीमित ऊर्जा-भंडार,
वायु-घर्षण से बचाव, एकमात्र उपाय।
सब उड़ते बनाकर, 'V' आकार,
बारी-बारी से झेलते, पवन-प्रहार।

कितना श्रम, कितना साहस,
लक्ष्य-साथी, अद्भुत सूझ-बूझ! (लाख)
सबसे ऊपर है आत्म-विश्वास,
वही करता उनका बेड़ा पार।

वे हमें समझा और दर्शा जाते,
अथक श्रम, सूझ-बूझ, साहस,
व आत्म-विश्वास के साथ-साथ,
सामूहिक प्रयास करे चमत्कार!

"The Valour of the Small"

Composed and translated by: "Loquacious doctor" Dr. P. N. Sharma

---

Nature harbours many wonders;
each of its creations is unique and promising.
Even a small bird can cross,
an ocean that is vast and monstrous.

The Golden Plover* is a tiny bird;
its only aim is to escape the severe cold.
A flock undertakes the flight from Alaska;
their destination is Hawaii, very, very far.

Over a thousand miles, across the open ocean;
the journey is continuous and arduous.
There are dark nights, and the weather is often brutal;
there is no map, no food, no water, and no rest.

Their bodies have limited energy reserves;
the only way out is to avoid air-drag.
They all fly in a 'V' shaped formation,
taking turns to bear the brunt of the winds.

What exemplary hard work, what exceptional courage!
A million partners, with amazing understanding.
But above all else, is their enormous self-confidence;
that is what carries them across to the other side.

They show us and teach us this lesson:
tireless hard work, understanding, courage,
and self-confidence, when combined with,
collective effort, can perform miracles.

गोल्डन-प्लोवर एक छोटा पक्षी है, जो अपने प्रवास के लिए प्रसिद्ध है। हर साल यह समुद्र के ऊपर, अलास्का से हवाई-द्वीप तक 4,000 किलोमीटर की उड़ान भरता है। यह सबसे छोटा मार्ग है और यह बिना रुके 88 घंटे की उड़ान होती है। रास्ते में कोई द्वीप नहीं है और यह पक्षी तैर नहीं सकता; अतः यात्रा में कहीं भी आराम के लिए रुकना असंभव है।

अब, आप ही बताएँ, आप परमेश्वर (सर्वोच्च निर्माता) की शक्ति को कैसे नकार सकते हैं? हवाओं की दिशा की समझ? गंतव्य के सबसे छोटे मार्ग की शिक्षा? रात के अँधेरे और प्रतिकूल मौसम की स्थिति में इस छोटे पक्षी का मार्गदर्शन कौन करता है?

The Pacific Golden Plover is a small bird, famous for its migration. Every year, it flies about 4,000 kilometres over the open ocean, from the US state of Alaska to the Hawaiian Islands.

This is the shortest route available to it, a non-stop flight of about 88 hours. There are no islands on the way where this bird, which cannot swim, could possibly rest or eat during its journey.

Now, you tell me, how can one deny the power of God (the Supreme Creator)? The sense of the direction of the winds? The knowledge of the shortest route to the destination? Who guides this tiny bird in the darkness of the night and through adverse weather conditions?

Note: *While the American Golden Plover also undertakes a remarkable migration, it is the Pacific Golden Plover (Pluvialis fulva) that is known for the non-stop flight between Alaska and Hawaii.*

"रंगों की छटा"

स्वरचित: "वाचाल चिकित्सक" (डॉ. पी. एन. शर्मा)

हर क़िस्म के रंगों की छटा छाई,
इस बदरंग जहाँ के एक कोने में।
ऐसी जगहें सुकूँ और ख़ुशियाँ देती हैं,
वर्ना जीना मुहाल कर रखा है इंसाँ ने।

"A Splash of Colour"

Composed & translated by: "Loquacious doctor" Dr. P. N. Sharma

---

A splash of every kind of colour has appeared,
in one small corner of this colourless world.
Such places give us peace and happiness;
otherwise, human beings have made life unbearable.

"मैं "मेपल टहनी" हूँ (फुनगी)"

स्वरचित मूल लेख अंग्रेजी और अनुवाद: "वाचाल चिकित्सक" (डॉ. पी. एन. शर्मा)

मेरे नीचे से गुज़र रहे, ऐ बच्चे,
ऊँचे पेड़ के शीर्ष तक देख।
हाँ, मैं "मेपल पेड़ की टहनी" हूँ,
ऊँचाई पर सवार और स्वतंत्र।

मंद-मंद हवा में लहराते हुए,
तुम शायद मुझे देख न पाओ।
क्योंकि मेरी संतानों, पत्तों, फूलों ने,
मुझे चारों ओर से पूरा ढँक रखा है।

तुम सोचोगे कि यहाँ मैं अकेला हूँ,
लेकिन नहीं, मैं अपने पूरे कुनबे के साथ हूँ।
तना मेरे दादा हैं,
और शाखाएँ, मेरे माता-पिता।

जो उपलब्ध है, मेरे पिता उसकी आपूर्ति करते हैं,
और जो परदादा जड़ हैं, वह तो दिखाई भी नहीं देते।
फिर भी, उन्हें जो-जो करना है, वह करते रहते हैं,
इसका ख़याल किए बिना कि कुछ तारीफ़ मिले।

जंगल में जो कुछ भी उग रहा है,
सब मेरे रिश्तेदार हैं, निकट के या थोड़े दूर के।
कीट, पशु-पक्षी, सब हमारे साथी हैं,
और कभी-कभी राहगीर भी आते हैं, जैसे आप।

जब शरद ऋतु आती है,
पर्ण अपना रंग और श्रृंगार बदलते हैं।
लेकिन जल्द ही, वे एक-एक करके झर जाते हैं,
इससे मैं कुछ देर के लिए काफ़ी दुखी होता हूँ।

जल्द ही मैं नवागंतुकों की व्यवस्था शुरू कर देता हूँ,
ये मुझे सजाएँगे, कुछ महीनों के लिए ही सही।
यह मुझे आनंद और जीवन-शक्ति से भर देता है,
और मैं प्रभु के चक्र के समक्ष शीश नवा देता हूँ।

मुझे एहसास होता है कि मेरे पर्ण, जो नीचे गिर गए,
मातृ-प्रकृति में पिघल और घुल रहे हैं।
वे अपनी आणविक संरचना को पुनः ग्रहण करते हैं,
वहाँ की अथाह गहराइयों और धरती की गोद में।

एक बार फिर, तने के माध्यम से वे,
शीर्ष पर पहुँच, मेरा नया क़बीला बनते हैं।
पहले पर्ण आते हैं, फिर फूल खिलते हैं,
भँवरे निषेचन करते हैं, फल और बीज लाते हैं।

वहाँ पहुँच, वे सूर्य-प्रकाश इकट्ठा करते हैं,
और वायु-प्रदूषण, जो मनुष्य की पैदाइश है।
वे सभी के साँस लेने के लिए स्वच्छ हवा बनाते हैं,
हम पर ही पशु, पक्षी और मानव-जाति निर्भर हैं।

मैं आजीवन ख़ुशी-ख़ुशी अपना रस-स्राव देता हूँ,
वह स्वस्थ, प्राकृतिक और मिठास देने वाला।
मेरी जो लकड़ी है, वह बहुत उपयोगी है;
मैं यहाँ देने के लिए हूँ, लेने के लिए नहीं।

मेरा जीवन-चक्र वास्तव में बहुत-बहुत लंबा है,
जब तक कि आँधी या मानव द्वारा गिराया न जाऊँ।
ठीक है, यदि तुम्हें चाहिए मेरी ज़मीन,
कम-से-कम, कहीं और वृक्षारोपण तो करो।

"I am the Maple Twig"

Composed and translated by: "Loquacious doctor" Dr. P. N. Sharma

---

Hey, child, passing under me,
look up to the top of the tall tree.
Yes, I am the "twig of the Maple tree,"
at the perch, riding high and free.

Swaying in the gentle breeze,
you may not notice me with eaze.
My progeny, the blooms and the blades,
cover me fully, from all sides.

You might think that here I am alone,
but no, I am with my whole clan.
The trunk is my grandfather,
and the branches, my parents.

Grand-Pa & Pa, supply me with what I need,
while my great-grand-pa, the root, is not even visible..
Yet they carry on doing what they have to do,
without a thought for a word of praise or two.

All that is growing in the forest,
are my relatives, near or a bit distant.
The birds and the animals are my companions,
and a few passers-by, just like you.

When the Autumn approaches,
the blades change their shades.
But soon, they fall, one by one;
it saddens me quite, for a while.

Soon I start arranging for the arrivals new,
Who will adorn me, through months a few.
This fills me with renewed joy and vitality,
and I submit to the cycles of the Almighty.

I realise that my blades fallen under,
are melting back into Mother Nature.
They re-assume their molecular structure,
in the depths and the lap of the earth there.

Once again, through the trunk,
they rise to the top and become my new clan.
First come the blades, then come the blooms;
bees fertilise them, and bring forth fruits and seeds.

Once there, they get busy, collecting the sunshine,
and the pollution in the air that humans create.
They make and release clean air for all to breathe;
on us, thrive the birds, the animals, and all humankind.

Lifelong, I bleed and gladly give my sap,
that healthy, natural sweetener.
The timber I make is very useful;
I am here to give, not to take.

I last a very, very long time in my cycle of life,
until I am felled by a storm, or by you.
It is alright, if you need the earth under me;
but at least plant my siblings, on some other site.

CHAPTER - 3

इतिहास, नायक

History & The Celebrity

महाराणा प्रताप: कालावधि

जन्म:९ मई, १५४०

राज्याभिषेक:२८ फ़रवरी, १५७२

हल्दीघाटी का युद्ध:१८ जून, १५७६

दिवेर का युद्ध:अक्टूबर, १५८२

पुण्य-तिथि:१९ जनवरी, १५९७

Maharana Pratap: A Timeline

Birth: 9 May 1540

Coronation: 28 February 1572

Battle of Haldi Ghati: 18 June 1576

Battle of Dewar: October 1582

Death: 19 January 1597

"महाराणा प्रताप"

स्वरचित: "वाचाल चिकित्सक" (डॉ. पी. एन. शर्मा)

हत कर राणा विक्रमादित्य, दासी-पुत्र बनवीर,
मेवाड़ हरा, रानी कर्णावती ने किया जौहर।
पन्ना धाय गूजरी ने किया निछावर स्व-सुत,
प्रताप-पिता, राणा उदय की प्राण-रक्षा अभिप्राय।

वीरता व जौहर-सजी वसुधा राजस्थान,
सिसोदिया राजपूत, मेवाड़-राज के वंश।
राणा उदय सिंह व जयवंता बाई के सुपुत्र,
१५४० में कुम्भलगढ़-किले में जन्मे प्रताप।

उनके जन्म के पूर्व ही राणा-वंशज मेवाड़,
हार गए कई क्षेत्र और राजधानी चित्तौड़।
कुलदेव "एकलिंगजी" ने तब लीला रची,
प्रताप को दी पूर्ण-विजय की ज़िम्मेदारी।

सात फ़ीट से भी ऊँची रौबीली काया,
तीखी मूँछें, बब्बर शेर की-सी छाया।
सौ किलो का जिनका कवच-ज़ंजीर,
अस्सी का भाला, दस की थी शमशीर।

राजपूताना आन-बान के वे प्रतीक बने,
घोड़ों के राजा, चेतक पर जो सवार हुए।
१५७२ में हो राजतिलक, मेवाड़-राणा बने,
राणा अनेक थे, महाराणा बस एक हुए।

अकबर-विरुद्ध, प्रताप अकेले खड़े थे,
दिल्ली-अरब-सागर के बीच में अड़े थे।
अकबर ने तब भेजे थे दूत अनेकानेक,
"ले लो आधा भारत, परंतु दे दो मेवाड़।"

"मेरी दासता स्वीकारो, दरबार में आओ,
शहंशाह अपना मानो, जागीर पाओ।"
प्रताप न माने, सर्वोच्च रखा निज मान,
न स्वीकारी अधीनता, बैर लिया ठान।

आपसी कलह, हिंद की सदा त्रासदी,
भाई जगमाल ने भी तो किया था घात।
जा मिला अकबर से, पाने को जागीर,
किया कलंकित राजपूतों का सम्मान।

सन् १५७६ को, पाँच-गुनी सेना सहित,
मुग़ल आ पहुँचे, उनको घुटनों पर झुकाने।
हल्दीघाटी पर डट गए, निडर प्रताप,
युद्ध-घोष हुआ, रक्त-पात अपूर्व हुआ।

"रामप्रसाद" मेवाड़ी हाथी ने मचाया ग़दर,
बारह मुग़ल हाथियों ने घेर कर बंद किया।
क़ैद में मौत स्वीकारी, अन्न-जल त्याग,
प्रताप का सेवक, था उन-सा मतवाला।

यह महाराणा प्रताप का ही बूता था,
सेनापति बहलोल ख़ान घोड़े सहित,
दो फाँक हुआ, एक वार से डाला काट।
फिर घिरे प्रताप, "चेतक" हुआ आहत।

"मान झाला" ने राज-छत्र धारण कर,
मुग़लों को भरमाया, भटकाया था।
वीर सेनापति ने प्राण निछावर कर,
इस तरह महाराणा को बचाया था।

चोटिल हुए प्रताप, घायल उनका घोड़ा,
चेतक भी चेतक था, कैसा अद्भुत दौड़ा!
जंगल, खेत और पहाड़ लाँघे, नाले फाँदे,
निकाल लाया स्वामी को, तब ही प्राण त्यागे।

हल्दीघाटी का दंश, स्वीकारा वनवास,
धरा थी बिछौना, शिला बनी सिंहासन।
घास की रोटी खाई, वे थे ही वैरागी-मन,
भीलों ने "कीका" नाम धर, दिया मान।

अरावली-पहाड़ियों में हुआ छापामार-रण,
मारने या मर-मिटने का उनका था प्रण।
था अजमेर-सूबेदार रहीम ख़ान-ए-ख़ाना,
अकबर का आदेश, "जीत लाओ मेवाड़।"

मेवाड़-सेनापति, कुँवर अमर सिंह युक्ति लगा,
पकड़ लाए समस्त ख़ान-ए-ख़ाना कुटुंब।
देख क़ैदियों को, लज्जित हुए प्रताप,
सादर सबको रिहा करवाया तत्काल।

सेठ भामाशाह ने तब किया अकूत दान,
प्रताप की ख़ाली झोली फिर भर दी थी।
सेना जुटा, १५८२ में हुआ दिवेर-रण प्रचंड,
जीता पुनः मेवाड़, राजधानी बनी चावंड।

अकबर उसके बाद सामने नहीं आया,
तब उन्नत हुआ मेवाड़, दिन-दूनी चाल।
सन् १५९७ में, शेर-आख़ेट-खेल दौरान,
ज़ख़्मी हो महाराणा गए स्वर्ग सिधार।

महाराणा के प्रयाण की सूचना पाने पर,
ऐसा सुना है, अकबर भी बहुत रोया था।
राजस्थानी भूमि पर, उनकी कितनी ही,
कहानी व गीत गाते, अब तक जन-जन।

"Maharana Pratap"

Composed and translated by: "Loquacious Doctor" Dr. P. N. Sharma

Having killed Rana Vikramaditya, the slave's son Banvir,
conquered Mewar; Queen Karnavati performed Jauhar[26].
The nursemaid, Panna Dai, sacrificed her own son,
with the intent to save Pratap's father, Rana Udai.

The land of Rajasthan is adorned with valour and Jauhar;
the Sisodia Rajputs, the line of the kings of Mewar.
The son of Rana Udai Singh and Jayavanta Bai,
Pratap was born in 1540 in Kumbhalgarh Fort.

Even before his birth, the Rana dynasty of Mewar,
had lost many territories and their capital, Chittor.
Then the family deity, "Eklingji," staged a divine play,
and gave to Pratap the responsibility of complete victory.

Over seven feet tall, an imposing figure,
with a sharp moustache, and the shadow of a lion.
His chain-mail armour weighed a hundred kilos;
his spear weighed eighty, and his sword weighed ten.

He became the symbol of Rajput honour and pride;
he who rode upon Chetak, the king of all stallions.
Crowned in 1572, he became the Rana of Mewar;
there have been many Ranas, but only one Maharana.

[26]Jauhar: The historical Hindu practice of mass self-immolation by women in parts of the Incian subcontinent, to avoid capture, enslavement and rape by any foreign invaders, when facing certain defeat during a war.

Against the Emperor Akbar, Pratap stood alone;
he stood stubbornly between Delhi and the Arabian Sea.
Akbar sent many envoys with an offer:
"Take half of India, but give me Mewar."

"Accept my suzerainty, come to my court;
accept me as your emperor, and receive an estate."
But Pratap did not agree; he held his honour supreme.
He did not accept subjugation, and instead vowed enmity.

Internal strife has always been the tragedy of India;
his own brother, Jagmal, also betrayed him.
He went and joined Akbar to get an estate,
and thus tarnished the honour of the Rajputs.

In the year 1576, with an army five times the size,
the Mughals arrived to bring them to their knees.
But the fearless Pratap stood firm at Haldi Ghati;
the cry of war was raised, and the bloodshed was unprecedented.

The Mewari elephant, "Ramprasad," created havoc,
until twelve Mughal elephants surrounded and captured him.
In captivity, he accepted death, refusing all food and water;
Pratap's servant was as defiant as his king.

Such was the might of Maharana Pratap,
that the commander Bahlol Khan, along with his horse,
was sliced in two with a single blow of his sword.
Then Pratap was surrounded, and his "Chetak" was wounded.

Man Singh Jhala, by wearing the royal parasol,
distracted and misled the Mughals.
The brave commander saved the Maharana,
by sacrificing his own life in the process.

Pratap was injured, and his horse was wounded,
but Chetak was Chetak; how amazingly he ran!
He crossed jungles, fields, and mountains, leaped over streams;
he brought his master to safety, and only then did he give up his life.

After the sting of Haldi Ghati, Pratap chose exile;
the earth was his bed, and a rock was his throne.
He ate bread made of grass, for he was a recluse at heart;
the Bhil tribesmen, in respect, named him "Kika."

In the Aravalli hills, a guerrilla war was waged;
his vow was to kill or be killed.
The subedar of Ajmer was Rahim Khan-i-Khanan,
and Akbar's order was, "Go and conquer Mewar."

Pratap's son, Amar Singh, devised a strategy,
and captured the entire family of Khan-i-Khanan.
But seeing the prisoners, Pratap was ashamed,
and had them all released immediately, with full honour.

The merchant Bhamashah then made a huge donation,
and Pratap's empty coffers were filled once more.
He gathered an army, and in 1582, the fierce Battle of Dewar was fought;
Mewar was retaken, and Chavand became the new capital.

After that, Akbar did not confront him again;
Mewar then progressed by leaps and bounds.
In the year 1597, while hunting a lion,
the Maharana was injured and passed into heaven.

Upon receiving the news of the Maharana's passing,
it is said that even Akbar wept a great deal.
On the land of Rajasthan, to this very day,
the people still sing his many stories and songs.

यह भारतीय युवाओं को हमारे गौरवशाली अतीत से, संक्षिप्त और रोचक तरीक़े से अवगत कराने के मेरे प्रयास का हिस्सा है।

मैं इस तरह के और लेख लिखने का इरादा रखता हूँ और आशा करता हूँ कि ये भारतीय मन को शिक्षित और प्रभावित करेंगे।

This is part of my endeavour to make the youth of India aware of our glorious past in a concise and interesting way.

I intend to write more such pieces, and I hope that they will educate and influence the minds of Indians.

"नवल-धवल हिंद-इतिहास"

स्वरचित: "वाचाल चिकित्सक" (डॉ. पी. एन. शर्मा)

पूर्व-लिखित, प्रायोजित, छद्म-इतिहास मिटा,
हम अपना इतिहास स्वयं लिखेंगे।
पुराने सफ़े फाड़, शौर्य, बलिदानों की असल गाथाएँ,
पुनः प्रचारित करेंगे।

अपनी दया, न्याय, स्वाभिमान, सामर्थ्य,
स्वातंत्र्य के गुणों का बखान करेंगे।
हाँ, कुछ स्याह पन्ने भी होंगे, वे ज़रूर चुभेंगे,
पर उन्हें भी स्वीकार अवश्य करेंगे।

देश-द्रोह, लोलुपता, कायरता, कालिख के क़िस्से,
भी नए पाठ में शामिल करेंगे।
प्रत्येक हिंदुस्तानी को आईना देखना और दिखाना,
भी अत्यंत ज़रूरी है।

हम अपनी हर बुरे पहलू, हर कमज़ोरी का सच्चा,
विश्लेषण कर, उसे दूर करेंगे।
तब ही तो जाकर, नवल, धवल, विनम्र पर सबल,
न्यायप्रिय हिंदुस्तान गढ़ेंगे।

"A New, Pure History of India"

Composed and translated by: "Loquacious doctor" Dr. P. N. Sharma

Erasing the previously written, sponsored, pseudo-history,
we will write our own history ourselves.
Tearing out the old pages, the true sagas of valour and sacrifice,
we will propagate them once more.

Our own qualities of kindness, justice, self-respect, and strength,
and the virtue of our freedom, we will praise.
Yes, there will be some dark pages, and they will certainly sting,
but we will surely accept them too.

The stories of treason, greed, shame and cowardice,
will also be included in the new treatise.
For every Indian to see themselves in the mirror, and to show it to others,
is also extremely important.

We will truthfully analyse every bad aspect, every weakness,
and we will remove it.
Only then will we be able to build,
a new, pure, humble but strong, and just Hindustan.

Lata Mangeshkar (1929–2022)

Lata Mangeshkar was a legendary and revered singer from India, who was lovingly titled the "स्वर-कोकिला (Swar Kokila)," meaning the Nightingale of songs. Over a career spanning eight decades, she recorded thousands of songs, mostly in Hindi but also in a great number of other Indian languages. The recipient of the Bharat Ratna, India's highest civilian honour, she was the most sought-after and respected female playback singer of her time.

"लता मंगेशकर को श्रद्धा-सुमन"

स्वरचित: "वाचाल चिकित्सक" (डॉ. पी. एन. शर्मा)

किसी ने कहा

स्वर्ग कहाँ है, कैसा है,
किसको है ख़बर?
जहाँ है, जैसा है,
आज से सुरीला है!

मैंने कहा

वाह कहूँ, या भरूँ आह,
आपने कहा, सही कहा।
जहाँ से, जन्नत छीन के,
जन्नत को जहाँ दे दिया।

उसे क्या कह कर कोसूँ,
उसके जहाँ, जन्नत दोनों।
उसने कभी इसको दिया,
उसने कभी उसको दिया।

अजब इत्तिफ़ाक़ है, कभी-कभार ही होता है,
विधाता के मन को कौन जान सकता है?

आज ही था जन्म-दिवस कवि प्रदीप का,
"ऐ मेरे वतन के लोगों" के रचयिता का।

क्यों आज को ही चुन के, किया महाप्रयाण,
"स्वर-कोकिला" जिसने गीत में फूँके प्राण?

"A Tribute to lata Mangeshkar"

Composed and translated by: "Loquacious doctor" Dr. P. N. Sharma

Somebody said:

Where is heaven, and what is it like?
Who has such knowledge?
But wherever it is, and whatever it is like,
from today onwards, it is more melodious.

I replied:

Should I say "bravo," or should I let out a sigh?
What you have said, you have said truly.
He has snatched paradise from the Earth,
and given the Earth to paradise.

What can I say to Him, why should I curse Him?
Both the Earth and paradise belong to Him.
At one time, He bestowed her upon the one;
this time, He has bestowed her upon the other.

It is a strange coincidence, one that happens only in ages;
who can understand the designs of the Creator?

Today was the birthday of the poet Pradeep,
the author of "Ae Mere Watan Ke Logon.[27]"
Why did she choose this very day for her great departure?
The "Nightingale of Song," who breathed life into that song.

[27] "Ae Mere Watan Ke Logon" (O, the People of My Country) is one of India's most famous patriotic songs, written by Kavi Pradeep and famously sung by Lata Mangeshkar. Her moving live performance of the song in 1963, in the aftermath of the Sino-Indian War, is an iconic moment in Indian cultural history.

"उषा उत्थुपः भारतीय पॉप-महारानी"

स्वरचित: "वाचाल चिकित्सक" (डॉ. पी. एन. शर्मा)

चेहरे पर अब भी ग़ज़ब नूर है,
उत्थुप की बिंदी बदस्तूर है।
"कांजीवरम" साड़ी में सजी, पॉप-गायिका,
अनोखी, भारी आवाज़, विशिष्ट पहचान है।

प्रशंसक हमेशा उन्हें घेरे रहते हैं,
और उनके गानों के दीवाने हैं।
उनके लिए दीवानगी ऐसी कि,
बढ़ती ही जाती है।

जीवन ने थकाया कुछ ज़रूर,
शरीर तो हुआ कुछ कृशकाय।
पर दिल में भावना-ज्वार है,
ले रहा शब्दों, गीतों में आकार है।

बढ़ी उम्र, तेरी ऐसी की तैसी!
उनके हौसलों ने ली मुक्त-उड़ान है।
अब शुरू की है दूसरी पारी,
वो दोस्तों, पागल श्रोताओं के नाम है।

"Usha Uthup: The Indian Pop Queen"

Composed and translated by: "Loquacious doctor" Dr. P. N. Sharma

Upon her face, there still shines a wonderful glow;
Uthup's bindi[28] is still as large and bright as ever on her brow.
A pop singer, clad in an Indian "Kanjivaram" saree,
her unique, husky voice is her distinct identity.

Her fans always throng around her,
and they are crazy for more of her songs.
The passion for her and for her singing,
is such that it just keeps on growing.

Life has certainly taken its toll, a little bit;
her body looks somewhat weaker and more tired now.
But a tide of emotion keeps bubbling in her heart,
and it is taking the shape of words and new songs.

As for old age, to hell with it!
Her spirits have taken a free flight.
Now she has started her second innings;
one that is dedicated to her friends and her crazy fans.

[28]Bindi: A decorative dot worn on the forehead, a signature part of Usha Uthup's iconic look.

"एमबीए दाल-रोटी वाली"

स्वरचित: "वाचाल चिकित्सक" (डॉ. पी. एन. शर्मा)

छोटी-सी जान,
ऊँचे हैं अरमान।
ये है नया भारत,
बहती नई बयार।

असफलता से,
अविचलित रह।
सफलता की,
ज़िद पाल ले।

दुर्ग की कमसिन बाला,
छोटी-सी कली।
एमबीए रोटी वाली,
दुर्गा बनना ठान ले।

स्वरोज़गार और,
रोज़गार-प्रदाता बन।
अनजानी राह का,
दामन थाम ले।

दाद दूँ इसको,
मैं क़ाबिल नहीं।
इसका जज़्बा,
ला-मुक़ाबिल सही।

सलाम तुझको,
मैं होता कौन हूँ,
क़सीदे पढ़ूँ तेरे?
क़ाबिल ही नहीं!

"The MBA Food-Stall Entrepreneur"

Composed and translated by: "Loquacious doctor" Dr. P. N. Sharma

A young, small girl,
nurturing high aspirations.
This is a new India,
a new wind is blowing.

She remains unperturbed,
by setbacks and by failures.
She is stubborn in her determination,
to succeed.

A tender, young girl from Durg,
small, still a bud.
The MBA bread-seller,
is resolved to become Durga[29].

She chose self-employment,
and became an employment provider.
She has taken hold of the hem,
of an unknown path.

To praise her,
I am not worthy.
Her passion,
is truly without rival.

I salute you,
but who am I,
to sing your praises?
I am not worthy at all.

[29]Durga: The Hindu goddess of strength, war, and protection.

CHAPTER - 4

खेलकूद

Sports

"टोक्यो ओलंपिक के रणबांकुरे"

स्वरचित: "वाचाल चिकित्सक" (डॉ. पी. एन. शर्मा)

टोक्यो, जापान में रणभूमि सजी,
आधुनिक खेल-युद्ध की भेरी बजी।
संसार-भर के रणबांकुरे जुटे थे,
सब प्राण-प्रण से श्रेष्ठता हेतु भिड़े थे।

डगर कँटीली, प्रतिद्वंद्विता निर्मम,
राष्ट्र-प्रमुख से अंत्य-नागरिक तक।
शुभकामनाएँ, सब की अपेक्षाएँ,
स्वयं के दावों और वादों का भार।

उत्तर से दक्षिण, पूरब से पश्चिम,
खेत-खलिहान, अभाव की उपज।
राम की भूमि, राम के ही वंशज,
हृदय में अगन, सपनों-भरे नयन।

अपनों से दूर, संन्यासी-सा जीवन,
वर्षों तक मेहनत, प्रशिक्षण गहन।
दृढ़-निश्चय, साधना, कठिन श्रम,
विशिष्ट आहार व संयत व्यवहार।

ट्रैक-और-फ़ील्ड का मुक़ाबला,
जिसने आज तक वंचित रखा।
राणा "नीरज" का था वो भाला,
जिसने स्वर्ण-लक्ष्य भेद डाला।

"मीराबाई चानू" की बलिष्ठ भुजा,
भार उठा, जीता था स्वप्निल रजत।
दंगल में "रवि" ने खेले चपल दाँव,
जीत रजत, रखा पोडियम पर पाँव।

"सिंधु" की ऊर्जा और करारे शॉट,
"बजरंग" का यादगार मल्लयुद्ध।
"लवलीना" के दमदार मुष्टि-प्रहार,
बल से कांस्य किया अपने नाम।

"पुरुष-हॉकी" की युक्ति, टीम-भाव,
चार दशक की प्रतीक्षा का घाव।
तिरंगा फहरा, गूँजा जन-गण-मन,
काँसे से सजे-सँवरे, गर्वित बदन।

कितने ही नज़दीकी से चूक गए,
अश्रु बेलगाम बहे, दिल टूट गए।
हासिल हुई प्रशंसा और अनुभव,
लेकिन उन्नत भविष्य की भी जगी आस।

"The Indian Stalwarts of the Tokyo Olympics"

Composed and translated by: "Loquacious doctor" Dr. P. N. Sharma

The battlefield was set in Tokyo, Japan;
the trumpet of modern sporting war was blown.
Warriors from all over the world had congregated;
each was fighting with all their might for supremacy.

The path was thorny and the rivalry was ruthless.
From the head of state to the last citizen,
there were everyone's best wishes, everyone's expectations;
and the burden of one's own claims and promises.

From north to south, from east to west;
from the fields and barns, the products of scarcity emerge.
From the land of Lord Rama, the descendants of Rama;
with fire in their hearts and eyes full of dreams.

Far from their loved ones, they lived the life of a hermit;
years of hard work, and intense training.
Firm determination, meditation, and hard labour;
a special diet and restrained behaviour.

The contest of track and field,
in which we had been deprived until today.
But that was the spear of the warrior, **Neeraj**,
which pierced the golden target.

The mighty arms of **Mirabai Chanu**,
won a dream-like silver by lifting the weights.
Ravi Kumar Dahiya played agile moves in the wrestling,
and won the silver, placing his foot upon the podium.

The energy and powerful shots of the shuttler, **P.V. Sindhu**;
the memorable wrestling match of **Bajrang Punia**.
The powerful, fisty punches of **Lovlina Borgohain**;
with their strength, they claimed the bronze their own.

The strategy and team spirit of the **Men's Hockey** team,
healed the smarting wound of four decades of waiting.
The Tricolour was hoisted, the national anthem echoed;
their proud bodies, adorned and decorated with bronze.

So many others missed out by a narrow margin;
tears flowed uncontrollably, hearts were broken.
But they gained praise and experience,
and the hope for a brighter future was rekindled.

"नीरज का स्वर्णिम भाला (टोक्यो ओलंपिक)"

स्वरचित: "वाचाल चिकित्सक" (डॉ. पी. एन. शर्मा)

पंक में नीरज उपजता,
सेना ने सँवारी सीरत।
राष्ट्र-गौरव बन उभरा,
यह भारत माँ का लाल।

दृढ़ता का उच्च सोपान,
समर्पण की सीमा चरम।
देखो कैसे ख़ून-पसीना,
रूप बदल, बनता सोना।

"Neeraj' s Golden Javelin (Tokyo Olympics)"

Composed and translated by: "Loquacious doctor" Dr. P. N. Sharma

Neeraj (literal meaning Lotus) grows in the slushy mud;
the army groomed his character.
He emerged as the pride of the nation,
this beloved son of Mother India.

The highest step of determination;
the extreme limit of dedication.
See how blood and sweat,
change their form and turn into gold.

Note: Neeraj, the name of the Indian Gold Medallist at the Tokyo Olympics, literally means "lotus."

"हिमा दास, हिमा दास"

स्वरचित: "वाचाल चिकित्सक" (डॉ. पी. एन. शर्मा)

हिमा दास, हिमा दास।

पी. टी. ऊषा ने देखा था जो सपना,
कहलाई थीं जो, "पय्योली-एक्सप्रेस।"
अब आई "डिंग-एक्सप्रेस", हिमा दास,
वर्षों बाद, साकार किया सपना।

हिमा दास, हिमा दास।

भारतीय उड़न-परी, ये हिमा दास,
भरती उड़ान, हमारी हिमा दास।
प्रथम भारतीय, ट्रैक-स्वर्ण जीत,
वर्ल्ड-गेम-विजेता, ये हिमा दास।

हिमा दास, हिमा दास।

सुदूर खेतिहर-परिवार से उपजी,
हिम्मत की दास्तान है, हिमा दास।
खिलाड़ियों के लिए प्रेरणा, हिमा दास,
जीवित पारस-स्पर्श है, हिमा दास।

हिमा दास, हिमा दास।

राष्ट्र-गौरव, राष्ट्रीय बिटिया, हिमा दास,
तोड़ सामाजिक बेड़ियाँ, ये वर्जनाएँ।
सारे अवरोध, प्रतिरोध और उलाहने,
उठ खड़ी होती हैं, सारी हिमा-दास।

हिमा दास, हिमा दास।

"Hima Das, Hima Das"

Composed and translated by: "Loquacious doctor" Dr. P. N. Sharma

---

Hima Das, Hima Das.

The dream that P. T. Usha[30] had once seen,
she who was lovingly called the "Payyoli Express."
Now has come the "Dhing Express," Hima Das;
years later, she has made that dream come true.

Hima Das, Hima Das.

The Indian flying-angel, this Hima Das;
she takes flight, our Hima Das.
The first Indian to win a world track gold,
a world champion, our Hima Das.

Hima Das, Hima Das.

She arose from a remote farming family;
she is a story of courage, this Hima Das.
An inspiration for all Indian athletes, Hima Das;
a living legend[31], our Hima Das.

Hima Das, Hima Das.

The pride of the nation, the nation's daughter, Hima Das,
she breaks the social chains, these taboos.
Overcoming all obstacles, resistance, and rebukes,
all our other Hima Dases now stand up tall.

Hima Das, Hima Das.

---

[30]P. T. Usha: A retired Indian track and field athlete, often called the "queen of Indian track and field."
[31]The original text uses "पारस-स्पर्श (paras-sparsh)," which refers to the mythical philosopher's stone that turns everything it touches to gold. "A living legend" is a fitting English equivalent.

CHAPTER – 5

परिवार

Family

"आज माँ-पिताजी बहुत याद आए"

स्वरचित: "वाचाल चिकित्सक" (डॉ. पी. एन. शर्मा)

आज माँ-पिताजी बहुत याद आए।

जिसे पहले पहचाना, वो थी माँ,
तत्पश्चात् परिचित हुए पिताजी।
रहती थी साथ हर क़दम तो माँ,
मिलते केवल ढलती शाम, पिताजी।

आज माँ-पिताजी बहुत याद आए।

जहाँ सिखाते अनुशासन पिताजी,
लाड़-प्यार ख़ूब लुटाती थी माँ।
डाँटने-डपटने वाले भी थे पिताजी,
पकवान बनाती, लोरी सुनाती माँ।

आज माँ-पिताजी बहुत याद आए।

समझाते, दिखाते राह पिताजी,
राह के काँटे चुनती थी माँ।
खिलौने, किताबें लाते पिताजी,
तो वहीं स्वेटर बुनती थी माँ।

आज माँ-पिताजी बहुत याद आए।

राग-प्यार स्पष्टतः दोनों को ही था,
पर जाने क्यों छिपा जाते थे पिताजी?
घोड़ा बन पीठ पर बैठाते थे पिताजी,
खुलकर गोद में दुलारती थी माँ।

आज माँ-पिताजी बहुत याद आए।

सफ़ल होते तो हर्षित होते दोनों,
पर हाँ, कुछ अंतर तो ज़रूर था।
जहाँ शुभ-आशीर्वाद देते थे पिताजी,
वहीं सीने से लिपटा लेती थी माँ।

आज माँ-पिताजी बहुत याद आए।

विफलता पर क्रोधित होते पिताजी,
पर साथ सदा खड़ी होती थी माँ।
कैसे भी शांत करा कर पिताजी को,
पुनः पटरी पर ले ही आती थी माँ।

आज माँ-पिताजी बहुत याद आए।

घर छोड़ जब पढ़ने निकले बाहर,
उत्साहित और निर्देश देते पिताजी।
छिप कर भर-भर आँसू रोई माँ,
अनमनी-सी सामान बाँधती माँ।

आज माँ-पिताजी बहुत याद आए।

आज़ाद हो, हम बहुत ख़ुश हुए,
जीवन में माता-पिता से दूर हुए।
फिर अपना घर बसा, व्यस्त हुए,
ख़याल न आया, अब कैसे हैं वे?

आज माँ-पिताजी बहुत याद आए।

भूला बैठे थे कि सदा न रहेंगे वे,
जब यह हुआ, हैरान हो गए हम।
कितना कहना-सुनना बाक़ी था,
धरा रह गया सब मन-ही-मन में।

आज माँ-पिताजी बहुत याद आए।

"I Missed You, Mom and Dad, So Much Today"

Composed and translated by: "Loquacious doctor" Dr. P. N. Sharma

---

I missed you, Mom and Dad, so much today.

The first person I recognised was Mom;
I became acquainted with Dad only later on.
Mom was with me at every step of the way;
I would meet my Dad only at the end of the day.

I missed you, Mom and Dad, so much today.

While Dad taught me discipline,
Mom used to pamper me in abundance.
It was Dad who would scold me on my slips,
while Mom would cook delicacies and had songs on her lips.

I missed you, Mom and Dad, so much today.

Dad would explain things and show me the way;
Mom would pick the thorns strewn upon that way.
Dad would bring me toys and educational books;
Mom would sit and knit the sweaters that gave me joy.

I missed you, Mom and Dad, so much today.

The love and affection was clearly there from both sides,
but I don't know why Dad used to hide.

Dad used to kneel and give me a horse ride;
Mom would openly caress me openly by her side.

I missed you, Mom and Dad, so much today.

When I succeeded, both of them would be happy,
but yes, there was certainly a small difference.
While Dad would give me his blessings and advices right,
Mom would just clasp meto her chest tight.

I missed you, Mom and Dad, so much today.

At my failures, Dad would get really angry,
but Mom would always stand up for me.
Somehow, she would always calm Dad down,
and get him back on track again.

I missed you, Mom and Dad, so much today.

When I left home to go out and study,
Dad was excited and gave me instructions.
Mom in her secret space, tears she shed.
and packed my things, reluctant and sad.

I missed you, Mom and Dad, so much today.

Feeling free, I was very happy;
in my life, I had moved away from my parents.
Then I settled down, got busy with my own house,
and it never occurred to me to wonder how they were

I missed you, Mom and Dad, so much today.

I had forgotten that they would not last forever;
and when it happened, I was left in shock.
There was so much left to say, so much left to hear;
everything remained, unsaid, within my heart.

I missed you, Mom and Dad, so much today.

“माँ माँ ही थी, पिता थे पिताजी”

स्वरचित: “वाचाल चिकित्सक” (डॉ. पी. एन. शर्मा)

बहुत पहले की है यह बात,
तब, जब मैं छोटा बच्चा था।
मैंने पिता से पूछा एक बार,
“मैं बड़ा हो कर, क्या बनूँगा?”

उन्होंने कुछ देर सोचा, गुना,
और पूर्ण गंभीरता से कहा:
“पढ़ा-लिखा, तो होगे नवाब;
न पढ़े, तो बस होगे ख़ाक।”

मैं घबरा गया, आँसू आ गए,
माँ भी वहीं पास में बैठी थीं।
देख मेरा म्लान, उदास चेहरा,
वे तत्काल डर भाँप गईं मेरा।

बोलीं वे, “तुम जो भी बनो,
एक बात गाँठ में बाँध लो।
रहोगे सितारे सदा हमारे,
तुम यह विश्वास पाल लो।

मन लगा, मेहनत करो बेटा,
मेहनत का फल होगा मीठा।
क़दम-क़दम पर, प्रत्येक द्वारे,
हम दोनों साथ होंगे तुम्हारे।”

दोनों ने बात वही कही थी,
और सच्ची बात कही थी।
पिता ने कड़वा सच बोला,
माँ ने उसमें गुड़ भी घोला।

"Mother was Mom, Father was Father"

Composed and translated by: "Loquacious doctor" Dr. P. N. Sharma

This happened a long time ago,
back when I was a small child.
I asked my Father once,
"What will I become when I grow up?"

He thought for a while, he pondered,
and then said with complete seriousness:
"If you study well, then you will be a prince;
if you do not, you will be reduced to dust."

I got scared, and tears came to my eyes;
Mom was also sitting nearby.
Seeing my sad, faded face,
she immediately sensed my fear.

She said, "Whatever you become,
tie this one thing in a knot:
You will always be our star;
you must hold on to this belief.

Put your heart into it, and work hard, my son;
the fruit of hard work will be sweet.
At every step, at every door,
we will both be there with you."

They had both said the same thing,
and they had both spoken the truth.
Father had told the bitter truth;
Mother mixed jaggery[32] in it.

[32]Jaggery: A traditional, unrefined cane sugar, used here metaphorically to mean she sweetened the harsh reality.

"ईमानदार पोता"

स्वरचित: "वाचाल चिकित्सक" (डॉ. पी. एन. शर्मा)

शान ने बिफ़र कर गुस्से से कहा,
"वान, तू इतना झूठ क्यों बोलता है?"
दुखी वान ने सिर झुका कर कहा,
"हाँ, मैं बोल देता हूँ, पर पता नहीं क्यों।"

"The Truthful Grandson"

Composed and translated by: "Loquacious doctor" Dr. P. N. Sharma

---

Shaan, getting angry, said furiously,
"Vaan, why do you lie so much?"
A sad Vaan bowed his head and said,
"Yes, I do, but I don't know why."

"चुन्ना को"

स्वरचित: "वाचाल चिकित्सक" (डॉ. पी. एन. शर्मा)

शिक्षित और मेहनती, प्यारा बेटा,
आसमान में चमकता और ज़िम्मेदार बेटा।
इससे ज़्यादा और क्या चाहिए, बेटा?
इससे बेहतर नहीं हो सकता कोई बेटा।

हमेशा ख़ुश और सफल रहो, बेटा,
सदा दयालु और उदार बने रहो, बेटा।
अपने परिवार का हमेशा अच्छा नेतृत्व करो, बेटा,
इस दुनिया में न्यायपूर्ण रास्ते पर चलो, बेटा।

जन्मदिन की शुभकामनाएँ, २०२२
तुम्हारा गौरवान्वित पिता

"To Chunna, My Son"

Composed and translated by: "Loquacious doctor" Dr. P. N. Sharma

A learned and laborious, loving son,
a shining and a caring son.
I couldn't have asked for more, son,
I couldn't have had a better son.

Be happy and an achiever, always, son,
be kind and generous, forever, son.
Lead your family well, always, son,
walk the just path in this world, son.

Happy Birthday, my son. 2022
Your Proud Dad

"टूटू के लिए"

स्वरचित: "वाचाल चिकित्सक" (डॉ. पी. एन. शर्मा)

आज हमेशा की तरह सूर्योदय हुआ,
लेकिन यह बहुत अलग, शुभ दिन है।
सालों पहले, इसी दिन,
सर्वशक्तिमान ने हमें हमारा,
प्यारा-सा दूसरा बेटा दिया।

तुम पीछे-पीछे, मेरे अगल-बग़ल चले,
यह एक अनूठी, सुखद अनुभूति थी।
जब तुम लंबे, मज़बूत और समझदार हुए,
और अपने पिता, मुझ से, आगे निकल गए,
तब अन्य पिताओं जैसे, मैंने भी गर्व महसूस किया।

तुम अपने दम पर लक्ष्य हासिल करते हो,
और मैं तुम्हें दूर से देखता हूँ।
अधिकांश समय, आत्मविश्वास के साथ;
पर हाँ, मैं चिंतित हो जाता हूँ, कभी-कभी,
लेकिन विजेता बन, तुम हमेशा उभरते हो।

मेरा छोटा, मगर बड़ा बच्चा
जन्मदिन की हार्दिक शुभकामनाएँ

"To Tutu, My Son"

Composed and translated by: "Loquacious doctor" Dr. P. N. Sharma, 2022

Today rose the sun, in the usual way,
but it is a very auspicious day.
Years back, on this very day,
the Almighty bestowed upon us,
our sweet little second son.

You followed me at my heel;
it was a strange, pleasant feel.
When you grew taller, stronger,
wiser, and dwarfed your Dad,
like other Dads, I felt proud.

You achieve your targets on your own,
and I watch you from a distance.
Most of the time, with confidence;
yes, I do get concerned at times,
but a victor, you always emerge.

My younger, but big baby,
Happy, Blissful Birthday

CHAPTER – 6

"मित्र और मित्रता"

Friend and Friendship

Author's Note

When I undertook this project, I didn't realise what I had thrust my neck into. The challenge of incorporating 150 names into a smoothly flowing and meaningful poem seemed attractive, but it soon turned into an unfathomable nightmare. My unending torture continued for months. After many failures and attempts at giving it up altogether, the project still churned compulsively and silently in the back of my mind.

Once I discovered "the very obvious," things streamlined. Indian, particularly Hindu names, aren't just a bunch of letters; they are auspicious, meaningful, literary words, most often having a religious connotation. Hindus have hundreds of thousands of Gods and Goddesses—from trees, animals, rivers, and mountains, to celestial bodies, to Gods in heaven or who came down to earth. What is more, each of them has tens to hundreds of synonyms, by-names, or co-names attributable to some of their attributes or their associations with places, persons, or events.

It was still a mammoth task, though. When I finished, my wretched mind played a trick yet again. It prompted me to translate it into English. As the names are proper nouns, they lose their identity once translated. At times, I managed by incorporating their English translation alongside the name, or by adding the prefix "Lord." In other places, I have put the translated meaning instead of the actual name, leaving the job of interpretation up to the readers.

Please enjoy it as a normal poem, sidelining its basic intent.

“मेरे सहपाठी (जबलपुर-७१ पुराण)”

स्वरचित: “वाचाल चिकित्सक” (डॉ. पी. एन. शर्मा)

१.

पीयूष रचे पद्य, कर श्री-**गणेश**-नमन,
करे जबलपुर-इकहत्तर का गौरव-गान।
सपन है साथी-नामों का समायोजन,
नवीन कविता का बस यही प्रयोजन।

२.

ये मित्र **परम, सुबोध, प्रवीण** और **सुशील** थे,
नवल मैत्री, अतुल जीवन का काल था।
प्रमोद, विनोद, रंजन और **ममता**-मय था,
हम दोस्ती व इंसानियत की मिसाल थे।

३.

पढ़ाई के **राजेन्द्र**, खेलों में **अजय, नील** (चैंपियन) थे,
कला, संस्कृति, संगीत के **रसिक** थे।
मन **अमित, असित**, शैतान कम न थे,
प्रतिद्वंद्विता थी, तो भी हम हमदम थे।

४.

व्यवहार जुदा-जुदा, पर मन से एक थे,
कुछ प्रखर, कुछ मुखर, या कुछ चुपचाप।
नर्म या गर्म, कोई धीर, कोई अधीर,
कोई सुस्त, कोई चुस्त-चंचल यार थे।

५.

नम्र-मन **सरला, रीता, नमिता, अनीता**,
सुंदर **मंजू** और मधुर **मधु.** हमारी सहपाठी थीं।
सुशीला, रेखा, पुष्पा, ज्योति की **शोभा** भी साथ थीं,
दबंग थीं हमारी "३०३" **बीरबाला** ठकुराइन।

६.

हिंदू-महासभा तो, जैन-बौद्ध पीछे न थे,
आबिद, ग़ौस, नज़त-जमाल, सलीम मुस्लिम थे।
मावी, गोगिया, ढींगरा, अवतार सरदार,
डॉली, जेस्सी, सैमसन, टाइटस जैसे मेरे थे यार।

७.

मयंक, शशांक, शशि, चंद्र, तो **दिवाकर**-सूर्य,
अनिल-वायु, **राम** थे **राघवेंद्र**, **जय-रमन।**
ओमेश चला था ज्ञान-आध्यात्म के पथ,
धन्य भाग्य हमारे, **भाग्यलक्ष्मी** स्वयं आईं थीं।

८.

कथा धरा की, विद्यालय **भवन** जहाँ,
योगेंद्रशंकर विराजे **गिरीश-कैलाश।**
प्रसन्नमन निरखें, **आभा-भारती** की,
प्रकाश-वान जबलपुर निहारा होगा।

९.

अशोक-महान का अनमोल राष्ट्र हिंद,
जगदीश ने यहाँ लिए कितने अवतार!
राम-जनम प्रथम, पीछे आए थे कृष्ण,
सुरेंद्र, सुरेश खड़े, तिन सेवा-अभिप्राय।

१०.

बालकृष्ण-लीला से गोकुल है निहाल,
गौ-सेवा कर के, वे कहलाए थे **गोपाल।**
मोहन, रमेश, श्याम, कृष्ण के दूजे नाम,
धरा पर कृष्ण-**रुक्मिणी** का साथ था।

११.

कृष्ण पर मन हारे, **अमल** हुए **विजित,**
शिव-रूप थे **सतीश, मुकेश, अविनाश,**
नटराज, सदाशिव और **ओमप्रकाश।**
विष्णु-रूप **बद्री, सत्येंद्र, महेंद्र** साथ थे।

१२.

माँ दुर्गा के प्रतिनिधि, **भवानीशंकर,**
हरीश में समाहित दोऊ विष्णु-शंकर।
सुखदेव सुख के, **वीरेंद्र** वीरों के राजा,
मदन, प्रीतम, प्रेम-प्रतीक थे हमारे संग।

१३.

वसंत आए, छाएँ **सुमन, कुसुमलता,**
मध्य सरोवर उपजें **राजीव** और **अरविंद।**
अमृत-सदृश मधु एकत्र करें **मिलिंद,**
मृदुल समीर सबके तन-मन हरषाए।

१४.

जब **अंशुमान** प्रकटते, हो जाता **प्रभात,**
ऊषा-किरण से **अरुण**-रंग रंगता गगन।
जब **रवि** होते ओझल, आते **शशि-संध्या,**
प्रदीप-भू-**चंद्रप्रकाश** से, **दीपक** से कुटीर।

१५.

मूलचंद की सच्चाई, **सुनील** की चमक,
विजया का प्रेरणा-दायक प्रयास अथक।
अलका, हसीना, सुंदर बालाओं का रूप,
पावन **विमला, सावित्री**, यमुना का साथ।

१६.

उत्तम भावनाओं के उफनते सैलाब,
शब्दों की **विनय**-शील यह बाज़ीगरी।
धीरे-धीरे सबके दिलों को छूने लगी,
नए कवि उभरे, कई सोपान चढ़े पुराने कवि।

१७.

लगा **तिलक** माथे, **देवीप्रसाद** मिला,
फैले विश्व में, करी दुखियों की सेवा।
ज्ञान-विज्ञान को अद्भुत विस्तार दिया,
रौशन परिवार व देश का नाम किया।

१८.

कुछ साथी असमय साथ छोड़ गए,
नियति सहनी ही थी, तो हम सह गए।
न भूलेंगे उन्हें, न उनके साथ बिताए पल,
नत-शिर, अर्पित करते श्रद्धा-सुमन।

"My Batchmates: The Epic of the Jabalpur 1971 Batch"

Composed in Hindi and Translated by:
"Loquacious doctor" Dr. P. N. Sharma, 2022

1.

Peeyush composes this verse, paying obeisance to Lord **Ganesh**;
(The author **Peeyush** - *Necta*r)
he sings the glory of the Jabalpur Medico batch of 1971.
It is a *Dream* to include the names of all his 150 batch-mates; **(Sapan**)
this is the sole purpose of this *fresh* poetry. **(Naveen)**

2.

These friends were *Polite, supreme*, *wise,* and *proficient*;
(Sushil, Param, Subodh and **Praveen** in order),
it was a time of *new friendship* and a *matchless life*.
(Naval, Maitri, Atul, Jeevan in order**)**
It was full of *fun*, *humour*, *joviality* and *affection;*
(Pramod, **Vinod**, **Ranjan** & **Mamta** in order**)**
we were an example of friendship and humanity.

3.

King of academics, invincible and *champions* in sports,
(Rajendra, Ajay and **Neil** in order**)**
we were *connoisseurs* of art, culture, and music. **(Rasik)**
Our love was *limitless* and *unbounded*, still were no less naughty;
(Amit & **Asit** in order)
there was rivalry, yet we were all close companions.

4.
We were different in our behaviour, but unified in our hearts;
some were sharp, some outspoken, and some were quiet.
Some were **s**ober, some warm, some patient and some were impatient;
some were outright lazy, while others were agile and playful friends.

5.

The *humble-hearted* **Sarla** and **Namita**, the *beautiful* **Anita**,
honourable **Reeta**, *pretty* **Manju** and *sweet like honey* **Madhu**,
the *graceful* **Susheela**, **Rekha**, tender as a *flower* and bright as the *flame*;
(**Pushpa** Flower and **Jyoti** Flame);
dauntless "303" *warrior-heroine*, **Birbala,** all were our friends
(303 a rifle).

6.

While Hindus abounded, Jains and Buddhists did not lag behind:
there were **Abid**, **Gaus**, **Najat-Jamal**, and **Salim**.
Mavi, **Gogia**, **Dhingra**, **Avtar** were our Sikh friends,
and **Dolly**, **Jessie**, **Samson** and **Titus** were our Christian companions.

7.

Mayank, **Shashank**, **Shashi**, **Chandra** were Moon, **Diwakar** was Sun.
Anil was the Wind; **Ram** was in **Raghavendra** and **Jay-Raman**.
Omesh the *Lord of light* walked the path of knowledge and spirituality;
Blessed were our fortunes, for **Bhagya -Lakshmi** herself had come.
(**Bhagya-Lakshmi** the *Goddess of Opulence and fortune*).

8.

The story of the Earth, where our college *building* stands; **(Bhavan)**;
Lord **Yogendra-Shankar** sitting atop the *king of mountains*, *his abode*.
(Girish & mount **Kailash** in order**)**,
he must have watched with a Happy heart, the *aura* of *Mother India*
(**Aabha** and **Bharti** in order),
and gazed upon the glittering, glowing city of Jabalpur in *light* **(Prakash)**.

9.

In the precious nation India, the kingdom of ancient emperor **Ashok** the great,
Lord of the World has taken many *incarnations*. **(Jagdish** and **Avatar** in order)

Lord **Ram** was born first, and Lord **Krishna** came later;
Lord of Gods **Surendra** and the *Ruler of Gods* **Suresh** stood, intending to serve.

10.

With Lila the plays of *baby Krishna*, his village of Gokul was in delight;
(Balkrishna)
by *serving the cows*, he came to be called **Gopal**.
Mohan, **Ramesh**, **Shyam** were other names for *Krishna*;
and on this earth, **Rukmini** gave Lord **Krishna** company.

11.

Amal lost his heart to Krishna and was *vanquished* **(Bijit)**;
(Amal - To perform or to execute);
in the form of *Lord Shiva* were **Satish**, **Mukesh**, and **Avinash**;
also **Natraj**, **Sadashiv** and **Omprakash**.
Lord Vishnu was with us in the form of **Badri**, **Satyendra**, and **Mahendra**.

12.

The representative of *Goddess Durga* was **Bhavani-Shankar**;
in **Harish**, both *Lord Vishnu and Lord Shankar* were merged.
Sukhdev was the *god of happiness*, **Virendra** the *king of heroes*;
Madan and **Pritam**, the *epitomes of love*, were with us.

13.

Spring arrived, and with it, the *flowers* and *flowering Creepers*;
(**Vasant, Suman & Kusum-Lata** in order)
in the Lake, grew *lotuses* **(Rajiv**, and **Arvin**d).
the *Bumblebees* collect *honey* like Nectar; **(Milind & Madhu** in order**)**
and the *gentle breeze* makes every heart and mind cheerful.
(Mridul & **Sameer** in order**)**

14.

When the *Sun* arises, breaks the *Dawn* **(Anshuman** and **Prabhaat** in order**)**;
with the *rays of Dawn,* the sky gets adorned with *orange red* hue.
(Usha-Kiran and **Arun** in order)
When the *Sun* sets, the *Moon* and the *dusk* arrive;
(Ravi, Shashi and **Sandhya** in order**)**
the earth is *lit* by the *moonlight* and the hut by the *lamp*.
(Pradeep, Chandra Prakash & Deepak in order**)**

15.

The *truthfulness* of **Moolchand**, the *glitter* of **Sunil**;
the inspiring, tireless efforts of **Vijaya** the *Victor*.
The *beauty* of the maidens, **Alka** and **Hasina**;
and the company of the pious **Vimla**, **Savitri**, and Yamuna.

16.

A surging flood of *noble* feelings; (**Uttam**)
this jugglery and *modesty* of words; (**Vinay**)
slowly, it began to touch everyone's heart;
New poets emerged, and the established poets shone brighter.

17.

We received the sacred **Tilak** on our brow and the *Blessings of the Goddess;*
(Devi-Prasad)
we spread across the world and served the suffering of humanity.
We gave an amazing expansion to knowledge and science;
and brought fame to our families and our country.

18.

Some friends left us before their time;
it was our destiny to bear it, so we bore it.
But we will never forget them, nor the moments we spent with them;
with bowed heads, we offer them these flowers of tribute.

"जब-७१, मेरे बिछड़े साथी"

स्वरचित: "वाचाल चिकित्सक" (डॉ. पी. एन. शर्मा)

मैं बहुत miss करता हूँ।

पापा नवीन सोनी द्वारा हमारी चिंता,
वो देखभाल, हॉस्टल-मेस-मैनेजमेंट।
अनिल मिश्रा की चुस्ती, ज़िंदादिली,
अनिल के. मिश्रा के सुर, शैतानियाँ।

मैं बहुत miss करता हूँ।

दादा बिश्नोई की सीधाई, सज्जनता,
और दादागिरी का मिश्रण एक-साथ।
नटराज बोस का बेमिसाल फ़ुटबॉल,
छुट्टियों में मुरादाबाद की वे मुलाक़ातें।

मैं बहुत miss करता हूँ।

मोहम्मद ग़ौस अली ख़ान की शायरी,
ग्रुप में उसकी तह-ए-दिल से भागीदारी।
अरविंद 'इंडिया' गुप्ता, चेतन सिंह वर्मा की,
छत्तीसगढ़ में बैच-समागम के लिए मेहनत।

मैं बहुत miss करता हूँ।

प्रदीप वाजपेयी के मुँह में दबा पान,
उसकी मंथर चाल, बेफ़िक्र अंदाज़।
असित मुखर्जी की सौम्य 'बावा-गिरी',
छोटे-से **सुनील सचदेव** की बड़ी दोस्ती।

मैं बहुत miss करता हूँ।

अलका, हसीना, सुंदर बालाओं का रूप,
पावन **विमला, सावित्री**, यमुना का साथ।
पढ़ने में मेहनती, छोटी-सी **वी. विजया**,
संध्या जैन की सौम्यता से भरी मुस्कान।

मैं बहुत miss करता हूँ।

"Jab-71, My lost friends"

Composed and translated by: "Loquacious doctor" Dr. P. N. Sharma

I miss it all so much.

The concern for us in Papa **Naveen Sony's** heart;
that care, his management of the hostel mess.
Anil Mishra's energy and liveliness;
Anil K. Mishra's musical notes and his pranks.

I miss it all so much.

Dada **Vishnoi's** straightforward gentlemanliness,
and his bullying, all mixed in together.
Natraj Bose's unmatched football dribbling;
those meetings in Moradabad during the holidays.

I miss it all so much.

The poetry of **Mohammad Ghaus Ali Khan**;
his wholehearted participation in the group.
The hard work of **Arvind 'India' Gupta** and **Chetan Singh Verma**,
for the batch get-together in Chhattisgarh.

I miss it all so much.

The paan[33] pressed in **Pradeep Vajpayee's** mouth;
his slow gait, his carefree style.
Asit Mukherjee's gentle aristocracy;
big friendship with the little **Sunil Sachdev**.

I miss it all so much.

The beauty of the lovely girls, **Alka** and **Hasina**;
the companionship of the pious **Vimla**, **Savitri**, and Yamuna.
The diligent, hardworking, and tiny **V. Vijaya**;
Sandhya Jain's gentle, smiling face.

I miss it all so much.

[33]Paan: A stimulant, narcotic preparation of betel leaf chewed with areca nut.

"पुराने दोस्त"

स्वरचित अंग्रेजी और अनुवाद: "वाचाल चिकित्सक" (डॉ. पी. एन. शर्मा,

बुज़ुर्ग ने उदास मन से एक गीत गाया,
बीते सामर्थ्य, सफलता और आनंद पर।
अब उपेक्षित, रस-रंग-रहित जीवन पर,
अकेलेपन और अनिश्चितता के भाव पर।

पर आशा की एक किरण भी चमक रही है,
तुम्हें अँधेरे में टटोलने की ज़रूरत नहीं है।
तुम्हारे अपने, पुराने, प्यारे दोस्त मौजूद हैं,
तुम्हारी ही नाव पे सवार, सोने के दिल वाले।

"Old friends"

Composed by: "Loquacious doctor" Dr. P. N. Sharma

The old man sang a sombre song,
of the pain of things, gone away long.
Of feelings of loneliness and loss;
of neglect, bereft of all its gloss.

Yet, there shines a ray of hope;
in the dark, you need not grope.
You have your loving, old friends,
sailing in the same boat, with hearts of gold.

"ये क्या हो रहा है मुझे?"

स्वरचित: "वाचाल चिकित्सक" (डॉ. पी. एन. शर्मा)

आजकल मैं ख़ूब बोलने लगा हूँ,
मनचाहा लिखने, सुनाने लगा हूँ।
ज़माने की परवाह करता रहा हूँ,
अब बे-ख़ौफ़ मन खोलने लगा हूँ।

क्या हो रहा है मुझे, क्या कहूँ आपसे?
दोस्ती और अपनापन ही है आपसे,
जो मैं ख़ुद-ब-ख़ुद बे-पर्दा हो रहा हूँ;
वरना मैं बंद-गोभी-सा ही, बंद बंदा हूँ।

"What is Happening to Me?"

Composed and translated by: "Loquacious doctor" Dr. P. N. Sharma

---

These days, I have started speaking a lot;
I have started writing and reciting whatever I want.
I used to be so concerned about what the world thought,
but now I am opening my heart without any fear.

What is happening to me, how can I explain it to you?
It is only because of the friendship and sense of belonging I feel with you,
that I am revealing myself, layer by layer;
otherwise, I am a self-enclosed fellow, just like a cabbage.

OPEN

"मधुशाला"

स्वरचित अंग्रेजी और अनुवाद: "वाचाल चिकित्सक" (डॉ. पी. एन. शर्मा)

वो बेहद ही ख़ूबसूरत दिन थे,
अपने घनिष्ठ, प्रिय मित्रों के साथ।
हम सारा दिन आवारागर्दी करते,
और कभी-कभी "मधुशाला" भी जाते।

फिर हम एक चूहा-दौड़ में पड़ गए;
कार्य, आपाधापी और दौड़-धूप ने,
हमारे चिंता-मुक्त दिन बदल दिए,
और हम अपने प्रिय रास्ते से भटक गए।

सादगी ने अपना अर्थ खो दिया,
उसके बजाय कूटनीति आ गई।
क्यों हुआ, ऐसा क्यों होना था?
अजीब हैं दुनिया के तौर-तरीक़े।

जो होना था, सो तो हो चुका;
अब साठ पार, हम पुनः मुक्त हैं।
आओ, हम फिर मधुशाला चलें,
एक घूँट लें और उन्मुक्त हो हँसें।

"The Tavern"

Composed by: "Loquacious doctor" Dr. P. N. Sharma

Those were beautiful days,
with our close, dear friends.
We would loiter all day and,
once in a while, visit a tavern.

Then we got into the rat race;
the tasks and the schedules,
replaced our carefree days,
and we lost our dear old ways.

Simplicity lost its meaning;
in its place came scheming.
Why, oh why, did it have to be so?
Strange are the ways of this world.

What happened, has happened;
at 60-plus, we are free once more.
Let us all go to the tavern once more,
have a sip, and laugh aloud once again

“दिल मेरा, है आपका”

स्वरचित: “वाचाल चिकित्सक” (पीयूष/डॉ. पी. एन. शर्मा)

कहा तो था, “दिल मेरा, है आपका,”
यूँ ही मान लेते इस बात को।
क्यों कर झाँका था मेरे दिल में?
एतबार नहीं मुझ पर, आपको?

यूँ तो बजा फ़रमाया आपने,
दर-असल सवाल सिर्फ़ ये है,
ताका-झाँकी का सबब क्या था?
ऐतबार भी लाए होते हम पर।

“My Heart is Yours”

Composed and translated by: “Loquacious doctor” (Peeyush/Dr. P. N. Sharma)

I had told you, “My heart is yours”;
you should have just taken me at my word.
Why did you have to peek into my heart?
Do you not have any trust in me?

What you said in return was quite right,
but the real question is only this:
What was the reason for all that peeping?
You should have brought some trust with you.

"कवि-मित्र दीपक का धन्यवाद-ज्ञापन"

स्वरचित: "वाचाल चिकित्सक" (डॉ. पी. एन. शर्मा)

धन्यवाद दीपक

दीपक ने काव्य की राह रौशन की, वरना,
हम इस राह के राही तो न थे।
न ही राह कभी नज़रों में थी,
भटकते थे बस, यूँ ही यहाँ-वहाँ।

देख दीपक की राह, राह पकड़ी,
हम भी इस राह के राही हो गए।
भले ही हों हम ना-तजुर्बेकार,
तजुर्बा आते-आते ही आता है।

तुम तो आसमानों पर विराजे हो,
तुम्हारा ठौर महफ़ूज़, मुकम्मल है।
तुम्हारी अपनी बाज़ुओं का ज़ोर है,
किसी के गिराने से क्या गिरोगे?

हम नवागंतुक हैं, बाज़ू कमज़ोर हैं,
ज़रा हाथ बढ़ाओ, हमें खींच लो।
आस-पास हमारा भी ठौर कर लो,
हम भी देख लेंगे नज़ारे वहाँ के।

हम भी सितारे हैं उसी आसमाँ के,
जहाँ आप सब चमकते साथ-साथ।

आप सब की सोहबत ने,
सँवारी है ये हस्ती हमारी।
कुछ रौशनी इधर-उधर से,
वहीं थोड़ी-बहुत हमारी है।

दीपक रौशनी का बाइस है,
हम भी कुछ कह जाते हैं।
छोटी-सी बात बड़ी बनाना,
ज़र्रा-नवाज़ी है आपकी।

दोस्ती के तरानों से आगे,
कुछ भी नहीं इस जहाँ में।
इन गुलदस्तों में हैं सारे रंग,
हर सुगंध ज़माने-भर की।

कभी आप कहें, कभी हम,
बस सुने हरेक, दाद दे, न दे।
बस यूँ ही ख़ुशियाँ बँटें, बढ़ें,
यही रब से इल्तिजा हमारी।

न तुम आगे, न हम ही आगे,
साथ क़दम तुम्हारा-हमारा।
हम एक-दूजे के उत्प्रेरक हैं,
साफ़गोई से बात, बस ये है।

बहुत तेल है दीपक में,
जज़्बात लबालब तुझ में।
लफ़्ज़ों में ढालने इनको,
ज़रूरी हुनर भी ख़ूब है।

और क्या-क्या बोलें तुझ पे,
सबकी जान बसी है तुझमें।
सदा इसे सँभाल के रखना,
बड़ी क़ीमती है इस जहाँ में।

सारा ज़िम्मा दीपक का नहीं,
कुछ तो अपने ज़िम्मे भी लें।
साथ उसका अगर हम न दें,
फिर हम-आप, क्यों साथ हैं?

दीपक की एक मियाद है,
तेल डालना आपका काम है।
दीपक का एक दायरा है,
उसे बढ़ाना आपका काम है।

रौशनी से रौशनियाँ जोड़ें,
ये हमारा-आपका काम है।
काम व्यापक विस्तार का है,
हाथ-साथ मिलें, ये बात है।

"A Note of Thanks to My Poet Friend, Deepak (The lamp)"

Composed and translated by: "Loquacious doctor" Dr. P. N. Sharma

---

Deepak lit the path of poetry; otherwise,
I was never a traveller on this path.
Nor was the path ever in my sight;
I was just wandering aimlessly, here and there.

Seeing Deepak's trail, I took the cue;
I too became a traveller on this path.
I am surely inexperienced, but then,
experience comes only with time.

You are seated high up in the skies;
your place is secure and complete.
Your achievements are the result of your own strong arms;
how could you fall, even if someone tried to push you?

I am a newcomer, and my arms are weak;
just extend a hand and pull me up.
Make a place for me nearby,
so that I too can savour the sights from there.

I too am a tiny star in that same sky,
where all of you shine together.
The company of all of you,
has illuminated my very being.

Some light I borrowed from hither or thither,
and the little that is unaccounted for, is my own.

The lamp is the source of light;
I too say a few things, from time to time.
To praise my small attempt as if it were a great one,
that is your kindness.

Beyond the songs of friendship,
there is nothing in this world.
In this bouquet are all the colours,
and every fragrance of the entire world.

Sometimes you recite, and sometimes I
everyone just listens, whether they praise it or not.
Let happiness be shared and be kept growing;
this is my only prayer to the Almighty.

Neither are you ahead, nor am I;
our steps fall in time with each other.
We are each other's catalyst;
frankly, that is all there is to it.

There is a lot of oil in your lamp;
you are filled to the brim with emotions.
And to mould them into words,
you do have an awesome skill.

What else should I say about you?
The life of everyone dwells within you.
Always keep that spirit safe;
it is very precious in this world.

All the responsibility does not fall upon the lamp;
some of it should be shared by us.
If we do not support him,
then why are we all together?

A lamp has a limited time;
it is our job to pour oil to fill it.
A lamp has a limited range;
it is our duty to spread its light farther.

It should be our effort to connect our individual lights,
one with the other.
The work is one of comprehensive expansion;
the point is for all our hands to join together.

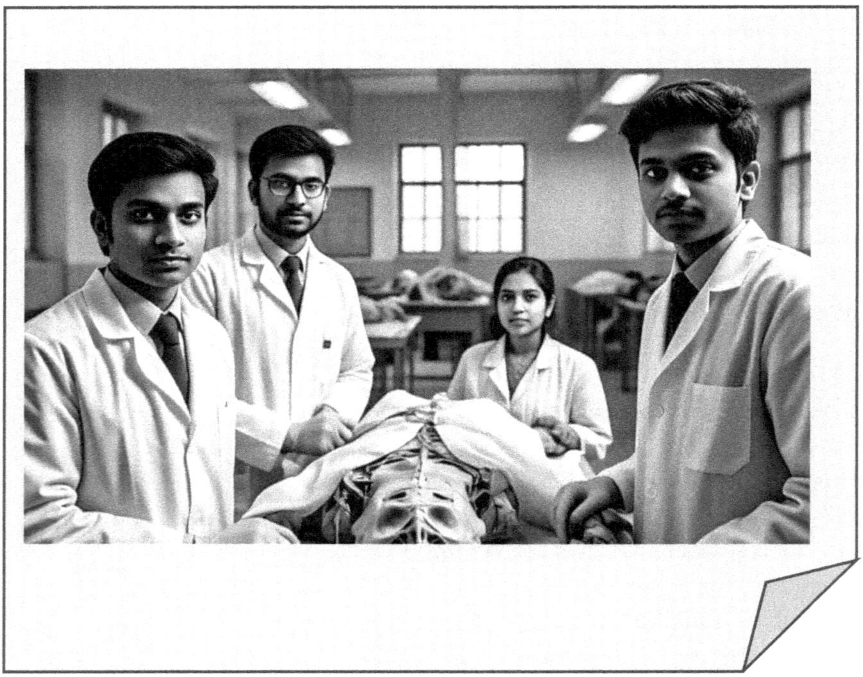

"ख़्वाब-से लगते, वे सोने-से दिन"

स्वरचित: "वाचाल चिकित्सक" (डॉ. पी. एन. शर्मा)

ख़्वाब-सा लगता सुनहरा काल,
कम नहीं, चला पूरे पाँच साल।
कैसे, कब गुज़रा, पता नहीं चला,
आज फिर से बहुत याद आया।

यूँ बचपन तो गुज़र चुका था,
बचपना अभी भी बाक़ी था।
तरुणाई का अनजाना ख़ुमार था,
जो अब धीरे-से सिर पे सवार था।

माता-पिता का साया अब दूर था,
अजब आज़ादी का एहसास था।
शिक्षक अब हमारे सरपरस्त थे,
उनका ख़ौफ़ भी था, सहारा भी।

"Those Dreamy, Golden Days"

Composed and translated by: "Loquacious doctor" Dr. P. N. Sharma

---

That golden era of our lives lingers like a dream;
it lasted for no less than a full five years.
We didn't realise how or when it passed;
today, I reminisced about it again, a great deal.

Though childhood had already passed,
a certain childishness still held its loosening clasp.
There was the ill-understood intoxication of youth,
that was now slowly taking over our thoughts.

The shadow of our parents was now distant;
there was a strange and wonderful feeling of freedom.
Our teachers were now our new guardians;
they were feared, but they were also our support.

"सोहबत पर तोहमत"

स्वरचित: "वाचाल चिकित्सक" (डॉ. पी. एन. शर्मा)

अक्सर किसी बिगड़ैल को देख के,
सारी तोहमत, लोग पता नहीं क्यों,
उसकी सोहबत पर चस्पाँ करते हैं।
औरों की बात और, मैं कैसे जानूँ?

मेरी ख़ताएँ, ख़ुद मेरी अपनी ही हैं,
नादाँ फ़ितरत मेरी, सच कह देती है।
ख़ुद में बिगाड़, मैंने ख़ुद ही किया,
किसी और की इतनी ज़ुर्रत कहाँ?

"Blaming the Friendship"

Composed and translated by: "Loquacious doctor" Dr. P. N. Sharma

---

Often, upon seeing a spoilt brat,
I don't know why, but people,
put all the blame on his company.
I cannot speak for others, how would I know?

My own mistakes are very much my own;
my foolish nature makes me speak the truth.
The flaws within me, I have made myself;
where would anyone else find such audacity?

"मेरे मित्र चेतन सिंह वर्मा"

स्वरचित: "वाचाल चिकित्सक" (डॉ. पी. एन. शर्मा)

मैं और मेरे मित्र, चेतन सिंह वर्मा,
हम दोनों एक ही प्रदेश के वासी।
रहते थे कुछ ही दूर, आस-पास,
पूरे काल, एक-दूजे से अनजान।

प्रभु के मन में था कुछ तो ख़ास,
ला मिलाया था हमें यक-ब-यक।
हम सब पहुँच गए एक साथ,
जबलपुर मेडिकल छात्रावास।

हममें से कई रहे अपने में मगन,
वह रहे अपनी पुस्तकों के संग।
कोई पाँच वर्ष का साथ रहा था,
वक़्त गुज़रते-गुज़रते गुज़र गया।

कभी-कभार बस 'हाय-हैलो' रही,
फिर अपने-अपने घरों को वापसी हुई।
कब हम आपस में फिर से मिले,
कैसे हम अंतरंग हुए, पता नहीं।

यह एक ग़ज़ब की कहानी हुई,
जैसे राम को अब जा पता चला,
कि "यह तो भरत है, मेरा छोटा भाई,"
और भरत भी राम को पहचान गया।

फिर पता नहीं कैसे, कहाँ-कहाँ से,
चेतन, प्रमोद, शशि, रामकृष्ण, अरविंद,
अमित, ओमेश, पीयूष जुटते गए,
पूर्व-सहपाठी, अब मित्र बनते गए।

फिर ऐसा एक स्वर्णिम काल चला,
जब हमने मित्रता का स्वाद चखा।
उन पाँच सालों का कुछ ऐसा असर,
कि हमारे मन को अब पास लाता गया।

मित्र चेतन कुछ अरसा पहले,
असमय हमसे विदा कह गए।
हर कथा का अंत निश्चित है,
पटाक्षेप होना था, सो हुआ।

अविश्वसनीय लगा, पर सत्य था,
इस दर्द को सहना था, सो सहा था।
पर मन में, वे अब भी जीवित हैं,
यूँ ही मंद-मंद मुस्कुराते, अब भी हैं।

"My Friend, Chetan Singh Verma"

Composed and translated by: "Loquacious doctor" Dr. P. N. Sharma

My friend, Chetan Singh Verma and I,
we were both from the same state.
We used to live nearby, a little distance away,
but all that while, we were unaware of each other.

God must have had something special in His mind,
for He brought us together all of a sudden.
We all arrived together, at the same time,
at the Jabalpur Medical College Hostel.

Many of us were lost in our own worlds;
he was mostly lost in his books.
We were together for about five years;
time just kept on moving, and passed us by.

A few times, we just said "hi" or "hello,"
and then finally, we returned to our homes.
When did we meet again?
How did we become so close? I cannot recall.

This is an amazing story;
it is as if Lord Rama suddenly came to know,
"This is Bharata, my younger brother,"
and Bharata, too, recognised Rama.

Then, God knows how, and from which corners,
Chetan, Pramod, Shashi, Ramakrishna, Arvind,
Amit, Omesh, and Peeyush all started coming together;
former classmates were now becoming friends.

Then such a golden period ensued,
when we tasted the flavour of true friendship.
Such was the effect of those five years together,
that it kept bringing our hearts closer and closer.

My friend, Chetan, some time ago,
left us untimely, without saying goodbye.
The end of every story is certain;
the curtain had to fall, and so it fell.

It felt unreal, but it was the truth;
this pain had to be endured, and so we endured it.
But in my mind, he is still alive;
he is still here, smiling softly, just like before.

"शातिर दोस्त"

स्वरचित: "वाचाल चिकित्सक" (डॉ. पी. एन. शर्मा)

प्यार की चाहत तो है हमें,
पर कभी इतना भी न चाहें,
कि हम ही आपे में नहीं रहें;
नाचीज़ थे और वही रहने दें।

शातिर दोस्तों की क्या कहें,
सफ़ाई से चुराया मेरा दिल,
किसी को पता भी न चला।
पर हम तो गए इस जान से!

"Cunning Friends"

Composed and translated by: "Loquacious doctor" Dr. P. N. Sharma

Yes, I do long to feel the feeling of being loved,
but please, do not love me so intensely,
that I lose my own perception of myself;
I was a nobody, so please just let me be.

What can I say about my cunning friends?
They stole my heart so cleanly, so cleverly,
that no one even got an inkling.
And as for me, I completely lost myself in the flow.

CHAPTER - 7

स्वर्णिमकाल, रजतबाल

Golden Age, Silver Hair

Prologue

As I wished my septuagenarian friend on his birthday, he gloomily blurted, "What birthday? It is just another one year gone away from my life."

प्रस्तावना

जब अपने ७०-वर्षीय मित्र को उनके जन्मदिन पर शुभकामनाएँ दीं, तो उन्होंने उदास हो कर कहा, "कैसा जन्मदिन? जीवन से एक और वर्ष और चला गया।"

"बूढ़े का जन्मदिन"

स्वरचित: "वाचाल चिकित्सक" (डॉ. पी. एन. शर्मा)

माना कल एक ईंट गिरी,
पर हर साल दरकती ईंटों से,
दीवार में छोटा-सा ही सही,
एक झरोखा बन गया है।

अब तलक बंद-बंद थे हम,
बेजा उलझनों में उलझे थे।
अब इत्मीनान से हैं, क्योंकि,
खुली हवा में साँस मिलने लगी।

सिक्के के दो पहलू होते हैं;
कोई एक पहलू देखता है,
तो दूजा, दूसरा पहलू।
सोच-सोच की बात है।

"The Birthday of an Old Man"

Composed and translated by: "Loquacious doctor" Dr. P. N. Sharma

Yes, a year has passed, akin to a brick falling from a wall;
but with the bricks that have fallen each year,
even if it is only a small one,
a window has opened up in that wall.

Until now, we were enclosed and restricted,
entangled in unnecessary complexities.
But now, we are at ease because,
we have finally begun to breathe the open air.

A coin always has two sides;
one person sees only one side,
while another sees the second.
It is all just a matter of how one sees things.

"मैं और वो"

स्वरचित: "वाचाल चिकित्सक" (डॉ. पी. एन. शर्मा)

मुझसे सालों दूर लगते थे जो, वो,
वो अब नहीं रहे; मैं भी, मैं नहीं रहा।
जो अक्स, मैं बुज़ुर्गों के देखता था,
आज हक़ीक़त में, मैं वो बन गया हूँ।

काल-सहज-चक्र का, खेल खेल गया,
वह काल कैसे, कब, कहाँ चला गया?
यकायक ही मुझसे मेरा 'मैं' ले गया।
कल तक की तो बात है, मैं ऐसा था:

भुजा में फड़क, पंजे में जकड़,
ग्रीवा में अकड़, वाणी से कड़क।
समाज पे पकड़, चुनौती से झड़प,
जीत की तड़प, हारने पर रड़क।

चौकस निगाहें, स्पष्ट सुनते कान,
सरपट चाल, लहराते घने, काले बाल।
जो ख़्वाहिशें, जो आग, मुझमें थी,
वो अधीरता, जो मेरा स्वभाव थी,

कब की तिरोहित हो चुकी हैं।
समय कैसे दबे पाँव तेज़ चलता है!
नियमाधीन वे अब चले गए, और,
विरासत के साथ, मुझे ये भी दे गए:

अपने रजत-बाल, वह सुस्त चाल,
गुमशुदा याददाश्त, कँपकँपाते हाथ।
चेहरे और बदन की झुर्री-भरी त्वचा
आँखों पर चढ़ा ऐनक, कर्ण में श्रवण-यंत्र।

उनकी ये विरासत,
अब मेरी हो चुकी है।
कल तक मैं, 'मैं' था;
अब मैं, 'मैं' नहीं, 'वो' हो गया हूँ।

इसका एहसास या आभास रहता,
तो शायद कुछ और भी करता।
कुछ और अभिलाषाएँ, शौक़ करता,
कुछ और ज़िम्मेदारियाँ पूरी करता।

पर कोई बात नहीं, हाँ, अब मैं:

मैं जो सबका था, अब मैं, ख़ुद मैं हूँ,
काँधे का बोझ उतार, फूल-सा हल्का।
निर्बाध, उन्मुक्त, परिंदे-जैसा उड़ता,
बेधड़क, बे-ख़ौफ़, चंचल बालक-सा।

लिबास से बे-परवाह, यायावर-आवारा,
मन-मर्ज़ी करने वाला, मन-मौजी हूँ मैं।
कँपकँपाती, बेसुरी आवाज़ में गाता,
लड़खड़ाते हुए, धुन से बे-मेल नाचता।

अंतिम पहर, रीतते जीवन का ये पहलू,
प्रभु की माया, जाने से पहले ये दिखाया।
मन-माफ़िक जीवन जीने का मौक़ा आया,
इस पहर की महत्ता है, चूकना मूढ़ता है।

"Me and They"

Composed and translated by: "Loquacious doctor" Dr. P. N. Sharma

"They," who seemed years away from me,
are gone now; and I, too, am no longer that "me."
The image that I used to see of my elders,
today, in reality, I have become "They."

The inevitable cycle of time has played its game;
when and where did that time go?
All at once, it stripped my "I" away from me.
It was only yesterday that I was like this:

A throb in my arms, a grip in my fists;
my neck erect with self-pride, a sternness in my tone.
A place in the world, a clash with every challenge;
a yearning for victory, a sting in every loss.

A sharp vision, and ears that heard clear;
a swift gait, and thick, waving black hair.
The wants and desires, the fire that was within me;
that impatience that was my very nature.

All these have disappeared long since.
How quickly and quietly time moves!
As per the laws of nature, they are now gone, and,
along with their inheritance, they have given me this as well:

Their silver hair, that lazy gait;
their fading memory, their shaky hands.
The wrinkled skin of their bodies and their faces;
eyeglasses on their eyes, and hearing aids in ears.

This inheritance of theirs,
has now become mine.
Yesterday, I was "me";
today, I am no longer "me," I have become "They."

Had I an inkling or a feeling of this,
then perhaps I would have done much more.
I would have fulfilled more wishes and desires;
I would have carried out more duties, fulfilled more vows.

But never mind; yes, there is good that has come of it, too.

I, who used to belong to everyone, now belong to no one but myself;
the burden is off my shoulders, and I am as light as a flower.
Unhindered, free, flying like a bird;
fearless, unafraid, like a playful child.

A wanderer, careless in my attire;
I do as I please, I am capricious and free-willed.
I sing in a dissonant, out-of-tune voice;
I stumble and dance, without any rhythm.

This aspect of the final watch of this emptying life,
this blissful period of God, He has shown me before I leave.
The opportunity to live life as I wish has arrived;
this moment has its own importance, and it would be foolish to miss it.

"रुख़सती का वक़्त"

स्वरचित: "वाचाल चिकित्सक" (डॉ. पी. एन. शर्मा)

"रुख़सती शानदार हो,

यही अब तुम्हारी ज़िम्मेदारी है।

"रुख़सती का वक़्त" आ चुकाहै,
ध्यान रखो, यह शानदार हो।
तुम्हारे अपने इसे झेल सकें,
रुख़सत ऐसी जानदार हो।

अपने दर्द जो भी हों, पी जाओ,
सबको भ्रम में डाल के चले जाओ।
उन्हें भी उनकी अनिवार्य रुख़सती के,
सही सलीक़े का पैग़ाम दे जाओ।

ज़िंदगी-भर तुमने दम दिखाया,
अब परीक्षा की घड़ी आई है।
क़ुदरत के समक्ष घुटने न टेकना,
वापस आओगे, यह स्मरण रखना।

किसी को दर्द दे कर जाना,
कहाँ तक तर्क-संगत है?
सबको समझा कर जाना,
यही अब तुम्हारी ज़िम्मेदारी है।

टूट कर जाना, समझदारी नहीं,
प्रभु के समक्ष शीश नवाना ही है।
नज़ीर बन, सबको राह दिखाओ,
यही अब तुम्हारी ज़िम्मेदारी है।

वरिष्ठ बोले या अबोले गए हों,
अपना अंतिम कार्य, कर के ही जाओ।

"The Time to Depart"

Composed and translated by: "Loquacious doctor" Dr. P. N. Sharma

---

"Let the departure be splendid;

this is now your responsibility."

The "time to depart" has arrived;
take care that it is a splendid one.
May your loved ones be able to bear it well;
let your departure be a lively event.

Whatever your own pains may be, swallow them;
leave everyone in a state of confusion as you go.
Give them a message about their own inevitable departure;
show them the right manner in which to face it.

You have shown your mettle throughout your life;
now the hour of your testing has arrived.
Do not bend your knee before Nature;
remember that you will come back again.

To leave, while leaving others in pain—
how far is that logical?
To explain the matter to everyone before you depart,
that is your responsibility now.

To go broken-hearted is not wisdom;
one must simply bow one's head before God.
Become an example, and show the path to everyone;
that is your responsibility now.

Whether your elders have spoken of this or not,
you must perform your final obligation before you leave.

CHAPTER - 8

सुभाषितानि

Motivational, Proverbs

"उसका वजूद"

अहमियत और तसल्ली का फ़लसफ़ा
स्वरचित: "वाचाल चिकित्सक" (डॉ. पी. एन. शर्मा)

यूँ तो वो आया नाक़ाबिल, अनगढ़, तन्हा,
वैसे ही, जैसे सब ही आते हैं तन्हा।
उसे ख़ानदान, दोस्त, उस्ताद मिले,
वैसे ही, जैसे बाक़ी सब को भी मिले।

फ़र्क़ कहाँ हुआ, क्या हुआ?
हाँ, कुछ फ़र्क़ तो ज़रूर हुआ।
कोई कुछ हुआ, कहीं पहुँचा;
वो भी कुछ हुआ, कहीं पहुँचा।

तराश और मौक़ों में फ़र्क़ लाज़मी है,
सो हासिल बुलंदी में ऊँच-नीच रहती है।
जहाँ का सामना किस शिद्दत से किया,
दर-असल, बहुत फ़र्क़ तो इसी से पड़ा।

सबका अपना-अपना नसीब है,
यही रिवाज़ है, यही मुनासिब है।
अब वो कैसे मन को समझाए,
वो कैसे मन में अमन-चैन लाए?

अहम सवाल जो है, तो वो है,
उसके किरदार ने क्या किया, न किया।
उसकी इस कायनात के जानिब,
शिरकत क्या कुछ मुफ़ीद रही?

गर वो नीचे देखे, तो तसल्ली है;
अगरचे वो ऊपर देखे, तो प्रेरणा है।
कोई रंज न हो, कोई ग़ुरूर न हो;
जो है, सो है, उसका अपना ही है।

"His Existence"

(A Philosophy of Self-Fulfilment)
Composed and translated by: "Loquacious doctor" Dr. P. N. Sharma

He came into this world inept, unpolished, and alone;
just as everyone else comes, alone.
He had his share of family, friends, and teachers;
just as everyone else gets them.

Where did the difference occur? What happened?
But yes, there surely was some difference.
Everyone became something, everyone reached some height;
he, too, became something, he, too, reached some height.

A difference in the carving and in the opportunities is natural,
so the heights of achievement are bound to be different, high or low.
The determination with which the world he faced;
in fact, that is what made all the difference.

Everyone has their own destiny, and so did he;
this is the natural way, and this is what is appropriate.
But now, how does he explain this to his own psyche?
And how can he attain peace for his dejected mind?

The most important question is this:
what did character do, or not do?
In his participation in this universe,
was his contribution of any worth?

I say, if he looks at those below him, there is contentment;
and if he looks at those above him, there is inspiration.
There should be no remorse, and there should be no pride;
whatever it was, it was his own.

"दुर्योग"

स्वरचित: "वाचाल चिकित्सक" (डॉ. पी. एन. शर्मा)

काली बिल्ली रास्ता काट गई,
मेरे बढ़ते हुए क़दम थाम गई।
टूटा आसमान में क्या सितारा,
आशंका से मन यूँ धड़क गया।

किसी ने पीछे से जो टोक दिया,
राह चलते-चलते मैं ठिठक गया।
ज्योतिषी ने लकीरें बाँच, बक दिया,
मैंने लिखित विधान ही मान लिया।

दिया क्या बुझा, मन ही बुझ गया;
चूड़ी टूटी, वैधव्य ही दिखने लगा।
वेदी गिरी, क्रुद्ध देव नज़र आ गए;
ये कैसे-कैसे विचार मुझे आने लगे!

क्यों संयोग को दुर्योग मानता हूँ?
मेरी अक़्ल पर ये कैसा पर्दा पड़ा?
इतनी शिक्षा का बेड़ा-ग़र्क़ किया,
ख़ुद के पाँवों को बेड़ियों में जकड़ दिया।

नींबू-मिर्च लटकाने से क्या होगा?
काला टीका भी क्या कर सकेगा?
डर तो बस दिमाग़ में बसता है,
आत्म-बल ही मुक्ति का रास्ता है।

"Superstitions"

Composed and translated by: "Loquacious doctor" Dr. P. N. Sharma

---

A black cat crossed my path;
my advancing steps came to a halt.
A shooting star fell from the sky;
my heart skipped a beat in apprehension.

Someone interrupted me from behind;
I lurched to a stop as I was walking.
The astrologer read the lines on my palm and said something;
I accepted it as my written fate.

The lamp went out, and my mind went blank;
a bangle broke, and the scene of widowhood loomed.
The altar fell, and I believed I had angered the Gods;
what kind of silly thoughts were these that came to me?

Why do I consider a coincidence to be bad luck?
What kind of veil has fallen over my wisdom?
I have made a mockery of my own education;
I have shackled my own feet in chains.

What will happen by hanging a lemon and chillies?
What can a black dot painted on the face even do?
Fear resides only in our own minds;
self-confidence is the only way to liberation.

"हे कृष्ण, मर्म अब समझ आया"

स्वरचित: "वाचाल चिकित्सक" (डॉ. पी. एन. शर्मा)

दूध को पेय बनने, पहले उबलना पड़ेगा;
स्वर्ण को आभूषण बनने, तपना पड़ेगा।
माटी को लौह बनने, पिघलना पड़ेगा;
सैनिक को वीर कहाने, लड़ना पड़ेगा।

ये ज़िंदगी आसान नहीं है, यारों,
यहाँ पग-पग पर जूझना पड़ेगा।
मन हताश हो, या पाँव में पड़ें छाले,
यारों, चलना तो फिर भी पड़ेगा।

हर ख़ुशी, हर सफलता के पीछे,
ग़मों, विफलताओं की दास्ताँ है।
सतत संघर्ष, खींचा-तानी होगी,
इन्हें दर-किनार कर, चलना पड़ेगा।

प्रयास के अपेक्षित प्रतिदान का भी,
शायद लंबा इंतज़ार करना पड़ेगा।
हाथ ख़ाली या अपर्याप्त रह जाएँ, तो,
कृष्ण-वाणी का मर्म समझना होगा।

कवि बनना है तो, रात जागना पड़ेगा,
दिल जब बोले, तभी लिखना पड़ेगा।
आलस किया, तो ये फुर्र हो जाएगा,
फिर से याद करने, तड़पना पड़ेगा।

"कर्मण्येवाधिकारस्ते मा फलेषु कदाचन।
मा कर्मफलहेतुर्भूर्मा ते सङ्गोऽस्त्वकर्मणि॥"

"O Krishna, Now I Understand"

Composed and translated by: "Loquacious Doctor" Dr. P. N. Sharma

Milk must boil before it can be drunk;
gold must bear the heat to become jewellery.
Clay has to melt to become iron and steel;
to be called a soldier, one must first go to war.

This life is not easy, my friends;
at every step, you will have to struggle.
Whether your mind is dejected, or your feet are blistered,
my friends, you will still have to walk on.

Behind every happiness, behind every success,
there is a story of sorrows and of failures.
There will be a constant struggle, a tug-of-war;
you will have to ignore them and move on.

For the desired reward for your efforts,
perhaps you will have to wait for a very long time.
If your hands remain empty or short of your expectations,
then you must understand the essence of Krishna's words.

If you want to be a poet, you have to spend sleepless nights;
you have to write as and when your heart speaks.
If you get lazy, then the idea will vanish in a flash,
and you will have to toil hard to recall it once again.

"You have a right to perform your prescribed duties, but you are not entitled to the fruits of your actions. Never consider yourself to be the cause of the results of your activities, and never be attached to not doing your duty."

—The Bhagavad Gita, 2.47

"कर्म, प्राप्ति, प्रेरणा, संतोष"

स्वरचित: "वाचाल चिकित्सक" (डॉ. पी. एन. शर्मा)

सतत कर्म बिन मिले न प्राप्ति,
प्राप्य पर संतोष बिन, न शांति।
तुमसे बेहतर चहुँ-ओर बिखरे,
अहंकार से बड़ी नहीं भ्रांति।

ख़ुद से श्रेष्ठ जनों से लो प्रेरणा,
अपने से कमतर देख, करो संतोष।
निर्बल न मानो तिरस्कार का पात्र,
सहयोग कर बढ़ाओ, आगे की राह।

कहे "वाचाल", कभी न तजो धर्म-मार्ग,
अधर्म रुष्ट करे, जननी, जनक, गुरु, ब्रह्म।
सबको चाहिए निज सर पर वरद-हस्त,
तरोगे इह-लोक, बाधाएँ चाहें हों सहस्त्र।

श्रेष्ठ से स्पर्धा, बिन ईर्ष्या, बिन द्वेष;
स्पर्धा जनती श्रेष्ठता और विकास।
द्वेष-युक्त अंध-स्पर्धा, जने विकार,
वंचित पर करुणा, बनो अवलंब।

"Deed, Achievement, Inspiration, Satisfaction"

Composed and translated by: "Loquacious doctor" Dr. P. N. Sharma

There can be no achievement without continuous action;
there can be no peace without satisfaction in what has been achieved.
People better than you are scattered all around you;
there is no greater misconception than ego.

Take inspiration from people who are better than you;
looking at those less successful, feel contentment.
Do not consider the feeble as worthy of contempt;
cooperate with them and help them upon their way.

Says the "Loquacious One," never abandon the path of righteousness;
unrighteousness angers your mother, your father, your Guru, and God.
Everyone needs a blessing hand over their heads;
you will conquer this world, even if there are a thousand obstacles.

Compete with the best, but without jealousy and without hatred;
competition breeds excellence and development.
Blind competition, filled with malice, only creates disorders;
have compassion for the deprived, and become their support.

"क्या हुआ जो दिन ढला"

स्वरचित: "वाचाल चिकित्सक" (पीयूष/डॉ. पी. एन. शर्मा)

"क्या हुआ जो दिन ढला", रात हुई?
चंद्र प्रकाश का बे-पनाह हुस्न,
दिन ढलने के बाद ही बे-पर्दा होता है।
फ़लक पे चाँद, अचला पर दीपक;
साथ में अगर हो पीयूष[34] का पान,
तब धरा पर मधु-एहसास होता है।

इन चार दिनों से ख़ौफ़ज़दा न हो,
जो फैला है, उससे ग़मज़दा न हो।
हम जो पढ़े, न पढ़े; किया, न किया,
अगली जवान क़ौम के पल्ले डाल।
तू तो बस बुढ़ापे में घोल बचपना,
मन में जो रह गया, अब कर डाल।

सब को सीमाओं का पता है,
ऐसा भ्रम और डर क्यों पाल?
तू मन की सारी गाँठें खोल दे,
जो मन कहे, लिख या बोल दे।

हमारे प्रोत्साहन का मान करो,
अपनी क्षमताओं का भान करो।
कब तलक अज्ञात डर से डरोगे?
हमारा साथ रहेगा, विश्वास करो।

---

[34]पीयूष = अमृत = सुरा

"What if the Day has Ended?"

Composed and translated by: "Loquacious doctor" (Peeyush/Dr. P. N. Sharma)

"What if the day has ended," and it is now night?
The infinite beauty of the moonlight,
is revealed only after the day has taken flight.
With the moon in the sky and a lamp upon the ground,
if there is a goblet of Peeyush[35] (nectar or wine) to go along with it,
then a sweet feeling on this earth abounds.

Do not be scared of these few remaining days;
do not be saddened by the events all around.
Whatever we studied or did not, whatever we did or did not do,
let us hand that over to the younger generation.
You just mix a little childishness into your old age;
whatever desires remained in your heart, fulfil them now.

Everyone knows their own limitations;
so why do you nurture such fears and illusions?
Untie all the knots that are in your mind;
whatever your heart says, write it down or speak it aloud.

Respect our support and encouragement;
be aware of your own capabilities.
How long will you be afraid of the unknown?
Believe us, we will always be by your side.

[35]Peeyush = Nectar = Wine

"ध्यान किस पे दें"

स्वरचित: "वाचाल चिकित्सक" (डॉ. पी. एन. शर्मा)

पावों के छाले यकीनन दर्द देते हैं,
राह मुश्किल, चाल सुस्त होती है।
उसूल पे चलना, सुकूने दिल भी है,
ये आप पे है, ध्यान किस पे देते हैं।

"What Should One Pay Attention To"

Composed and translated by: "Loquacious Doctor" (Peeyush/Dr. P. N. Sharma)

Blisters on the feet definitely cause pain,
the tread becomes difficult & the gait slow.
Walking the path of truth, gives the heart peace too,
it is up to you, what you pay attention to.

"बुनियाद के पत्थर"

स्वरचित: "वाचाल चिकित्सक" (डॉ. पी. एन. शर्मा)

नज़र में आते ही कहाँ हैं,
बुनियाद में लगे हुए पत्थर?
वे ज़मीं में दब, गुम हो गए,
मंज़िलें उन पे सवार हो गईं।

बोझ तो बुनियाद ढोती है,
तारीफ़ इमारत ले लेती है।
अजब-सा दस्तूर है, जनाब,
पर यहाँ का यही रिवाज़ है।

"The Foundation Stones"

Composed and translated by: "Loquacious Doctor" Dr. P. N. Sharma

---

Never are they ever visible,
the stones that are laid in the foundation?
They get buried in the earth and are lost from view;
the floors ride high and shine above them.

The foundation bears all the load,
but the building takes all the praise.
It is a strange custom, sir,
but that is what is customary over here.

"ऊँचे मक़ाम बैठ, इतराने वाले"

स्वरचित: "वाचाल चिकित्सक" (डॉ. पी. एन. शर्मा)

ऐ ऊँचे मक़ाम पर बैठ इतराने वाले,
पीछे मुड़ कर भी कभी देख ले।
कौन तेरे वजूद का बाइस बना?
किसने तुझे चलना सिखाया?
और किस-किस ने राह दिखाई?
किसने ठोकर लगने पर थामा?
किसने साथ दिया, हौसला बढ़ाया?
किसने पोंछे, बे-साख़्ता बहते आँसू?
वो कौन थे, जिन्होंने तुझे हँसाया?

तेरी कहानी तो तब ही पूरी होगी,
जब उन पर डालेगा कभी नज़र,
जिनके काँधे पर पाँव रख ऊपर उठा।
किन-किन को पैर-तले कुचला तूने?
किन्हें तूने रुलाया कभी, आँसू दिए?
किनका दिल तूने तोड़ दिया कभी?
किनसे मुँह फेर, तू बढ़ गया आगे?
किसको तूने धोखे और ज़ख़्म दिए?
किस-किस के अरमान तोड़ दिए?

"Those Who are Perched on High and Boast"

Composed and translated by: "Loquacious Doctor" Dr. P. N. Sharma

---

O you who are perched on high and boast,
turn around and look back, sometime.
Who was the support for your existence?
Who taught you how to walk?
And all those who showed you the path?
Who held you when you stumbled?
Who supported you and boosted your morale?
Who wiped away your uncontrollable tears?
Who were those who made you laugh?

Your story will be complete only when,
you cast a glance at those,
on whose shoulders you placed your feet to rise.
Whom did you trample under your feet?
Whom did you make sad and to shed tears?
Whose heart did you break?
From whom did you turn your face and move ahead?
Whom did you betray and hurt?
Whose dreams did you shatter?

"ख़ुद को, ख़ुद से ही ख़ुश रखें"

स्वरचित: "वाचाल चिकित्सक" (डॉ. पी. एन. शर्मा)

ख़ुद को, ख़ुद से ही ख़ुश रखें;
ये ज़िम्मेदारी कोई और न लेगा।
काँटा आपके पाँव में लगा है,
यक़ीनन दर्द भी आपको ही होगा।

अगर भीड़ लग भी जाए कभी,
आपकी ग़ुरबत, बदहाली पर,
जान लें, ज़माने की फ़ितरत;
अधिकतर तमाशबीन ही होंगे।

अजब दुनिया है, जनाब;
ठीक से ध्यान दीजिएगा।
सब एक-दूजे के हैं और एक-दूजे से हैं,
फिर भी एक-दूजे के हैं नहीं।

"Keep Yourself Happy, by Yourself"

Composed and translated by: "Loquacious Doctor" Dr. P. N. Sharma

Keep yourself happy, by yourself;
no one else will take this responsibility.
The thorn is stuck in your foot;
certainly, only you will feel the pain.

If a crowd ever gathers by chance,
to witness your deprivation and your plight,
then know the nature of this world;
most of them will just be spectators.

It is a strange world, sir;
please pay close attention.
Everyone belongs to each other, and is from each other,
and yet, they do not stand for each other.

"जड़ से जुदा दरख़्त"

स्वरचित: "वाचाल चिकित्सक" (डॉ. पी. एन. शर्मा)

जड़ों से जुदा, वो पेड़ कैसा?
कहाँ और कैसे होंगे फूल?
ऐसे पेड़, जो ख़ुद काटें जड़ें,
वो पेड़ न देखे आज तलक।

पर ये ज़माना आ गया ऐसा,
कि ये देखना भी मयस्सर हो गया।
और क्या देखना रहा बाक़ी,
पूरी झाँकी दिखा, ऐ ज़िंदगी!

मुझे माफ़ करो, भाइयो,
मय सच कहलवा देती है।
ये भी उसने ही अता की है,
इसमें शर्म, क्यों और कैसी?

"The Tree Severed from its Roots"

Composed and translated by: "Loquacious doctor" Dr. P. N. Sharma

What kind of tree is that, severed from its roots?
Where and how will its flowers bloom?
Trees that cut their own roots—
I have never seen such a tree, until today.

But the times are such now,
that I have seen even this.
What else now remains to be seen?
Show me the whole spectacle, O dear Life!

Forgive me, my brothers,
but wine makes one tell the truth.
It is He who has bestowed this upon us, too;
so why should I, or why should you, feel embarrassed about it?

"हसरतें और उत्तरदायित्व"

स्वरचित: "वाचाल चिकित्सक" (डॉ. पी. एन. शर्मा)

काश मैं होता एक पखेरू,
उड़ता उन्मुक्त गगन में।
काश मैं होता एक दरख़्त,
झूमता, लहराता पवन में।

काश मैं होता एक कच्छप,
इठलाता व्यापक जलधि में।
काश मैं होता एक हिरण,
घूमता स्वच्छंद कानन में।

इनकी परेशानियाँ, जोखिम,
कुछ-कुछ जानता हूँ मैं।
पर इनकी जैसी ख़ुशियाँ,
देखी नहीं कभी जीवन में।

क्या हक़ बनता हमारा?
राग, विद्वेष, लोभ, मूढ़ता,
भोग, उपभोग से अपने,
डालें संकट में ये धरा?

अवगुणों को त्यागें हम,
समझदारी से काम लें।
ताकि प्रकृति के पैमाने पे,
बनें और उतरें हम खरे।

"Desires and Responsibilities"

Composed and translated by: "Loquacious doctor" Dr. P. N. Sharma

I wish I were a bird,
flying free in the sky.
I wish I were a tree,
swaying in the soothing breeze.

I wish I were a turtle,
strutting in the vast oceans.
I wish I were a deer,
roaming at will in the wilderness.

Their hardships and their perils—
I know a little something of them.
But a happiness like theirs,
I have never seen in my own life.

What right do we have,
with our attachments, hatred, greed and our foolishness,
with our indulgence and our consumption,
to put this whole world in jeopardy?

Let us abandon our vices,
and let us act with wisdom,
so that, on the scale of Nature,
we may be judged and found to be true.

"मदहोश होश"

स्वरचित: "वाचाल चिकित्सक" (डॉ. पी. एन. शर्मा)

मैं होश में हूँ या मदहोश हूँ,
कोई फ़र्क़ नहीं पड़ता मुझे।
अपना किया तुम भुगतोगे,
मेरा किया मैं ही भुगतूँगा।

वक़्त में ही इसका जवाब है,
तुम देखोगे, मैं भी देखूँगा।
चाहें हम यहाँ रहें या वहाँ,
हमारा किया सामने होगा।

मैं तो शर्मसार नहीं हूँगा,
तुम अपना भी सोच लो।
वहाँ किससे, कैसे मिलोगे,
नज़र नीचे या ऊपर होगी?

"Intoxicated Consciousness"

Composed and translated by: "Loquacious doctor" Dr. P. N. Sharma

Whether I am oriented or intoxicated,
it does not matter to me at all.
You will suffer for your own misdeeds;
I will suffer for mine.

Time itself holds the answer to this;
you will see it, and I will see it, too.
Whether we are here on this earth or there in the heavens,
our deeds will be laid out before us.

I will not be embarrassed,
but you should think about yourself.
Whom will you meet there, and how?
Will your gaze be cast up, or down?

"श्वेत-श्याम का खेल, ज़िंदगी"

स्वरचित: "वाचाल चिकित्सक" (डॉ. पी. एन. शर्मा)

जब तलक शोर न हो,
ख़ामोशी में मज़ा कहाँ?

जब तलक बदसूरती न हो,
सौंदर्य में दीवानगी कहाँ?

जब तलक ग़म न हों,
ख़ुशियों में शिद्दत कहाँ?

जब तलक नाक़ामी न हो,
कामयाबी में रस कहाँ?

जब तलक जुदाई न हो,
नज़दीकियों में रूह कहाँ?

जब तलक बेवफ़ाई न हो,
वफ़ा की अहमियत कहाँ?

श्वेत-श्याम का खेल है ज़िंदगी,
चाहे तो झेल, चाहे जी ले ज़िंदगी।

"Life is a Game of Black and White"

Composed and translated by: "Loquacious doctor" Dr. P. N. Sharma

---

As long as there is no noise,
where is the joy in silence?

As long as there is no ugliness,
where is the madness in beauty?

As long as there is no sorrow,
where is the intensity in happiness?

As long as there is no failure,
where is the taste in success?

As long as there is no separation,
where is the soul in proximity?

As long as there is no infidelity,
where is the value of loyalty?

Life is a game of black and white;
you can either endure it, or you can live it.

CHAPTER - 9

"कोरोनाकाल"

"Corona"

My Poems on Corona

Author's Note

This is a very simple composition, and this is perhaps its final form. However, I believe that it is a novel experiment in Hindi poetry. In every line, I have used a word in Hindi which we all customarily pronounce twice in a row, like "बार-बार" (again and again) or "कुछ-कुछ" (a little bit). I do not know how the grammar of the language defines the use of words in such a way.

This is hard to replicate in English, except in a couple of sentences. In other sentences, I have decided to use the "Power of 2" symbol, like "Far away^2."

"कोरोना, कैसी ये बला?" (1 of 4)

स्वरचित: "वाचाल चिकित्सक" (डॉ. पी. एन. शर्मा)

वक़्त तो है बीमार-बीमार,
सारा जहाँ भी है बंद-बंद।
सभी अपने हैं दूर-दूर,
मन रहे हर-दम बुझा-बुझा।

ज़िंदगी हुई फीकी-फीकी,
अरमान हुए धुआँ-धुआँ।
समय सरकता धीरे-धीरे,
ख़तरा मुस्काए मंद-मंद।

एक-दूजे को निरखें डरे-डरे,
लगी हर दिल में धक-धक।
मोबाइल पे बातें लंबी-लंबी,
मिलती हिम्मत थोड़ी-थोड़ी।

जीवन के नियम नए-नए,
सब ही रहें अलग-अलग।
सब रखें चेहरे ढँके-ढँके,
हाथों को धोएँ बार-बार।

हाँ, कोई एक है साथ-साथ,
उम्मीदें हैं ज़रूर, कुछ-कुछ।
अब दिखने लगा साफ़-साफ़,
कल समाँ होगा बदला-बदला।

हम ख़ुद ही सँभलें, सँभालें,
सावधानियाँ बरतें, बरतवाएँ।
रास्ता यही, समझें, समझाएँ,
और बीती को भूलें, भुलवाएँ।

"Corona, What a Menace?" (1 of 4)

Composed and translated by: "Loquacious doctor" Dr. P. N. Sharma

---

The times are sick^{2};
the whole world has shut down^{2}.
Everyone we hold dear is locked far away^{2};
the spirit is always frustrated^{2}.

Life has become drab^{2};
desires have gone up in smoke^{2}.
Time is slipping by slowly, slowly;
the threat is smiling menacingly^{2}.

We look at each other with suspicion^{2};
in fear, every heart is pounding^{2}.
The talks on our mobile phones are long^{2};
but it gives us courage, little by little.

The rules of life are now new^{2};
everyone must stay isolated^{2}.
Everyone should keep their faces covered^{2};
and wash their hands, again and again.

Yes, someone is still here, side-by-side;
there is still some hope, a little bit.
Now it can be seen clearly^{2};
tomorrow, the situation is bound to change^{2}.

We must ourselves be careful, and take care of others;
we must take precautions, and make others take them.
This is the way; we must understand it, and explain it.
The past we must forget, and make others forget it.

स्वागत २०२१ (Swagat 2021)

Author's Note

The dreams expressed in my poem written to welcome the arrival of 2021 were shattered by the end of March. So, I am presenting that poem again, after adding a few more paragraphs.

"स्वागत २०२१" (कोरोनाः दूसरी लहर)

स्वरचितः "वाचाल चिकित्सक" (डॉ. पी. एन. शर्मा)

अब आख़िर २०२० चला गया,
पर ढेरों रिसते ज़ख़्म दे गया।
सारे तौर-तरीक़े बदलवा गया,
नए नियम-क़ायदे बनवा गया।

पूरी ज़िंदगियाँ उलट-पुलट गया,
अकेलेपन को हिस्सा बना गया।
मिलना-मिलाना दूर की कौड़ी हुई,
जो जहाँ था, वहीं फँसा रह गया।

आना-जाना, कमाना-धमाना छुड़वा गया,
क़ैद क्या है, यह परिचय करवा गया।
हँसना, गुनगुनाना भुलवा गया,
परिवार टूटे, संगी-साथी भी छूटे।

विद्रूप हँसी हँसता, व्यंग्य कसता,
सारी ठसक धूल में मिलागया।
सबको निज बौनापन दिखा गया,
प्रकृति की ताक़त दिखा गया।

अब आया नया साल, २०२१;
वैक्सीन आईं, जश्न मनने लगा।
बुझी उम्मीदों की कोंपलें फूटीं,
क़ैद से आज़ादी आती दिखी।

पर न जाने क्यों, सुरक्षा आई पर,
उँगलियों के पोरों को छू, फिसल गई।
और मुट्ठियाँ रीती-की-रीती रह गईं,
आती मुस्कान, आते-आते रह गई।

ये तो नीम-चढ़ा करेला निकला,
फिर से उसी दौर में ढकेल दिया।
फिर से छा गए अँधियारे बादल,
इंतज़ार का सिलसिला बढ़ चला।

"Welcome, 2021" (Corona: The Second Wave)

Composed and translated by: "Loquacious doctor" Dr. P. N. Sharma

---

Now, at last, 2020 has gone,
but it has left behind many seeping wounds.
It changed all the ways of life;
it made us make unprecedented new rules.

Entire lives were turned upside down;
loneliness became a part of life.
Socialising became a distant dream;
wherever one was, one got stuck there.

It stopped all movement and all economic activity;
it made us understand what a prison is.
It made us forget how to laugh and how to hum;
families broke apart, and friends were forgotten.

Laughing grotesquely, and mocking us,
it rubbed all our pride into the dust.
It made us all realise our own smallness;
it showed us the true power of Nature.

Now the new year, 2021, has arrived;
the vaccines have come, and the celebrations have begun.
The extinguished flames of hope have been rekindled;
freedom from our captivity seems imminent.

But I don't know why, though safety came,
it touched our fingertips and slipped away.
And our fists remained as empty as they were before;
the smiles that were surfacing, vanished once again.

It turned out to be a *bitter gourd coated in neem*[36];
it pushed us back into the same era of despair.
Dark clouds have loomed over us once again;
the long process of waiting has begun anew.

---

[36]A Hindi idiom meaning something that was already bitter has been made even more so.

कोरोना से जंग पर व्यंग्य (Corona se Jang par Vyangya)

An Author's Note

A satire on the war against Corona, accompanied by my poetry.

"विपक्ष की वैक्सीन" (कोरोनाः ३/४)

स्वरचितः "वाचाल चिकित्सक" (डॉ. पी. एन. शर्मा)

कोरोना-काल, ऊपर से चीन का घात,
पी.एम. की परीक्षा, क्या करेगा चौहान?
विरोधियों के लिए है सुनहरा अवसर,
समझ गए, अब आया ऊँट पहाड़-तले।

पी.एम., तूने लॉकडाउन क्यों करवाया?
लॉकडाउन करा, तो देर से करवाया?
मासूमों को सरे-आम, चौराहे पिटवाया,
ख़ास कर तबलीग़ियों पर ज़ुल्म ढाया।

"जान है तो जहान है", क्यों कर कहा?
स्कूल, व्यापार, आवागमन बंद करा,
कारोबार सारा-का-सारा चौपट करा?
क्यों फ़र्ज़ी कोरोना का यह राग गढ़ा?

पहले "ताली और थाली" क्यों बजवाई?
"गो कोरोना गो", गाना क्यों सुनवाया?
फ्रंट-वर्कर्स पर बरसवाए फूल, क्यों?
मोबाइल पर महानायक की ट्यून, क्यों?

क्या कोरोना इन तदबीरों से जाएगा?
कोई मानेगा, ये सब उत्प्रेरक क़दम थे?
हे प्रधान, इस युग में, कैसे तू जीता है?
ये सब, तेरी खाल खींचने में ही लगे हैं।

सबको “जहाँ हैं, वहीं रहें”, ऐसा कहा,
किसी ने भी सुना, जो कुछ तूने कहा?
किसने “माइग्रेंट-वर्कर्स” का मान किया?
कई ने तो उन्हें भागने हेतु मजबूर किया।

फिर मजबूर मज़दूरों की तस्वीरें दिखाईं,
दास्तानें दुख-दर्द की सबको सुनाईं।
तेरी औक़ात तुझे, सारे जग को बताई,
पर था तेरे समक्ष, एक कुआँ, दूजी खाई।

फिर तूने कहा, “जान भी, जहान भी,”
पेट्रोल, डीज़ल, दारू का दाम बढ़ाया।
जनता का ख़ून चूसा व काम चलाया,
किसी ने देखना चाहा, जो सहायता दी?

किसने साथ दिया? पर तू चलता गया,
ऐसी हिम्मत और लगन कहाँ से पाई?
गरल-पान की कुछ तो सीमा भी होगी?
तू तो बस बेहिसाब पीता ही चला गया।

साइंटिस्ट, डॉक्टरों का ही तो काम था,
वैक्सीन-फ़ैक्ट्री का भ्रमण तूने क्यों करा?
तेरा योगदान ऐसा इसमें था ही क्या,
जो श्रेय में भागीदारी तूने यूँ झटकी?

इस बहाने टी.वी. पे निज चेहरा दर्शाया,
ऐसे, जैसे तेरे बिना हो सकता ही क्या!
हाँ, वैक्सीन बनने में देर तो तूने करी,
फिर पूरे ट्रायल हुए ही बिना मंज़ूरी दी।

ये बी.जे.पी. की वैक्सीन है, छोड़ो यार,
इसी बहाने करते हैं सरकार पर वार।
इस जनता का क्या, कोई रहे, न रहे,
हम बनें और बने रहें, है यह असल बात।

जनता को तो ख़तरनाक वैक्सीन दी,
पर ख़ुद मुँह छुपा कर घर में बैठ गया।
लगवाई तो 'बायोटेक' की ही लगवाई,
क्या राज़ है इसका, इससे पूछो, भाई!

पी.एम., तुमने तब क्यों नहीं लगवाया?
पी.एम., तुमने अब क्यों वैक्सीन लगवाया?
सबेरे क्यों लगवाया, सब तो सो रहे थे?
दिन में लगवाते, सारा जग भी देखता।

लगवाया तो, टी.वी. पे क्यों दिखाया?
तुमने चुपचाप ही क्यों नहीं लगवाया?
लगवाया, तो गमछा पहन क्यों लगवाया?
मलयाली, पुडुचेरी-नर्स से लगवाया?

क्या सबको लगेगी, कब तक लगेगी?
बिहार में फ़्री, बाक़ी जगह नहीं, क्यों?
बताओ तूने दुनिया-भर में बाँटी, क्यों?
ये क्यों, वो क्यों, भ्रमित किया जन को।

भाइयो, किसी को कुछ समझ में आया?
पी.एम. के विरोधी कहना क्या चाहते हैं?
ये कोरोना नहीं, तुझ पर जय चाहते हैं,
हर बात को इसी कारण से चलाते हैं।

"The Opposition's Vaccine" (Corona: 3 of 4)

Composed and translated by: "Loquacious doctor" Dr. P. N. Sharma

The time of Corona, and on top of that, China's snare;
a test for the PM; what will the Chauhan do?
It is a golden opportunity for his adversaries;
they understand that now, *the camel is trapped under the mound.*[37]

"PM, why did you impose a lockdown?
And if you did, why did you do it so late?
You had innocent people beaten up in public, at the crossroads;
you especially tortured the Tablighis."

"Why did you say, 'If you have life, you have the world'?
You shut down schools, businesses, and transportation;
why did you ruin all the businesses?
Why did you create this fake corona hoax?"

"First, why did you make us clap and beat our plates?
Why did you make us listen to the song, 'Go Corona Go'?
Why did you have flowers showered on the frontline workers?
Why is there a celebrity's caller tune on our mobiles?"

"Will Corona go away with these measures?
Will anyone believe that these were catalytic steps?
Hey, Prime Minister, in what era do you live?"
All of them are busy skinning you alive.

You told everyone to "stay where you are";
did anyone even listen to what you said?
Who respected or cared for the migrant workers?
Many, in fact, forced them to flee.

---

[37] A Hindi idiom meaning that a person has finally met their match.

Then they showcased the pictures of the helpless labourers;
they told their tales of pain and suffering to the whole world.
They showed you your true place, and the whole world, too;
but before you, there was a well, and behind you, a ditch.

Then you said, "Life, and the world, too,"
and you increased the price of petrol, diesel, and liquor.
You sucked the people's blood and managed the show;
did anyone care to see the support you provided?

Who supported you? And yet, you kept moving ahead.
From where did you get such courage and resolve?
There must be some limit to consuming poison, no?
You just kept silently and limitlessly gulping it down.

It was the job of the scientists and the doctors;
so why did you visit the vaccine factory?
What was your contribution to it,
that you snatched a share of the credit like this?

With this excuse, you showed your face on TV,
as if nothing could have happened without you!
Yes, you were the one who delayed the production of the vaccine;
and then you gave your approval without the full trials being completed.

"This is the BJP's vaccine, so forget it, friends";
on this pretext, they attack the government.
As for the public, who cares whether they live or die?
"We must come to power and stay in power," that is the real issue.

You gave a dangerous, untried vaccine to the public,
but you yourself hid your face and sat securely at home.
When you did get vaccinated, you took the Bharat Biotech vaccine;
what is the secret behind this? Ask him, brothers!

"PM, why didn't you get vaccinated then?
PM, why did you get vaccinated now?
Why did you get vaccinated at dawn, when everyone was asleep?
If you had done it during the day, the whole world would have seen!"

"If you got vaccinated, why did you show it on TV?
Why didn't you just get it done quietly?
And when you got it, why did you wear a scarf?
Why did you take the shot from a Malayali nurse from Puducherry?"

"Will everyone get it? When will it be available?
Why is it free in the state of Bihar, but not elsewhere?
Tell us, why did you distribute it all over the world?"
"Why this, why that?"—they only confused the public.

Brothers, did anyone make any sense of any of this?
What do the PM's opponents really want to say?
They do not want victory over Corona, but over you;
and for that reason, they keep raising all these issues.

"कोरोनाः तीसरी लहर" (4 of 4)

स्वरचित: "वाचाल चिकित्सक" (डॉ. पी. एन. शर्मा)

सवार हुए तेरी रज़ा से, तेरी ही थी नाव;
वक़्त हुआ, थपेड़ों में डोलती रही है नाव।
तट नज़र में, फिर भी भटकती रही नाव;
प्रभु, इस बार तो पार लगा दे मेरी ये नाव!

दो-दो तूफ़ान झेल चुकी तेरी ही ये नाव;
देख, किस क़दर टूट-फूट चुकी है ये नाव!
सितम तेरा ही, कब तक झेलेगी ये नाव?
तीसरी लहर न भेज, सह न पाएगी नाव!

ख़तावार गर मैं, फिर क्यों झेले ये नाव?
कितने ही मासूम भी हैं सवार इस नाव!
देख, इंसाफ़ तुझी से माँगे तेरी ही नाव;
कम-से-कम बख़्श मासूमों को, कहती है नाव।

"Corona: The Third Wave" (4 of 4)

Composed and translated by: "Loquacious doctor" Dr. P. N. Sharma

I boarded this boat with Your nod; it was Your boat, after all.
It has been some time now, and the boat has been rocking in the waves.
The shore is in sight, and yet the boat keeps wandering;
O Lord, please help my boat reach the other side, this time!

This boat of Yours has already weathered two storms;
look, how shattered and broken this boat is!
This torture is from You alone; how long will this boat have to endure ?
Do not send a third wave; the boat will not be able to stand it!

If I am the sinner, then why this boat has to suffer?
There are so many innocents riding on this boat!
Look, your own boat asks for Your mercy;
"At least pardon the innocents," pleads the boat.

CHAPTER – 10

स्वरचितउर्दूशायरीनज़्म

Self-Composed Urdu Poetry Nazm

"मेरे ही, बेगाने-से अल्फ़ाज़"

स्वरचित: "वाचाल चिकित्सक" (डॉ. पी. एन. शर्मा)

आजकल, मेरे अल्फ़ाज़ भी बोलने लगे हैं;
यक-ब-यक निकल पड़ते हैं, पूछते भी नहीं।
गुस्ताख़ ऐसे कि रोको, तो रुकते भी नहीं;
तबीयत की ऐसी मिसाल, ज़माने में नहीं।

सकते में हूँ मैं, इनके मिज़ाज को जान कर;
कमबख़्त हैं ऐसे, मिरे ही दिल को छू लेते हैं।
मुझे ही अपने इश्क़ की गिरफ़्त में ले रखा है;
इन्होंने मेरा हाल ऐसा बे-हाल कर रक्खा है।

इंतिहा-ख़ामोशी से मिरी गुज़र-बसर रही थी;
लोग मिरे मिज़ाज से अनजान हुआ करते थे।
लफ़्ज़ मेरे अंदर छिपे थे, मैं ही बे-ख़बर था;
यकायक बाहिर आ, सब पर ज़ाहिर हो गए।

ऐसा हुआ क्या आख़िर, कब, क्यों हो गया?
मुझे पता भी नहीं चला; ऐ यारब, तू ही बता!
क्या ये मेरे ही अल्फ़ाज़ हैं, दूसरे के तो नहीं?
कैसे अपना मानूँ? अपने लगते भी तो नहीं!

जनाब, अल्फ़ाज़ों के असरात संगीन होते हैं;
ये नश्तर और शमशीर से ज़्यादा पैने होते हैं।
कौन जाने कब और क्यों किसे घायल कर दें?
आपके ही लफ़्ज़, आप ही को बे-पर्दा कर दें।

ये 'मिडास-टच' है, जनाब, आप में घर कर ले;
जो छू लें, चाहें न चाहें, सोना बन कर रहेगा।
खाना, पीना, जीना, सब हो जाता है हराम;
क्या करें, क्या नहीं, मग़ज़ को सूझता ही नहीं!

"My Own, Yet Alien-Sounding Words"

Composed and translated by: "Loquacious doctor" Dr. P. N. Sharma

---

Nowadays, even my words have started speaking;
they come out suddenly, they do not even ask.
They are so arrogant that if you try to hold them back, they do not listen;
such an example of a temper is unparalleled in this world.

I am shocked to see this high-handedness of theirs;
they are so wicked, they even touch my own heart.
They have taken me under the spell of their own love;
they have made my condition utterly miserable.

I was happily living in a state of extreme anonymity;
people were ignorant of my temperament.
The words dwelled silently within me, and I myself was unaware;
but they poured out suddenly and exposed me to everyone.

What happened, after all? When and why did it happen?
I did not even come to realise it; O God, you alone must tell me!
Are these words really mine, and not someone else's?
How can I accept them as my own? They do not even feel like they are.

My dear sir, the consequences of words are serious;
they are sharper than the lancet and the sword.
Who knows when, why, or whom they will injure?
Your own words can expose you, yourself.

This is the "Midas touch," my dear sir; it can take you over completely.
Whatever you touch, whether you like it or not, will turn into gold.
Eating, drinking, living—everything becomes difficult;
what to do, what not to do—the mind cannot even discern.

"क़िरदार हमारा इस जहाँ में"

स्वरचित: "वाचाल चिकित्सक" (डॉ. पी. एन. शर्मा)

मैंने ये कभी न चाहा कि मिरे नाम के,
पत्थर लगें किसी तरफ़, किसी चौराहे।
ख़्वाहिश है, जैसे आए, वैसे रुख़सती हो;
बस गुमनाम-सा मिरा इक मुक़ाम हो।

हमें भेजा, कुछ तो मक़सद होगा रब का;
हमें फ़र्ज़ दिए हैं, अंजाम देना लाज़िमी है।
कुछ मुकम्मल होंगे, और कुछ रह जाएँगे;
पर न मग़रूर होंगे, न मलाल ले के जाएँगे।

इस दौर में, कुछ ख़्वाब भी देखे हमने;
कुछ मुकम्मल हुए, बाक़ी बिखर गए।
यूँ सफ़े थे बहुत, ज़िंदगी की किताब में;
कुछ रंगीन हुए, बाक़ी कोरे ही रह गए।

कुछ लोग चाहेंगे, सँभालेंगे और तराशेंगे;
हमारा फ़ैसला करने वाले भी कम न होंगे।
हिस्से में इज़्ज़त और तौहीनी भी आएगी;
बाइस-ए-ख़ुशी होंगे, अश्क़ भी न बख़्शेंगे।

कुछ याद रखो, करो नज़र-अंदाज़ बाक़ी;
यही फ़लसफ़ा था हमारा, ता-ज़िंदगानी।
सही था या ग़लत था, ये हमें मालूम नहीं;
हमारी ठीक गुज़री, शायद साधे तुम्हारी।

आए हैं, तो कुछ-न-कुछ लेन-देन तो होगा;
तय है कि कुछ दिलों में गुज़र होगी हमारी।
हाँ, कुछ बरसों की ही तो बात होगी फ़क़त;
वे भी रहेंगे आख़िर, इस जहाँ में कब तलक?

फिर बाक़ी हमारा, न नाम, न निशाँ होगा;
ये जहाँ मौजूद है, रहेगा गुलज़ार बदस्तूर।
आख़िर, इक सराय-सा है क़िरदार इसका;
ये किसी की भी मिल्कियत, क़तई नहीं।

"Our Role in This World"

Composed and translated by: "Loquacious doctor" Dr. P. N. Sharma

I never wanted that in my honour,
plaques should be erected at any intersection.
I only wish to leave the way I came;
may my only introduction be as an unknown being.

God must have had some purpose in sending me here;
He has given me duties, and it is necessary to fulfil them.
Some will be fulfilled, and some will not be;
but I will neither be proud, nor will I leave with any regrets.

During this time, I also saw some dreams;
some of them materialised, while the rest got scattered.
There were so many pages in the book of my life;
some became colourful, while the rest remained blank.

Some people will love me, will care for me, and will carve me;
but those who judge me will also be more than a few.
My share will include both respect and insults;
some will be the cause of my happiness, while others will not spare my tears.

Remember a few things, and ignore the rest;
this was my philosophy, all through my life.
I do not know whether it was right or wrong,
but I had a good time; perhaps it will help you, too.

If one exists, then there will surely be some transactions;
it is certain that I will live on in at least a few hearts.
Yes, it will only be a matter of a few years, after all;
and even those people, how long will they remain in this world?

Then there will be no name or trace of me left;
but this world, which exists now, will continue to bloom as before.
After all, its character is like that of an inn;
it is most definitely not the possession of anyone.

"वफ़ाः आशु-शायरी"

स्वरचित: "वाचाल चिकित्सक" (डॉ. पी. एन. शर्मा)

ऐसी क्या बात थी हमारे नसीब में,
क्यों ऐसा होता आया हर दफ़ा?
कम न थी कभी भी मेरी वफ़ा,
जो हाथ आया, ख़ाली लिफ़ाफ़ा।

क़ुसूर हमारा कुछ भी तो न था,
हुज़ूर ख़ामख़ाह रहे हमसे ख़फ़ा।
क्या करते, कोई चारा भी न था,
सहते रहे ज़माने-भर की ज़फ़ा।

अहमियत-ए-शायरी का अंदाज़ा न था,
दिल जो टूटा, इसी ने मरहम लगाया।
जो छिपा था मुद्दतों, लबों पे आया,
बे-पर्दा हुए जज़्बात, छिपा न पाया।

आज इस पे यक़ीं हो गया,
कि चराग़-तले अँधेरा होता है।
जो होता है यहीं आस-पास,
उसे हम दूर तलक ढूँढ़ते हैं।

"Loyalty: An Extempore Poem"

Composed and translated by: "Loquacious doctor" Dr. P. N. Sharma

What was it that was written in my fate?
Why did this have to happen to me, every single time?
My loyalty was never in any doubt,
but I always received an empty envelope.

It was no fault of mine at all,
and yet, for no reason, you remained upset with me.
What could I do? There was no other option,
but to bear the atrocities of the world.

I had no inkling of the power of poetry;
when my heart was shattered, it was this that applied the healing balm.
What had been under wraps for so long, finally came to fore;
my emotions were bared in the open, and I could not hide them.

Today, I have become convinced of this:
that it is always darkest beneath the lamp.
The one for whom we are searching is always nearby,
but we keep searching for them far and wide.

CHAPTER - 11

"समय (Samay), ऐ ज़िंदगी (Ae Zindagi)"

(Time, O life)

"ऐसे ही गुज़रा करती हैं, ज़िंदगी"

स्वरचित: "वाचाल चिकित्सक" (डॉ. पी. एन. शर्मा)

"ऐसे ही गुज़रा करती है, ज़िंदगी";
कम तो कभी, बे-पनाह मिलता है।
इसमें गुलों की ख़ुशबुएँ होती हैं,
बाज़-वक़्त, वक़्त नासूर भी देता है।

ख़ुशबुएँ यक़ीनन सबब-ए-सुकूँ हैं,
ज़िंदगी बा-सबब हसीन बने है।
ज़ख़्मों के भी बड़े फ़ायदे होते हैं,
शायरी को यही तो ज़ुबान देते हैं।

अच्छा किया, दिल खोल दिया,
दर्द सैलाब बन कर बह निकला।
अब तो काफ़ी जगह बन गई है,
शायद सुकूँ वहाँ मुक़ाम बना ले।

अपने-आपको अदना-सा पाता हूँ;
कितना ही, और कुछ भी कह लूँ,
आपकी अज़ीम शायरी की शान में,
इंसाफ़ कर पाऊँ, दम नहीं मुझ में।

"Life Goes by Like This"

Composed and translated by: "Loquacious doctor" Dr. P. N. Sharma

---

"Life goes by like this";
sometimes the returns are small,
and sometimes they are overwhelming.
It bears the fragrance of flowers,
but at times, time also gives you wounds that never heal.

The fragrances are definitely a source of comfort;
they are the reason that life becomes beautiful and meaningful.
But the wounds also have their own great benefits;
it is these that give a voice to your poetry.

You did well to open up your heart;
the pain flooded out like a great deluge.
Now there is ample free space within;
perhaps tranquillity will find a place to settle there.

I feel so insignificant;
no matter what, and no matter how much I say,
in honour of your own great poetry,
I do not have the capability to do it justice.

"अजीब-ओ-ग़रीब है, तू ज़िंदगी"

स्वरचित: "वाचाल चिकित्सक" (डॉ. पी. एन. शर्मा)

"अजीब-ओ-ग़रीब है, तू ज़िंदगी,"
एक पहेली-जैसी तू, ऐ ज़िंदगी!
जब तक बूझें तुझे, ऐ ज़िंदगी,
ख़ुद ही रीत चली है, तू ज़िंदगी!

हम रह गए तमन्नाओं के फेर में,
तमन्नाएँ ही छूट गईं, ऐ ज़िंदगी!
ना-मुराद, बे-मुरव्वत है तू, ज़िंदगी,
हम तो ठगे गए तुझसे, ऐ ज़िंदगी!

जब तक समझे हम नाते-रिश्ते,
जुदा हो गए वे हमसे, ऐ ज़िंदगी!
जब तक समझे हम ज़िम्मेदारी,
वे और काँधे बैठ गए, ऐ ज़िंदगी!

"You are Strange and Confusing, O' Life"

Composed and translated by: "Loquacious doctor" Dr. P. N. Sharma

"You are strange and confusing, O' Life,"
you are like an unsolved puzzle, O' Life!
By the time I could understand you, O' Life,
you yourself were nearly over, O' Life!

We remained trapped by our own desires;
and now the desires themselves are gone, O' Life!
You are unkind and uncaring, O' Life;
oh dear, we were cheated by you, O' Life!

By the time we understood our relationships,
they had vanished from us, O' Life!
By the time we understood our responsibilities,
they had shifted to younger shoulders, O' Life!

"बूझा खुशगवार थी जिंदगी"

स्वरचित: "वाचाल चिकित्सक" (डॉ. पी. एन. शर्मा)

आगे रहस्यमय तिमिर पसरा,
आगत कैसा है, भान ही नहीं।
गत धूमिल, और छटा मद्धम है;
चलो, चहल-क़दमी करें वहाँ।

चाहें तो आप भी साथ चलें;
आप अपनी देखें, मैं अपनी।
करें बखान अपने क़िस्सों का;
चाहें तो कुछ पे पर्दा-दारी रखें।

खोले तस्मे, गर्द को साफ़ करा,
देखने लगी मुझे मेरी ही ज़िंदगी।
कितने क़िस्से बँधे हैं इस गठरी में!
यह पता नहीं था मुझे ता-ज़िंदगी।

कितना कुछ हसीन हुआ था;
कुछ दर्द से लबरेज़ लम्हे थे।
कुछ तो हैरत-अंगेज़ भी हुए;
कितने रंग देखे मैंने, ऐ ज़िंदगी!

जो भी हुआ था इस ज़िंदगी में,
सब मेरा ही था, मेरी ज़िंदगी।
कितने अपने, कितने यार मिले;
भरपूर सम्मान, तुष्टि, प्यार मिला।

हाँ, कुछ अय्यार ज़रूर मिले थे;
सबक़ लिया, दर-किनार किया।
रंगों पर जमी हुई गर्द की परत,
साफ़ हुई, बाक़ी रंग चमक उठे।

कुछ हैं, तो कुछ चले गए;
पोथी में कितने नाम मिले!
लेखा-जोखा करने बैठा जब,
"बूझा, ख़ुशगवार थी ज़िंदगी।"

कुल-मिला के, ख़ुशगवार थी ज़िंदगी।

"I Realised, Life Was Actually Fine"

Composed and translated by: "Loquacious doctor" Dr. P. N. Sharma

A mysterious darkness envelops the path ahead;
I do not even know what the future is like.
The past is foggy, and its shades are dim;
come, let us take a stroll over there.

You can come along, too, if you wish;
you can revisit your past, while I revisit mine.
We can tell the stories of our lives,
and if you want, you can keep some of them under wraps.

I opened the files and dusted them clean,
and my own life began to look back at me.
How many stories are tied up in this bundle!
I was unaware of this, all my life.

So many beautiful things had occurred;
there were also some moments that were filled with pain.
Some moments were absolutely surprising;
oh, how many colours I have seen, O' my Life!

Whatever had happened in this life,
everything was mine; it was my life.
So many relatives, so many friends I met;
I received so much love, respect, and satisfaction.

Yes, a few frauds and bullies also crossed my way;
I learned my lessons, and then I cast them aside.
The layer of dust that had settled on the colours,
was cleaned away, and the remaining colours began to shine.

Some are still with me, while some are gone;
I came across so many names in the file!
And when I sat down to take stock of it all,
"I realised, that life was actually fine."

And overall, life was filled with happiness.

"समयः विगत, वर्तमान, आगत"

स्वरचितः "वाचाल चिकित्सक" (डॉ. पी. एन. शर्मा)

लोग अक्सर अतीत में गोते लेते हैं,
सुखद यादों पर गुनगुनाते दिखे हैं।
हासिल ऊँचाइयों पर इतराते दिखे हैं,
उनके बीतने पर आँसू बहाते मिले हैं।

मैं कहता हूँ सुनो, चाहो तो मान लो,
समय बदलता है, सो तो बदलेगा ही।
यह निश्चित है, विधि का ही विधान है,
यदि न बदला, तो तड़प गहन होगी।

वर्तमान को वर्तमान ही रहने दो,
उसे अतीत के पैमाने पे न परखो।
यूँ न गँवाओ, जैसा है, वैसा जियो;
गुज़र गया, तो बस गुज़र जाएगा।

फन है कि आप समय के साथ बदलें,
समय से क़दम और चाल का मेल करें।
स्मरणीय विगत को स्मरण रखें ज़रूर,
आगत सँवारने की तैयारी करें भरपूर।

सुझाव पर अमल सुगम तो है नहीं,
पर बदलाव भी असंभव, क़तई नहीं।
कठिन को साधना ही तो पुरुषार्थ है,
समय साधो, यही जीवन का मंत्र है।

"Time: Past, Present, and Future"

Composed and translated by: "Loquacious doctor" Dr. P. N. Sharma

People often delve into their past,
humming over their happy reminiscences.
They are seen to be proud of the heights they achieved,
and they are found shedding tears upon their passing.

I say, listen, and if you agree, then adopt this:
time has to change, and so it will.
This is certain, it is a law of nature;
if you do not change with it, your anguish will only deepen.

Let the present be the present;
do not judge it by the scale of the past.
Do not waste it by brooding; live it as it is.
If it passes, it will forever be lost.

The art is that you must change with time;
you must match your steps and your moves with time.
You must certainly remember the memorable past,
but you must also prepare thoroughly for the time to come.

It is not easy to implement this suggestion,
but change is most absolutely not impossible.
To pursue what is difficult is the essence of human effort;
so master time—this is the mantra of life.

"वक़्त और भरोसा"

स्वरचित: "वाचाल चिकित्सक" (डॉ. पी. एन. शर्मा)

कभी एक ऐसा भी समय था,
लोग होते थे उन्मुक्त व निडर।
कम थे समर्थ, पर ख़ुशहाल थे,
एक-दूजे पर भरोसा बहाल था।

वह समय भी क्या समय था,
क्या उस समय के लोग थे!
उस ज़माने की बात न कर;
गुज़र गया, उसे गुज़रना था।

वक़्त ने सब-कुछ बदल दिया;
वक़्त करता, तो क्या करता?
लोग बदले, वक़्त बदल गया,
उसके पास चारा ही क्या था?

"Times and Trust"

Composed and translated by: "Loquacious doctor" Dr. P. N. Sharma

There once was a time,
when people were free and fearless.
They were less prosperous, but they were happy;
their trust in each other was complete.

What a time that was!
And what kind of people they were!
But do not cry over that bygone era;
it has passed, as it was meant to pass.

Time has changed everything;
but what could Time itself have done?
The people changed, and so did the times;
what other choice did it have?

"वक़्त"

स्वरचित: "वाचाल चिकित्सक" (डॉ. पी. एन. शर्मा)

वक़्त वो शय है, जो आता-जाता है;
वक़्त, हर वक़्त, एक नया वक़्त है।
वक़्त का भी अपना एक वक़्त है;
एक बीता, एक है, एक आगत है।

अच्छा वक़्त सुंदर उड़ान देता है,
तो कठिन वक़्त घुटने ला देता है।
न ये वक़्त, न वो वक़्त, अक्षुण्ण है;
वक़्त है, वक़्त से गुज़र जाता है।

अच्छा-बुरा वक़्त सबके हिस्से आए,
विव्हल होने से कभी न बदले वक़्त।
प्रभु-प्रदत्त है वक़्त, समझो वक़्त को,
वक़्त रहते करो, वक़्त-अनुरूप आचार।

ग्रंथ कहें, सत्-कर्म अच्छा वक़्त लाएँ,
दुष्कर्म से तो बुरा वक़्त ही पाएँ।
वक़्त न देता कभी असीमित वक़्त,
वक़्त है, वक़्त रहते चुनें सही पथ।

जहाँ वक़्त में हैं असीम संभावनाएँ,
वहीं वक़्त में ही हैं अपार चुनौतियाँ।
वक़्त-वक़्त की बात है, जो है, वो है;
जो वक़्त के रोके से भी न रुके, वही वक़्त है।

गत-वक़्त के ज़ख़्मों को भुलाना होगा,
आगत-वक़्त को भी जीना ही होगा।
वह वक़्त फूल लाए, चाहे लाए काँटे,
जो वक़्त अब है, जी ले उसे इसी वक़्त।

"Time"

Composed and translated by: "Loquacious doctor" Dr. P. N. Sharma

---

Time is a thing that comes and goes;
time, every time, is a new time.
Time, too, has its own time;
one has passed, one is here, and one is coming.

Good times give you a beautiful flight,
while difficult times bring you to your knees.
Neither this time, nor that time, is permanent;
it is time, and with time, it passes.

Good and bad times come to everyone;
but time will never change by getting anxious.
Time is a gift from God, so understand time;
while there is still time, behave in a way that suits the time.

The scriptures say that good deeds bring good times,
while with bad deeds, you will only get bad times.
Time never gives you unlimited time;
there is still time, so choose the right path in time.

Where there are infinite possibilities in time,
there are also unlimited challenges in time.
It is all a matter of time; what is, is.
That which cannot be stopped by time is Time itself.

The wounds of the time that has passed will have to be forgotten;
the time that is coming will also have to be lived.
Whether that time brings flowers or whether it brings thorns,
the time that is here now—live it, right now.

"उम्र के पड़ाव"

स्वरचित: "वाचाल चिकित्सक" (डॉ. पी. एन. शर्मा)

बचपन और तारुण्य,
सतही, उन्मुक्त, अल्हड़ होते हैं।

सुंदर, बे-फ़िक्र, बे-ख़ौफ़,
उम्र के आनंद-दायी पड़ाव होते हैं।

परिपक्वता व उत्कृष्टता,
बढ़ती उम्र का एक तक़ाज़ा है।

यह किसी एक की नहीं,
लगभग सभी की यही कहानी है।

यौवन यूँ छीज जाता है,
रोज़-दर-रोज़ की आपा-धापियों में।

जीवन में ठहराव आता है,
सारा ज़माना बीतने के बाद ही।

तब गंभीरता आती है,
समय भी अतिरेक होता है।

कला, साहित्य का मर्म,
अब जा कर मन को समझ आता है।

मन खिंचता, रीझता है,
सुनता है, अपनी भी कहता है।

जो छिपा था मन के भीतर,
अब खुल कर सामने आता है।

हर पड़ाव का आनंद है,
चक्र घूम, पूर्ण से संपूर्ण होता है।

"The Stages of life"

Composed and translated by: "Loquacious doctor" Dr. P. N. Sharma

Childhood and youth,
are superficial, free, and careless.

Beautiful, carefree, and fearless,
they are the joyous stages of life.

But maturity and excellence,
are the endowments of a growing age.

This is not the story of just one person;
rather, it is the story of almost everyone.

Youth simply gets wasted,
in the everyday routines and struggles.

A certain sobriety comes into one's life,
only after a whole lifetime has nearly passed.

Then, a new solemnity is bestowed,
and there is an abundance of free time, as well.

The essence and beauty of art and literature,
it is only now that the mind begins to understand.

The mind is drawn to them, and it takes delight in them;
it listens, and it also begins to narrate its own stories.

That which was hidden deep inside the mind,
now comes out into the open.

There is a joy in every stage of life;
the wheel turns, moving from the complete to the more-than-complete.

"मेरी एक भूमिका है, तुम्हारी अपनी है; मैं, मैं ही रहूँगा और तुम, तुम ही रहो।"

स्वरचित और हिंदी अनुवाद: "वाचाल चिकित्सक" (डॉ. पी. एन. शर्मा)

मेरी एक भूमिका है, तुम्हारी अपनी है,
लेकिन मैं, मैं ही हूँ, और तुम, तुम ही हो।
मैं, मैं ही बन सकता हूँ, और तुम, तुम ही रहो,
अनुराग ही मेरे-तुम्हारे बीच की कड़ी है।

भगवान ने मुझे पुरुष बनाया, और,
मैं वह हूँ, जिस मक़सद से मुझे बनाया।
भगवान ने तुम्हें स्त्री बनाया, और,
तुम वह हो, जिस मक़सद से तुम्हें बनाया।

मेरी सीमा के भीतर दख़ल न दो,
और न मैं तुम्हारी सीमा के भीतर दूँगा।
मैं, मैं ही बनूँगा और तुम, तुम ही रहो,
न तुम मुझे साधो और न मैं तुम्हें।

आइए, हम सब सद्भाव और प्रेम से रहें,
प्रभु की इच्छा और नियमानुसार।
क्योंकि उसने कुछ दायरे बनाए हैं,
आओ, हम अपने-अपने दायरे में रहें।

यह सब उनकी पावन इच्छानुसार है,
चाहे आप उसे किसी भी नाम से बुलाते हों।
मानवता, सद्भाव और प्रेम को पल्लवित होने दें,
इस जन्नत में, जो यह पृथ्वी ही है।

उसने त्वचा का रंग प्रदान किया,
भाषाएँ और आस्थाएँ हमने बनाईं।
पृथ्वी पर सीमाएँ भी हमने खींचीं;
विविधता उनकी इच्छा है, हमें पालन करना चाहिए।

उन्होंने हमें प्यार से बहुत कुछ दिया,
आइए, आनंद लें, न कि विनाश करें।
हम सब उन्हीं की तो रचनाएँ हैं,
क्या निर्माता, कृति का विनाश चाहेगा?

वनस्पति, पशु एवं पखेरू,
सागर, पर्वत, कानन, मरु,
वे सभी उन्हीं की ही रचनाएँ हैं,
उन्हीं के कैनवस के चित्र हैं।

विविधता-पूर्ण दुनिया में डग भरना,
निश्चित ही कई बार कठिन होता है।
आइए, हम विश्वास और धैर्य रखें,
और कम-से-कम इसे आज़माएँ।

कुछ लचीलापन रहने दें,
बदलते समय के अनुसार।
उनके मन में कुछ यक़ीनन होगा,
परमात्मा की अवहेलना सही नहीं।

निःसंदेह, मैं तुम नहीं हो सकता,
और तुम, मैं नहीं हो सकते।
आओ, भिन्नता का सम्मान करें,
तुम मुझे, मैं तुम्हें, जैसे हैं, स्वीकार करें।

सह-अस्तित्व, सौहार्द या प्रेम—कहानी एक ही है;
समझौता और अनुकूलन ही, इस खेल का नाम है।
स्वीकार करें और हरेक को अपने तरीक़े से चलने दें,
और पता लगाएँ कि प्रेम तब भी कैसे बना रह सकता है।

तुम अपनी धुन पर नाचो, मैं अपनी पर,
चलो, उनका मेल करें, भले ही वे बे-मेल हों।
विविधता, समानता और समावेशन (डी.ई.आई.),
वर्तमान समय की पुकार है।

"You Have a Role, And So Have I; I'll Be Me, And You Be You."

Composed and translated by: "Loquacious doctor" Dr. P. N. Sharma

I have a role, and so have you;
but I am me, and you are you.
I'll be me, and you be you;
love is the link between me and you.

God made me a man, and,
I am what I am meant to be.
God made you a woman, and,
you are what you're meant to be.

Don't rein me in, beyond a point;
and I won't rein you in, beyond yours.
I will be me, and you be you;
don't bind me tight, and I won't bind you.

Let us be in harmony and in love,
as per God's wishes and His dictate.
As He has drawn some lines,
let us remain within our own confines.

It is all in His holy design,
whatever name you call Him by.
Let humility prevail,
in the heaven that is this soil.

The skin colours, He provided;
the languages and faiths, we created.
The boundaries on the earth, we drew;
diversity is His wish, so let's comply.

He gave us so much, with much love;
let us enjoy it, and not knock it all down.
We are all His creations;
would He like to see them torn down?

The animals, the birds, and the vegetation;
the seas, the mountains, the jungles, and the deserts;
they are all His own creation.
It is He who painted them on the canvas.

To tread a path in this diverse world,
is surely difficult, many a time.
Let us have faith and tolerance,
and let us at least give it a try.

Let there be some flexibility,
as per the changing times.
He must have His reasons,
and let us not defy the divine.

For sure, I cannot be you,
and you cannot be me.
Let us respect the variance,
and love you as you, and me as I.

Coexistence, amity, love—the story is the same;
compromise and adaptation is the name of the game.
Let us accept, and let everyone be, in their own way,
and figure out the ways that love can still stay.

You dance to your tune, and I to mine;
let us meld them, even if they are out of rhyme.
Diversity, Equity, and Inclusion (DEI),
is the call of the present time.

"भगवान का मानव"

स्वरचित: "वाचाल चिकित्सक" (डॉ. पी. एन. शर्मा)

जिस भी शक्ति ने सृष्टि बनाई थी,
वह शक्ति यक़ीनन एक ही तो थी।
पता नहीं कौन थी, किसकी थी,
पर जो हो, वह एक ही शक्ति थी।

यदि भगवान ने ब्रह्मांड बनाया,
भगवान यक़ीनन एक ही थे, जो नाम लो।
उन ने ही आकाश-गंगाएँ बनाईं,
तारों, ग्रहों, उपग्रहों से सजाईं।

सबकी एक उम्र भी तय कर दी,
उनको अनवरत, तीव्र गति दी।
उनके भ्रमण की योजना रची,
सब खगोलीय-नियमाधीन रखा।

दिन, रात और मौसम बनाए,
सब-कुछ नियंत्रित चलता गया।
फिर कहीं-कहीं जीवन रचा गया,
उसे विकास की आज़ादी मिली।

जीव असंख्य प्रकारों में ढले,
यूँ तो सब थे अलग-अलग ही।
पर थे एक-दूसरे से गुँथे हुए,
ऐसा अनंत-काल चलता गया।

एक दिन मानव विकसित हुआ,
खगोलीय एक छोटे-से काल बाद ही।
यह मानव अब ईश्वर को गढ़ने लगा,
कोई तो स्वयं को ईश्वर ही कहने लगा।

नस्ल, रंगत, नाक-नक़्श, वाणी,
जैसे कि इतने अंतर काफ़ी न थे,
कि नए-नए संप्रदाय बनते गए,
जिससे फ़ासले और बढ़ते गए।

देव की धरती पर रेखाएँ खिंचीं,
बारंबार मिटाई और बदली गईं।
अहम् से अहम् टकराते ही रहे,
धरा घायल, रक्त-रंजित होती रही।

मानव को अ-मानव कहें या दानव,
भगवान को धता बता, मानव खड़ा।
एक अजब-सा ये सिलसिला चला,
चला तो यूँ ही, चलता चला गया।

इस प्रवृत्ति का क्या अंजाम मिलेगा?
इसका कोई उपचार है भी या नहीं?
या यह रोग ऐसे ही चलता रहेगा?
चलेगा तो, यूँ कब तक चल पाएगा?

यूँ कब तक चल पाएगा?

"God's Man"

Composed and translated by: "Loquacious doctor" Dr. P. N. Sharma

Whichever power created the universe,
that power was definitely only one.
I do not know what it was, or whose it was,
but whatever it was, it was only one.

If God created the universe,
then God was surely one, whatever name you give Him.
It is He who created the galaxies,
and decorated them with stars, planets, and moons.

The age of every celestial body was also fixed,
and He gave them a relentless, spiralling pace.
He planned the speed and course of their trips;
everything was kept under astronomical principles.

He created the day, the night, and the seasons;
everything went on just as planned.
Then, somewhere, life was created,
and it was given the freedom to evolve.

Organisms evolved into innumerable forms;
though each one was different and unique,
they were still intertwined with each other,
and this went on for almost an eternity.

One day, human beings evolved,
after only a short astronomical period.
And this human being now started creating Gods;
some even started calling themselves God.

Race, complexion, features, language—
as if these differences were not enough,
new sects and new divides came to the fore,
due to which the distances widened even further.

Lines were drawn on God's own land;
they were frequently erased and altered.
Egos kept clashing with other egos;
the Earth was repeatedly wounded and bled.

Should we call human beings inhuman, or demons?
Man stands there, defying God Himself.
This strange sequence of events has continued;
it has just kept going on and on.

What will be the outcome of this trend?
Is there any remedy for this, or not?
Or will this disease continue on like this?
And even if it does, how long can it go on?

How long can it go on like this?

"ज़िंदगी का एक फ़लसफ़ा है"

स्वरचित: "वाचाल चिकित्सक" (डॉ. पी. एन. शर्मा)

कभी आँखें बरबस बरस जाएँ,
या कभी मन झूम-झूम जाए।
न ग़मज़दा हों, न ऐंठ जाइए,
वक़्त की बात है, भूल जाइए।

ज़िंदगी का एक फ़लसफ़ा है:
न वो रहता है, न ये रहता है।
वो भी गुज़रा, ये भी गुज़रेगा,
मन को समझाने की बात है।

आपने जज़्बातों को हवा दी,
मन अचानक-से कुछ बोला।
यूँ कुरेदते रहेंगे आप,
तो सहर यूँ ही बीतेगी।

चलिए, अब बस करते हैं,
ज़िंदगी में और भी काम हैं।

"There is a Philosophy of life"

Composed and translated by: "Loquacious doctor" Dr. P. N. Sharma

Sometimes your eyes may shed their tears,
or sometimes your heart may dance with joy.
Do not be sad, and do not feel proud;
it is all a matter of time, so just forget about it.

There is a philosophy of life:
neither did that feeling last, nor will this.
That one has passed, and this one, too, will pass;
it is all a matter of convincing your own mind.

You have fanned the flames of my emotions,
and so my mind has suddenly uttered something.
If you keep probing like this,
the whole morning will pass by, just like this.

Come, let's take a break now;
there are other things to do in life.

"अतीत"

स्वरचित और हिंदी अनुवादः "वाचाल चिकित्सक" (डॉ. पी. एन. शर्मा)

अपना अतीत, मैं देखता और समीक्षा करता हूँ,
पर इसे बदल या नवीनीकृत नहीं कर सकता।
अतीत कभी भी परिपूर्ण नहीं हो सकता,
तुम्हारा जो कुछ भी है, उसे ही स्वीकार करो।

अपने पछतावे मैं विस्मृत नहीं कर सकता,
लेकिन सबक़, ज़रूर ले सकता हूँ।
अतीत सबसे मूल्यवान शिक्षक है,
उज्ज्वल भविष्य के निर्माण के लिए।

समय आपको निखार ज़रूर सकता है,
और यह आपको बाँधता भी नहीं है।
अतीत को अपना बंधन न बनने दें,
आगे बढ़ें और नए अध्याय जोड़ें।

दुख हमेशा बने रहते हैं, यह उनकी प्रकृति है,
जीवन के मार्ग का यह एक अपरिहार्य हिस्सा है।
वे आपको पीड़ा देंगे, आपको रुलाएँगे;
उन्हें दर-किनार करें—कम-से-कम कोशिश तो करें!

ख़ुशियाँ हैं, वे भी याद में बनी रहती हैं,
छोटी या शायद गिनती की ही क्यों न हों।
उनका रसास्वादन करें, उन्हें विस्मृत न करें,
क्योंकि वे ही आपको उत्साह से भर देंगी।

"The Past"

Composed and translated by: "Loquacious doctor" Dr. P. N. Sharma

My past, I view and I review,
but I can't change it or renew.
The past can never be perfect;
whatever you have, you must accept.

My Regrets, I cannot correct,
but from their Lessons, I can surely learn.
They are a most-valued Teacher,
to help you try and build a flawless future.

Time can surely refine you,
and it does not confine you.
Do not let the past shackle you;
go ahead and add chapters new.

Sorrows do stay, just as they are,
an inevitable part of life's way.
They will pain you, they may make you cry;
but put them aside—*At Least, You Must Try*.

There are JOYS, and they, too, stay,
small they may be, or maybe only a few.
Brush them, so they may shine anew,
because they are what will invigorate you.

CHAPTER - 12

आँसू और मुस्कान

Pains, Tears & Smiles

"बेबस मुस्कान"

स्वरचित: "वाचाल चिकित्सक" (डॉ. पी. एन. शर्मा)

जज़्बात की शिद्दत ही कुछ ऐसी थी,
कि बे-साख़्ता ही मेरे अश्क़ निकल पड़े।
वरना दिल में रहते हैं ज़ब्त, जज़्बात मेरे,
किसी को कानों-कान ख़बर नहीं होती।

करूँ क्या, ऐसी पत्थर-दिल है ये दुनिया,
अश्क़ किसी को भी क़तई पसंद नहीं।
"बेबस मुस्कान" ओढ़े रहते हैं लब मेरे,
ऐसे बे-दिल लोगों को भरमाने के लिए।

"Helpless Smile"

Composed and translated by: "Loquacious doctor" Dr. P. N. Sharma

Such was the intensity of my emotions,
that my tears rolled out, uncontrollably.
Otherwise, my feelings remain suppressed within,
and no one ever comes to know of my plight.

What can I do? This world is so ruthless;
no one likes or cares about tears at all.
My lips keep wearing a "helpless smile,"
just to hide myself from such heartless people.

"उफ़, ये अश्क़!"

स्वरचित: "वाचाल चिकित्सक" (डॉ. पी. एन. शर्मा)

ग़म के हों, या चाहे हों ख़ुशी के,
अपने ही अश्क़ ना-पसंद हैं मुझे।
यों, क़ुसूर उनका सिर्फ़ एक ही है,
कि सरे-बाज़ार मुझे बे-पर्दा कर देते हैं।

"Ugh, These Tears!"

Composed and translated by: "Loquacious doctor" Dr. P. N. Sharma

---

Whether they are of sorrow, or of joy,
I dislike tears my own.
Their only offence is this:
that they expose me to one and all.

"बात बड़ी अजीब-ओ-ग़रीब है"

स्वरचित: "वाचाल चिकित्सक" (डॉ. पी. एन. शर्मा)

आग मिरे दिल में लगी है,
और अश्क़ आँखों से बह रहे हैं।
अब कैसे उम्मीद करूँ,
कि आग बुझ जाएगी?

"It is Such a Strange Thing"

Composed and translated by: "Loquacious doctor" Dr. P. N. Sharma

There is a fiery anguish in my heart,
but tears are flowing from my eyes.
So how can I nurture the hope, now,
that this fire will ever be doused?

"आँसू और मुस्कान"

स्वरचित: "वाचाल चिकित्सक" (डॉ. पी. एन. शर्मा)

मुस्कुराते चेहरे वाली तस्वीर मेरी,
दर्द छुपा कर वो, खिंचवाई जो थी।
मेरी बेबसी का बयाँ करती कहाँ थी,
आँसू न थे, तो लोग बधाई दे गए।

जो न कहा, चेहरा वो कह गया;
जो कहना चाहा था, वो रह गया।
बात का बतंगड़ बनना था, बन गया;
मैं मुँह बाए, अवाक देखता रह गया।

"Tears and Smiles"

Composed and translated by: "Loquacious doctor" Dr. P. N. Sharma

That picture of me, with a smiling face,
I got it taken while I was hiding the pain deep within.
How could it ever express my helplessness?
It lacked tears, and so people gave it their "likes."

What I had not intended to say, my face said;
what I had meant to say, remained unsaid.
It was bound to become a big mess, and so it did;
I was just left staring blankly, in total disbelief.

"अश्क़ों की क़ीमत"

स्वरचित: "वाचाल चिकित्सक" (डॉ. पी. एन. शर्मा)

मिरे अश्क़ों की कोई क़ीमत बाज़ार में नहीं,
फिर भी ये कमबख़्त, बे-शर्म, थमते क्यों नहीं?
जब-तब निकल पड़ते हैं, मानते भी नहीं,
ख़ामख़ाह मुझे टूटा हुआ साबित कर देते हैं।

ज़्यादातर हँस कर मेरा मख़ौल उड़ाते हैं,
कोई अफ़सोस कर, मुझ पे रहम खाते हैं।
मुझे दोनों ही, किसी हाल बर्दाश्त नहीं होते,
ये क्यों-कर मुझे मेरे हाल पर छोड़ते नहीं?

"Valueless Tears"

Composed and translated by: "Loquacious doctor" Dr. P. N. Sharma

My tears are of no value in the worldly market,
so why then does this shameless stream not stop?
Whenever they roll out, they do not even ask me,
and for no reason, they prove that I am broken-hearted.

Most people just laugh at, or they ridicule me;
others feel sorry for me and take pity on me.
I cannot tolerate either of these, at any cost;
so why do they not just leave me alone with my woes?

"बे-दर्द लोग"

स्वरचित: "वाचाल चिकित्सक" (पीयूष/डॉ. पी. एन. शर्मा)

बे-दर्द लोगों से तआरुफ़ क्या हुआ,
दर्द ज़िंदगी का हिस्सा हो गया।
क्या आए वे ज़िंदगी में पल-भर,
तमाम दिनों का फ़साना हो गया!

कहना तो बहुत कुछ था हमें,
न जाने क्यों, कहने से रह गए।
शायद उन्हें कुछ तो सुनना था,
नहीं कहा, तो ख़फ़ा-से हो गए।

ख़याल न किया दीवानगी का,
मुँह मोड़ कर वो तो चल दिए।
भौं-चक्के, मुँह बाए, उन्हें ताकते,
हम वहीं, खड़े-के-खड़े रह गए।

"Heartless People"

Composed and translated by: "Loquacious doctor" (Peeyush/Dr. P. N. Sharma)

When I came across heartless people,
pain became a part of my life.
They came into my life for just a moment,
and it became a story for a lifetime.

I had so much to say,
but I don't know why, I could not say.
Perhaps they expected to hear some words,
and when I did not say them, they got upset.

They did not care for my passion;
they just turned their face and walked away.
I just stood there, staring at their back,
with my mouth wide open, in a daze.

"दर्द सैलाब बन, बह निकला"

स्वरचित: "वाचाल चिकित्सक" (पीयूष/डॉ. पी. एन. शर्मा)

ज़िंदगी ऐसे ही गुज़रा करती है;
कम तो कभी, बे-पनाह मिलता है।
इसमें गुलों की ख़ुशबुएँ होती हैं,
बाज़-वक़्त, वक़्त नासूर भी देता है।

ख़ुशबुएँ यक़ीनन सबब-ए-सुकूँ हैं,
ज़िंदगी बा-सबब हसीन बने है।
ज़ख़्मों के भी बड़े फ़ायदे होते हैं,
शायरी को यही तो ज़ुबान देते हैं।

अच्छा किया, जो दिल खोल दिया,
दर्द सैलाब बन कर बह निकला।
अब तो काफ़ी जगह बन गई है,
शायद सुकूँ मुक़ाम बना ले वहाँ।

अपने-आपको अदना-सा पाता हूँ;
कितना ही, और कुछ भी कह लूँ,
आपकी अज़ीम शायरी की शान में,
इंसाफ़ कर पाऊँ, दम नहीं मुझ में।

"The Pain Became a Flood and Gushed Out"

Composed and translated by: "Loquacious doctor" (Peeyush/Dr. P. N. Sharma)

Life passes by, just like this;
at times you get little, and at others, your hands are full.
It has the fragrance of flowers,
but sometimes, it also gives you wounds.

The fragrances are definitely a source of comfort;
they make the life becomes beautiful and meaningful.
But the wounds, too, have their own great benefits;
it is these that give a voice to poetry.

You did well by opening up your heart;
the pain came out like a great flood.
Now there is ample vacant space,
so perhaps peace can bestow its grace there.

I feel so insignificant;
no matter how much or how well I may try to speak,
in honour of your own great poetry,
I do not have the class to do it justice.

CHAPTER – 13

मिश्रित

Miscellaneous

बहुत से लम्हे छोटे,
बहुत छोटे होते हैं।
अक्सर खो जाते हैं।
मुझे शौक़ है उन्हें जमा करने का।

—प्रेरणा-स्रोत: लेखक "अज्ञात"

Many moments are small,
very small.
They are lost, most of the time.
I have the habit of collecting them.

—Inspiration from an "Unknown" writer.

"लम्हे"

स्वरचित: "वाचाल चिकित्सक" (डॉ. पी. एन. शर्मा)

ज़िंदगी लाखों छोटे-छोटे लम्हों में होती है,
हर लम्हे का अलग एक मिज़ाज होता है।
कुछ खट्टे, कुछ मीठे, कुछ कड़वे होते हैं,
कुछ सबक़, आँसू, बाक़ी ख़ुश-गवार होते हैं।

हर शख़्स का नज़रिया भी अलग होता है,
यह आप पर है कि आप इसे कैसे लेते हैं।
इन्हें बिसरा दो, तो ज़िंदगी बे-रंग हो जाए;
याद करो और लिख दो, किताब हो जाए।

"Moments"

Composed and translated by: "Loquacious doctor" Dr. P. N. Sharma

---

Life consists of millions of little moments;
each and every moment has its own distinct flavour.
Some are sour, some are sweet, and some are outright bitter;
some are lessons, some are tears, and the rest are merry.

Every person's perspective is also different;
it is up to you, how you take them.
If you forget them, then life becomes colourless;
but if you recall and write them down, they become a book.

"अंगूर की बिटिया"

स्वरचित: "वाचाल चिकित्सक" (डॉ. पी. एन. शर्मा)

बहुत दिन के बाद दिल गुनगुनाया,
कैसे हुआ कि ये दिन आज आया?
ऐ दिल, किसने मचाई ये खलबली,
कि दिल की बात ज़ुबाँ पे चली आई?

मुद्दतों से छिपा था जो राज़ सीने में,
टीसता रहा था हर रोज़, सुबह-शाम।
क्यों वो पर्दा-फ़ाश हुआ ऐसे सरे-आम?
अंगूर की बिटिया का तो नहीं, ये काम?

"The Elixir of Grape"

Composed and translated by: "Loquacious doctor" Dr. P. N. Sharma

After a long period of quiet, my heart started humming;
how did it happen that this day came today?
O' my heart, who has created this turbulence,
that the secrets of my heart have poured out from my tongue?

The secret that had been dwelling silently in my chest for so long,
that had been aching every evening and every dawn,
why was it exposed so publicly, like this?
This couldn't be the work of the Elixir of Grape[38], could it?

[38]A common metaphor for wine in Hindi and Urdu poetry.

"शायर इस ख़ाक का" (एक वाकया)

स्वरचित: "वाचाल चिकित्सक" (डॉ. पी. एन. शर्मा)

हम तो नज़रें भी चुरा रहे थे,
कुलीन जमात के जो आप थे।
हैरत तो तब हुई, जब आपने
आगे बढ़ कर हाथ मिला लिया।

शेरो-शायरी तो गहरे पैबस्त है,
ज़र्रे-ज़र्रे इस ज़मीं हिंदोस्तान में।
शायर इस ख़ाक का हर शख़्स,
ये ख़ाकसार भी कोई जुदा नहीं।

माना, हमें अदब-ए-शायरी नहीं आता;
चलना हरेक ने सीखा है यहीं।
यूँ जवानी गुज़री इसके बिन,
ख़ैर हुई, बुढ़ापे में रंगत चढ़ गई।

"Poet of the Soil" (An Incident)

Composed and translated by: "Loquacious doctor" Dr. P. N. Sharma

I averted my gaze, for you belonged to the elite set.
The surprise was when you stepped forward and shook my hand.

Poetry is woven deep into every speck of this land, India.
Every child of this soil is a poet; this humble one is no different.

I admit I lack the graces of high verse; youth passed without it—
but thankfully, in my old age, colour has at last appeared.

क़द्रदान: एक धन्यवाद ज्ञापन

स्वरचित: "वाचाल चिकित्सक" (डॉ. पी. एन. शर्मा)

आप-से क़द्रदान कितने, और किसके होते हैं;
ख़ुशकिस्मती हमारी, कि हम आपके यार होते हैं।
रब से विनती—हम कहते रहें, आप सुनते रहें;
हमारा शग़ल रहे, आपका भी वक़्त कटता रहे।

"Admirers: A Thank-You Note"

Composed and translated by: "Loquacious doctor" Dr. P. N. Sharma

How many can boast admirers like you?
Lucky for me, I'm counted as your friend.
May I keep reciting and you keep listening—
my pastime lives on, and your time flows pleasantly.

"लोग अक्सर पूछते हैं, मुझ से"

स्वरचित: "वाचाल चिकित्सक" (डॉ. पी. एन. शर्मा)

"लोग अक्सर पूछते हैं, मुझ से,"
तुम इस उम्र में कवि कैसे बने?
ऐसा क्या था जो उत्प्रेरक बना,
तुम्हारी मूक जिह्वा को शब्द मिले?

वह दिन था, जब गलवान घटा—
देश की असीम पीड़ा व आक्रोश;
शहीद परिवारों का दूरस्थ क्रंदन—
निर्झर-झरना बन, मन फूट पड़ा।

"People Often Ask Me"

Composed and translated by: "Loquacious doctor" Dr. P. N. Sharma

"People often ask me,"
how I became a poet at this age.
What was the catalyst
that gave words to a silent tongue?

It was the day Galwan happened—
the country's immense anguish and anger,
the distant cries of martyrs' families—
my heart burst like a spring and spilled into words.

"सफ़र और बुलंदगी"

स्वरचित: "वाचाल चिकित्सक" (डॉ. पी. एन. शर्मा)

सफ़र तो परवाज़ भर चुका है,
कितनी बुलंदगी हासिल होगी?
सब समय के गर्भ में छिपा है,
समय ही तोलेगा, वही बोलेगा।

"The Journey and its Pinnacle"

Composed and translated by: "Loquacious doctor" Dr. P. N. Sharma

---

The journey has already taken its flight;
How high will it soar?
It is all hidden in the womb of time;
only time will weigh it, and only time will tell.

"काव्य, एक संत्रास या उल्लास?"

स्वरचित: "वाचाल चिकित्सक" (डॉ. पी. एन. शर्मा)

मैं वाक़ई बहुत लंबे समय तक एक आम इंसान था,
चिकित्सा-विज्ञान के अपने पेशे में रमा हुआ था।
फिर मेरे छठवें दशक में एक अप्रत्याशित मोड़ आया;
सहसा एक झंझावात ने मुझे अपनी जड़ों से उखाड़ दिया।

अब तक मेरे शांत रहे मन में विचार कौंधने लगे,
मुझे कभी भी सताने लगे, चाहे रात हो या दिन।
कभी-कभी वे मेरी क़लम तक बहुत तेज़ी से उतरते,
और कभी-कभी वे त्रास-दाई, बहुत लंबा समय लेते।

उत्प्रेरक कभी हाल की ही कोई घटना होती,
या काल में अंतर्निहित कुछ, या बस एक अजीब ख़याल।
जीवन के रंग, रंगों में जीवन, प्रकृति, बदलते मौसम,
कल्पनाएँ, परिवार, दोस्त, या कोई नामाकूल चीज़ भी।

मैंने कभी सोचा भी नहीं था कि मैं लिखूँगा,
कहानियाँ सरल, और तो और, कविताएँ क्लिष्ट।
लक्ष्य ऊँचे रखने चाहे, चाहे विषय-वस्तु, शब्द हों या भाषा,
फल-स्वरूप, अत्यंत पीड़ा-दायक तनाव जनमता रहा।

मेरा संघर्ष आगे भी जारी रहा, कभी तुकबंदी के साथ,
और कभी कठिनाई से समझी, एक कवि की स्वतंत्र चाल के साथ।
मैं अनवरत चलती घड़ी के ख़िलाफ़ दौड़ता रहा,
क्योंकि मन की शांति केवल अंतिम रेखा के पार ही थी।

आख़िरकार, प्रथम-द्दष्ट्या, काम पूरा हो ही जाता था,
लेकिन मैं अपने शातिर दिमाग़ के बारे में क्या कहूँ?
यह अनिवार्य रूप से और भी नई चुनौतियाँ जोड़ देता,
जैसे कविताओं का विदेशी भाषाओं में अनुवाद।

वास्तव में, मुझे यह भी कहना चाहिए कि हर पड़ाव पर,
तृप्ति, उपलब्धि और गर्व की मादक भावना मिलती रही।
तभी मैं छड़ी के छोर पर लटकी तृष्णा-गाजर के पीछे पड़ा रहा,
इसने मेरे बूढ़े दिमाग़ के लिए उत्प्रेरक का काम किया।

मैं कभी भी अख़बारों या किताबों में छपने,
ऑनलाइन देखे जाने और न ही मशहूरियत का इच्छुक था।
पर अगर मैं अनिश्चय या झिझक वालों को प्रेरित कर सकूँ,
तो मैं लोगों और समाज के लिए एक प्रेरक तो बनूँगा।

"Poetry: A Woe or a Bliss?"

Composed and translated by: "Loquacious doctor" Dr. P. N. Sharma

---

I had been a common man for long, very long,
engrossed in my profession of medical science.
Then came an unexpected turn in my mid-sixties;
it happened suddenly and swept me off my feet.

Ideas started flashing in my restful mind,
troubling me at any time, be it night or sunshine.
Sometimes they descended very fast to my pen;
at other times, they took a long, tortuous time.

Sometimes the catalyst was a recent happening,
or things embedded in time, or just a weird thought.
The Life, the Colours, Nature, an ushering-in season;
fantasies, family, friends, or any damn thing.

I hadn't even imagined that I would ever write
simple stories, or worse, verses so arduous.
I tried to set goals high, be it content, words, or language,
resulting in tormenting stresses, unduly high.

My struggle continued further, with the rhyming,
and with the ill-understood liberties of a poet.
I raced against the ever-ticking chime,
because only the finish line held the peace of my mind.

Eventually, the job always got done, at face value;
but what can I say of my wretched mind?
It would inevitably add more woes,
like translating the poems into foreign languages.

Indeed, I must add, every terminus brought with it
a feeling of satiety, accomplishment, and pride.
For these, I chased the carrot at the end of the line;
these were the boosters for my aged, tired mind.

I never wished to be printed in papers or in books,
or to be followed or be made famous online.
But I felt that if I could enthuse the tentative or the hesitant,
then I would be serving a noble purpose to the people.

"तेरी औक़ात, मेरी औक़ात"

स्वरचित: "वाचाल चिकित्सक" (डॉ. पी. एन. शर्मा)

तेरी औक़ात तू सँवारे,
तो अपनी औक़ात मैं।
कभी तीजा आगे गया,
तो चौथा पीछे न रहा।

बात कुछ भी बनी नहीं,
ज़िंदगी यूँ ही ढलती रही।
औक़ात के इस खेल में,
कैसे मानें, तू फ़ेल या मैं?

हाथ कुछ आया नहीं,
मुट्ठी से रेत-सी फिसली,
तुझसे तेरी ज़िंदगी,
मुझसे मेरी ज़िंदगी।

"Your Status vs. My Status"

Composed and translated by: "Loquacious doctor" Dr. P. N. Sharma

You were busy grooming your status,
and so was I, for mine.
At times a third one took the lead,
and a fourth one also joined the race.

Nothing came of it in the end;
life just frittered away, like that.
In this game of status,
how can we decide who has failed, you or I?

Neither of us got anything of any worth;
from our fists, life just slipped away, like sand.
Your life from you,
and my life from me.

"चना ज़ोर गरम"

स्वरचित: "वाचाल चिकित्सक" (डॉ. पी. एन. शर्मा)

चना ज़ोर गरम, बाबू,
मैं लाया मज़ेदार, चना ज़ोर गरम!

मैं लाया चना मज़ेदार,
मेरा चना है सबसे आला,
इसमें डले गरम-मसाला,
जो भी खाए, वो हो मतवाला,
खाए हर दिल-वाला,
अरे, खाए हर दिल-वाला!

चना ज़ोर गरम, बाबू,
मैं लाया मज़ेदार, चना ज़ोर गरम!

जिसने खाया एक भी दाना,
आया उसको दिल का लगाना।
आशिक़ इस पर एक ज़माना,
बाबू, तुम भी खाते जाना,
चटखारे लेते जाना,
अरे, तुम भी कहते जाना!

चना ज़ोर गरम, बाबू,
मैं लाया मज़ेदार, चना ज़ोर गरम!

इस चने में यादें लड़कपन की,
दोस्तों संग आवारा-गर्दी की।
स्कूल से भाग, चढ़ें चने के झाड़,
फ़िल्में देख, ख़ुद को समझें हीरो।
साइकल का हैंडल हाथ में थामे,
मोटर-साइकल के सपने मन में।

चना ज़ोर गरम, बाबू,
मैं लाया मज़ेदार, चना ज़ोर गरम!

मार-पीट, लड़ाई-झगड़े,
भूल सब, खाओ चने चटपटे!
नंबर कम आने के ग़म,
क्रिकेट-फ़ुटबॉल के क़िस्से,
चटखारे लो और कहो कहानियाँ,
चाहे सच्ची हों, या हों मिथ्या!

चना ज़ोर गरम, बाबू,
मैं लाया मज़ेदार, चना ज़ोर गरम!

सुंदर, साँवली छोरियों की,
मुहल्ले में आई नई गोरियों की।
जिनकी आँखें हैं कटीली,
जिनके गाल पे छाए लाली।
जिनकी बिंदी ने जान ले ली,
दिखतीं बड़ी छैल-छबीली।

चना ज़ोर गरम, बेबी,
मैं लाया मज़ेदार, चना ज़ोर गरम!

मेरा चना बना है आली,
जिसे खाती है मतवाली।
रहती है पास वाली गली,
उसकी ज़ुल्फ़ें लहरों वाली।
उसकी कमरिया लचीली,
जिसकी चाल है नशीली।

चना ज़ोर गरम, बेबी,
मैं लाया मज़ेदार, चना ज़ोर गरम!

इस चने में याद मायके की,
केवल अठन्नी में ज़ायक़े की।
सहेलियों संग ठहाके की,
आते-जातों से ठिठोली की।
शरारती क़िस्से-कहानियों की,
आस-पड़ोस के अफ़सानों की।

चना ज़ोर गरम, बेबी,
मैं लाया मज़ेदार, चना ज़ोर गरम!

"Spicy Roasted Gram Flakes"

Composed and translated by: "Loquacious doctor" Dr. P. N. Sharma

---

Spicy roasted gram flakes, O people!
I've brought you some delicious, spicy roasted gram flakes!

I've brought you some delicious gram,
my gram is the best of all!
It's filled with hot masala,
and whoever eats it becomes an avid fan!
Everyone with a heart relishes it,
O, everyone with a heart relishes it!

Spicy roasted gram flakes, O people!
I've brought you some delicious, spicy roasted gram flakes!

Whoever has eaten even a single grain,
could not avoid falling in love.
A whole generation is in love with it;
O sir, you too must eat it and give it a try!
You will never fail to relish it,
O, you too will keep on talking about it!

Spicy roasted gram flakes, O people!
I've brought you some delicious, spicy roasted gram flakes!

In this gram are the memories of boyhood,
of loitering around with one's mates.
Bunking off school, climbing the gram-bushes[39],
watching movies, and imagining we were the heroes.
Holding the bicycle-handle in our hands,
but with dreams of motor-cycles in our minds.

Spicy roasted gram flakes, O people!
I've brought you some delicious, spicy roasted gram flakes!

---

[39]From the Hindi idiom 'चने के झाड़ पर चढ़ाना (chane ke jhaad par chadhaana),' which means to praise someone excessively.

To forget all the fights and the flaws,
just eat these spicy, flaked grams!
The dejection of getting low marks,
the defeats in cricket and football—
enjoy the taste, and tell your stories,
whether they are true or whether they are false!

Spicy roasted gram flakes, O people!
I've brought you some delicious, spicy roasted gram flakes!

Of the beautiful, brown-skinned girls,
and the new, fair-skinned beauties in the area.
The ones whose eyes are sharp as daggers,
and whose cheeks are flushed with red.
The ones whose bindi has stolen my heart,
and who look so full of charm.

Spicy roasted gram flakes, O baby!
I've brought you some delicious, spicy roasted gram flakes!

My gram has a top-class flavour,
which the young damsel devours.
She lives in the nearby lane,
her hair is wavy and vinous.
Her waist is flexible and slim,
and her gait is intoxicating.

Spicy roasted gram flakes, O baby!
I've brought you some delicious, spicy roasted gram flakes!

In this gram are the memories of a mother's home,
of the taste you could get for only fifty paise.
Of the laughter with one's confidantes,
and of teasing the passers-by.
Of all the mischievous stories and tales,
and of the secret chronicles from the nearby locales.

Spicy roasted gram flakes, O baby!
I've brought you some delicious, spicy roasted gram flakes!

"शब्द-साधना"

स्वरचित: "वाचाल चिकित्सक" (डॉ. पी. एन. शर्मा)

बूझ सको तुम, तो बूझ लो,
मुझे आज तो माफ़ करो।
सही कहा या ग़लत कहा,
पता नहीं, मैंने कहा क्या।

मुझे सच-मुच लग रहा ऐसा,
जो भी कहा, सच ही कहा।
मैं अपने पूरे होश में ही हूँ,
शब्द शायद बहक गए हों।

शब्द बारंबार भटकते रहे,
री-टेक पर री-टेक होते गए।
इल्ज़ाम हम पर न लगाओ,
शब्द-साधना आसान नहीं।

"Taming the Words"

Composed and translated by: "Loquacious doctor" Dr. P. N. Sharma

If you can decipher it, then please do;
but for today, please forgive me.
I do not know whether I said right or wrong,
or even what it was that I said.

But I truly do feel
that whatever I said, I said the truth.
I am fully in my senses, I believe;
perhaps it was my words that went astray.

The words kept wandering,
and retakes kept happening, again and again.
So do not put the blame on me;
to tame the words is not so easy.

“हम ही उन्हें मुरीद मान लेते हैं”

स्वरचित: “वाचाल चिकित्सक” (डॉ. पी. एन. शर्मा)

आप ही हैं जो चूकते नहीं,
हर बार हौसला-अफ़ज़ाई से।
वरना कई दिल पसीजते नहीं,
“हम ही उन्हें मुरीद मान लेते हैं।”

“I Just Assume They are My Fans”

Composed and translated by: “Loquacious doctor” Dr. P. N. Sharma

You are the one who never fails
to encourage me, every single time.
Otherwise, many hearts do not melt,
and so, “I just assume they are my fans.”

"मुझे मेरा मोम-दिल मुबारक"

स्वरचित: "वाचाल चिकित्सक" (डॉ. पी. एन. शर्मा)

पाँवों के छाले यक़ीनन दर्द देते हैं,
राह मुश्किल, चाल सुस्त होती है।
उसूल पे चलना सुकून-ए-दिल भी है,
ये आप पे है, ध्यान किस पे देते हैं।

जो भी चाहे, अकड़ के चले,
मुझे किसी पे ऐतराज़ नहीं।
मुझे मेरा मोम-दिल मुबारक,
आपको शिकवा हो, तो हो।

अकड़े दिल में इंसानियत,
बसेरा कर ही नहीं सकती।
वो मोम-दिलों को ढूँढ़ती है,
अपना डेरा ज़माने के लिए।

मैं तो जो हूँ, सो सामने हूँ,
पर आपके दिल का मोम?
इतना मुलायम, कहाँ पाया?
ये बाज़ार में बिकता कहाँ है?

"I am Happy with My Wax-Soft Heart"

Composed and translated by: "Loquacious doctor" Dr. P. N. Sharma

Blistered feet surely give you pain;
the walking is difficult, and your gait is slow.
But to abide by one's principles is also the peace of one's heart;
it is up to you, what you choose to pay attention to.

Whoever wants to walk with arrogance,
I have no objection to that.
I am happy with my wax-soft heart;
if you have a complaint about it, then so be it.

Humanity can never reside
in an arrogant heart.
It searches for wax-soft hearts,
in which to set up its camp.

I am what I am, right here in the open;
but the wax-like softness of your heart?
So soft, where did you get it from?
Where is it sold in the market?

"ज़माने का इम्तिहाँ"

स्वरचित: "वाचाल चिकित्सक" (डॉ. पी. एन. शर्मा)

"ज़माने का इम्तिहाँ" लेने से क्या हासिल?
पहले से ही दौर-ए-ज़माना रहा है बदनाम।
इसने कई हीर-राँझों का ख़ून तो पिया,
कमाल ये है, न इसके लबों पे रंग चढ़ा।
न किसी ने ख़ूँ-रेज़ी का इल्ज़ाम ही मढ़ा;
तुम ख़ुद से ही अपने ज़ख़्म सहला लो।
न पहले किसी ने किसी का इलाज करा,
न अब भी कोई खुले-आम साथ आएगा।

"Why Judge the World?"

Composed and translated by: "Loquacious doctor" Dr. P. N. Sharma

---

What will you gain "why judge the world"?
The world has always been notorious.
It has quenched its thirst with the blood of lovers,
but what is amazing is that its lips were never stained.
No one has ever accused it of bloodshed;
you must soothe your own wounds, yourself.
No one has ever cared for anyone, in times gone by,
and no one will openly side with you now, either.

"अपने-से दिखते तो हो, पर हो नहीं"

स्वरचित: "वाचाल चिकित्सक" (डॉ. पी. एन. शर्मा)

अपने-से दिखते तो हो,
पर हो नहीं।

बातें जैसी करते हो,
वैसे हो नहीं।

कहते हो हम एक हैं,
पर हैं नहीं।

तुम मेरी राह चलो,
ऐसा होगा नहीं।

मैं तुम्हारी राह चलूँ?
क़तई नहीं!

अपनी असलियत कभी,
तुमने कही नहीं।

फिर क्या हम साथ रहें?
सोचा नहीं।

"You Look like Me, But You Are Not"

Composed and translated by: "Loquacious doctor" Dr. P. N. Sharma

---

You do look like me,
but you are not.

The way you present yourself,
you are not.

You say that we are one,
but we are not.

You will walk on my path?
That will not happen.

And should I walk on your path?
Never!

You have never revealed
your real self.

So, should we still stick together?
I have never thought about it.

"बे-हया मुहब्बत"

स्वरचित: "वाचाल चिकित्सक" (डॉ. पी. एन. शर्मा)

जलने वाले जलें, मुझे क्या?
मैं सही हूँ, बे-शक न मानें, मुझे क्या?
बे-शरम हूँ अपनी मुहब्बत में,
किसी को आग लगे, मुझे क्या?

दीवानगी यूँ ही नहीं होती,
कुछ बात भी होनी चाहिए।
हमें पागल कहो या दीवाना,
क़ुबूल है फ़रमान तुम्हारा।

हम तो, अब जहाँ हैं, वहाँ,
तुम्हारी बात नहीं पहुँचती।
तरस तो तुम पर आता है,
दर पे लिखी इबारत नहीं दिखती।

क्या पीड़ा है, जो बेचैन हो,
बीता तजने, तैयार नहीं हो?
आँखें खोल, देखो तो सही,
ज़माने में सही है, तो वही।

"Shameless love"

Composed and translated by: "Loquacious doctor" Dr. P. N. Sharma

Let those who are jealous be jealous; what do I care?
I am right, and if they don't agree, why should I care?
I am shameless in my love;
if someone gets angry and frets over it, what do I care?

This obsession does not just happen on its own;
for this, there must be some solid reason.
Call me mad or call me crazy;
I accept your assessment of me.

Where I am now,
your message cannot reach me.
I only feel pity for you,
for you cannot see the writing on the wall.

What is this pain that makes you so restless?
Are you not ready to let go of the past?
Just open your eyes and see;
if there is anything that is right in this world, then it is that.

CHAPTER - 14

प्रसिद्ध गानों का अनुवाद

Translation of Famous Songs

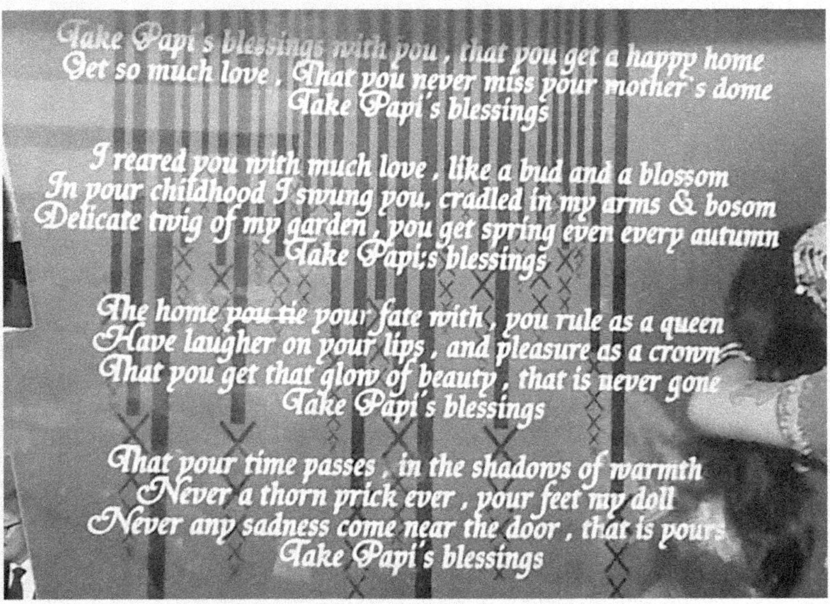

"बाबुल की दुआएँ"

मूल हिंदी सिनेमा गीत "नील कमल"

बाबुल की दुआएँ लेती जा,
जा, तुझको सुखी संसार मिले।
मैके की कभी न याद आए,
ससुराल में इतना प्यार मिले।

बाबुल की दुआएँ लेती जा।

नाज़ों से तुझे पाला मैंने,
कलियों की तरह, फूलों की तरह।
बचपन में झुलाया है तुझको,
बाँहों ने मेरी, झूलों की तरह।
मेरे बाग़ की ऐ नाज़ुक डाली,
तुझे हर पल नई बहार मिले।

बाबुल की दुआएँ लेती जा।

जिस घर से बँधे हैं भाग तेरे,
उस घर में सदा तेरा राज रहे।
होठों पे हँसी की धूप खिले,
माथे पे ख़ुशी का ताज रहे।
जिसकी ज्योत कभी न हो फीकी,
तुझे ऐसा रूप-सिंगार मिले।

बाबुल की दुआएँ लेती जा।

बीतें तेरे जीवन की घड़ियाँ,
आराम की ठंडी छाँव में।
काँटा भी न चुभने पाए कभी,
मेरी लाड़ली, तेरे पाँव में।
उस द्वार से भी दुख दूर रहे,
जिस द्वार से तेरा द्वार मिले।

बाबुल की दुआएँ लेती जा।

"Papa's Blessings"

Translated by "Loquacious doctor" Dr. P. N. Sharma

Take your Papa's blessings with you,
that you may find a happy home.
May you receive so much love,
that you never miss your mother's dome.

Take your Papa's blessings with you.

I reared you with such love,
like a bud and like a blossom.
In your childhood, I swung you,
cradled in my arm and bosom.
O delicate twig of my garden,
may you find a new spring, even in every autumn.

Take your Papa's blessings with you.

The home you tie your fate with,
may you always rule that as a queen.
May you have laughter on your lips,
and a crown of pleasure upon your brow.
May you receive a glow of beauty,
that is never gone.

Take your Papa's blessings with you.

May all the hours of your life pass,
in the cool shadows of warmth and comfort.
Never a thorn prick ever,
your feet, my doll.
Never any sadness come near the door,
that is now yours.

Take your Papa's blessings with you.

Thank you for this wonderful new chapter! This is a delightful addition to your book—a real-time, spontaneous exchange of poetry between friends, which captures the joy and camaraderie of a traditional *mushaira* (poetry gathering) but conducted over WhatsApp.

Editorial Team Walnut

CHAPTER - 15

व्हाट्स ऐप पर स्वतः-स्फूर्त तात्कालिक गुफ्तगू मुशायरा

Spontaneous Extempore Bantering & Musings on WhatsApp

व्हाट्सऐप पर स्वतः-स्फूर्त तात्कालिक गुफ्तगू

आशु-शायरी, मुशायरा

Spontaneous Extempore Chat

A Poet's Conference

Bantering & Musings on WhatsApp

ऑनलाइन तात्कालिक मुशायरा गुफ्तगू

Online Extempore Bantering & Musings

1. "क्या हुआ जो दिन ढला?"

डॉक्टर चंद्र-प्रकाश तिवारी (Dr. Chandra Prakash Tiwari): (स्वरचित / Self-composed)

कल ही तो ज़िंदगी की सहर हुई थी,
और लो, आज बे-वजह ही शाम हो गई।
कहते थे मिलती है चार दिन ज़िंदगी,
क़िबला, ये तो दो दिन में तमाम हो गई।
जीवन की किताब पूरी पढ़ ही न पाए,
करना था बहुत-कुछ, कर ही न पाए।
ये चौथा पन भी, बड़ा अजीब है, यारों;
फिर बचपन जीने का मन होता है, यारों।

पीयूषः "क्या हुआ जो दिन ढला?",

"क्या हुआ जो दिन ढला", रात हुई?
"चंद्र-प्रकाश" का बे-पनाह हुस्न,
दिन ढलने बाद ही बे-पर्दा होता है।
फलक पे चाँद, अचला पर "दीपक",
साथ में अगर हो "पीयूष" का पान,
तब धरा पर "मधु"-एहसास होता है।

इन चार दिनों से ख़ौफ़-ज़दा न हो,
जो फैला है, उससे ग़म-ज़दा न हो।
हम जो पढ़े न पढ़े, किया न किया,
अगली जवान क़ौम के पल्ले डाल।
तू तो बस, बुढ़ापे में घोल बचपना,
मन में जो रह गया, अब कर डाल।

डॉ. दीपक

मन में जो रह गया, अब कर डाल,
तू तो बस! बुढ़ापे में घोल बचपना।
बे-शक, न बर्बादी, न हो बे-इज़्ज़ती,
उम्र की गहराई का भी ध्यान रखना।

पीयूष

सब को सीमाओं का पता है,
ऐसा भ्रम और डर क्यों पाल?
तू मन की सारी गाँठें खोल,
जो मन कहे, लिख या बोल डाल।

हमारे प्रोत्साहन का मान करो,
अपनी क्षमताओं का भान करो।
कब तलक अज्ञात डर से डरोगे?
हमारा साथ रहेगा, विश्वास करो।

डॉक्टर प्रमोद

ख़ूब लिखा, सी.पी., पर बचपन जीने का मन मत करो—बचपन जियो। ज़िंदगी, ज़िंदा-दिली का नाम है। बहुत ख़ूब, पीयूष!

डॉक्टर सुरेंद्र

बहुत सुंदर रचनाएँ, सभी की। बहुत गहराई है। बहुत प्रेरणा देती हैं। जितनी तारीफ़ की जाए, कम है। कृपया जारी रखें।

1. "What if the Day has Ended?"

Bantering in Hindi & translated into English by
"Loquacious doctor" Peeyush / Dr. P. N. Sharma

Dr. Chandra Prakash Tiwari ("The Moonlight"):
(Self-Composed)

It was just yesterday that life had dawned,
and look, today it is already near its conclusion.
They said that we get four days of life,
but this life is ending in just two.
I could not go through the book of life to the end;
I had so much to do, but I could not do it.
This fourth phase of life is very strange, my friends;
I feel like living my childhood again, my friends.

Peeyush ("Nectar or wine"):
"What if the Day has Ended?"

"What if the day has ended," and it is now night?
The infinite beauty of the "Moonlight" (Chandra Prakash)
is revealed only after the day takes its flight.
With the moon in the sky and a "Lamp" (Deepak) on the ground,
if there is also a goblet of "Nectar" (Peeyush) to go along with it,
then a "sweet" (Madhu) sensation abounds on earth.

Do not be scared of these four days;
do not be sad about all that has unfolded around.
Whatever we have studied or not, done or not done,
hand over the job to the younger generation.
You just mix childishness into your old age,
and whatever craving remains unrealized, do it now.

Dr. Deepak (Lamp)

Whatever lingers undone in your mind, do it now.
You just do it! Mix childishness into your old age.
Of course, do not ruin yourself or earn a bad name;
you must take care of the sobriety that comes with age.

Peeyush:

Everyone knows their own limits;
why harbor such illusions and fears?
Untie all the knots in your mind,
and write or say whatever your heart desires.

Respect and honor our encouragement;
be aware of your own capabilities.
How long will you remain fearful of the unknown?
Believe us, we will always be there with you.

Dr. Pramod:

Well written, C.P., but do not just feel like living your childhood—live it!
Life is the name of liveliness. Well done, Peeyush!

Dr. Surendra:

Very beautiful creations, all of them. They have a lot of depth. They inspire a great deal. No amount of praise is enough. Please continue.

(25th August 2021)

2. कवि मित्र दीपक का धन्यवाद ज्ञापन

डॉ. दीपकः

मिल गया है दरख़्ते चना चढ़ाने को तुझे,
मेरे गिरने से तू खुश है, तो ये भी सही।

डॉ. प्रमोदः

लगे रहो।
कवियों की नोक-झोंक और
हमारा आनंद।

पीयूषः

धन्यवाद दीपक

दीपक ने राह रौशन की वर्ना,
हम इस राह के राही तो न थे।
न ही राह कभी नजरों में थी,
भटकते थे बस, यूं ही यहां-वहां।

देख दीपक राह, राह पकड़ी,
हम भी राह के राही हो गए।
भले ही हों हम नातजुर्बेकार,
तजुर्बा आते-आते ही आता है।

तुम तो आसमानों पर विराजे हो,
तुम्हारा ठौर महफ़ूज़ मुकम्मल है।
तुम्हारी अपनी बाजुओं का जोर है,
किसी के गिराने से क्या गिरोगे।

हम नवागंतुक हैं, बाजू कमजोर हैं,
जरा हाथ बढ़ाओ, हमें खींच लो।
आसपास हमारा भी ठौर कर लो,
हम भी देख लेंगे नजारे वहां के।

हम भी सितारे हैं उसी आसमां के,
आप सब चमकते जहां साथ-साथ।

आप सब की सोहबत ने,
संवारी है, ये हस्ती हमारी।
कुछ रौशनी इधर-उधर से,
वहीं थोड़ी बहुत हमारी है।

दीपक रौशनी का बाइस है,
हम भी कुछ कह जाते हैं।
छोटी सी बात बड़ी बनाना,
जर्रा-नवाजी है आपकी।

दोस्ती के तरानों से आगे,
कुछ भी नहीं इस जहां में।
इन गुलदस्तों में हैं सारे रंग,
हर सुगंध जमाने भर की।

कभी आप कहें, कभी हम,
बस सुने हरेक, दाद दे, न दे।
बस यूं ही खुशियां बंटे-बढ़ें,
यही रब से इल्तज़ा हमारी।

न तुम आगे, न हम ही आगे,
साथ कदम तुम्हारा हमारा।
हम एक-दूजे के उत्प्रेरक हैं,
साफगोई से बात, बस ये है।

डॉ. दीपक:
यार की यारी ने हौसला दिया मुझको,
वरना सिवा सांस के बाकी क्या था।

पीयूष:
बहुत तेल है दीपक में,
जज़्बात लबालब तुझ में।
लफ्ज़ों में ढालने इनको,
जरूरी हुनर भी खूब है।
और क्या क्या बोलें तुझ पे,
सबकी जान बसी है तुझ में।
सदा इसे संभाल के रखना,
बड़ी कीमती है इस जहां में।

डॉ. अतुल:
दीपक का काम ही है,
खुद जलकर रोशनी देना।

पीयूष:
सारा जिम्मा दीपक का नहीं,
कुछ तो अपने जिम्मे भी लें।
साथ उसका अगर हम न दें,
फिर हम आप, क्यूं साथ हैं?

दीपक की एक मियाद है,
तेल डालना आपका काम है।
दीपक का एक दायरा है,
उसे बढ़ाना आपका काम है।

रौशनी से रोशनियां जोड़ें,
ये हमारा-आपका काम है।
काम व्यापक विस्तार का है।
हाथ साथ मिलें, ये बात है।

स्वरचित मूल लेख (गुफ्तगू) हिन्दी, उर्दू
"वाचाल चिकित्सक" पीयूष — डॉक्टर पी. एन. शर्मा 19 जून 2021

2. Thank You Dear Poet Friend Deepak

Dr. Deepak:
You have found a "gram plant to seat me"—
If you're happy with my fall, then so be it.
(*Indian proverb: "to praise someone to the skies"*)

Dr. Pramod:
Keep it up: poets' banter and our joy.

Peeyush: Thanks, **Deepak (Lamp).**

Deepak (Lamp) lit the path—otherwise,
I never was a traveller of this track;
Nor was the way ever in sight,
I was just wandering, here and there.

Seeing Deepak's trail, I took the cue;
I too became a traveller of this trail, albeit of a few.
Sure, I am inexperienced,
but experience comes with time.

You are seated atop the skies,
your place is guaranteed and safe.
Your attainments come from strong arms—
You won't fall, even if someone tries real hard.

I am a newcomer, my arms are weak;
just extend a helping hand and pull me up.
Make a place for me nearby;
I want to savor the sights there too.

I too am a tiny star in that same sky,
where you all shine side by side.

The company of you all
has shaped this little existence of mine.
Some light, I borrowed here and there,
and a little unaccounted for, is truly mine.

The lamp is the source of light;
I too say a few things at times.
Praising a small attempt as big—
that is your kindness.

Beyond songs of friendship,
there is nothing in this world.
Bouquets have all the colors,
each fragrance that the world holds.

Sometimes you recite, sometimes I;
let each listen, whether they praise or not.
May happiness keep spreading and growing,
that is what I pray to the almighty.

Neither you lead, nor do I—
our steps match each other's.
We are each other's catalyst;
this is what truthfully matters.

Doctor Deepak (Lamp):
Friendship of my friend gave me courage,
otherwise, what was left except for breaths?

Peeyush:
There's a lot of oil in the lamp **(Deepak)**;
you are brimming full of emotion.
To pour them into words
you have a wonderful skill.

What else can one say about you—
everyone's soul is in you.
Keep it safe always;
it's so precious in this world.

Doctor Atul:
The work of the lamp is to burn and give light.

Peeyush:
All the responsibility isn't on the lamp **(Deepak)**—
some of it should fall to us as well.
If we don't support him,
then why are we together at all?

The lamp has a timespan;
it's our job to pour in the oil.
The lamp has a range—
it's our duty to help expand it further.

Let us connect light to light,
that's our shared task together.
The work is of broadening the shine—
let's join our hands; that's what matters.

Bantering in Hindi and translated into English by "Loquacious doctor"
PEEYUSH, Dr. P. N. Sharma, 19th June 2021

3. शब्द साधना

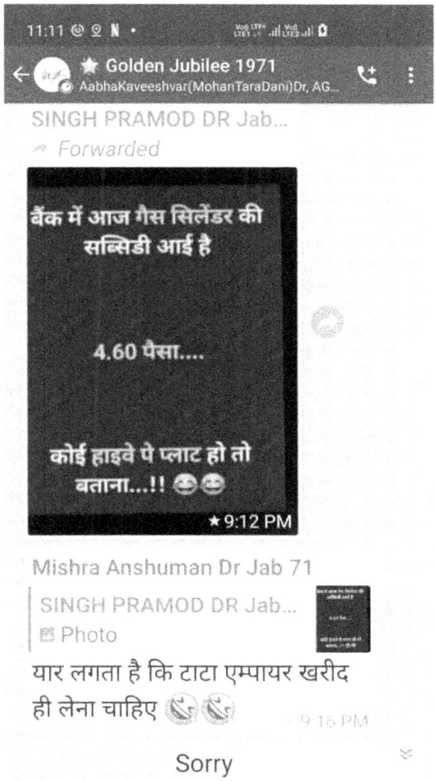

पीयूष:

बूझ सको तुम, तो बूझ लो,
मुझे आज तो माफ़ करो।
सही कहा या ग़लत कहा,
पता नहीं, मैंने कहा क्या।

मुझे सच-मुच लग रहा ऐसा,
जो भी कहा, सच ही कहा।
मैं अपने पूरे होश में ही हूँ,
शब्द शायद बहक गए हों।

शब्द बारंबार भटकते रहे,
री-टेक पर री-टेक होते गए।
इल्ज़ाम हम पर न लगाओ,
शब्द-साधना आसान नहीं।

डॉक्टर प्रमोद:
शब्द-साधना जिन्होंने नहीं की,
उनके लिए आसान नहीं। तुमने की है,
तत्काल शब्दों का जाल बुन देते हो,
तो आसान क्यों नहीं?

पीयूष:
हाईवे का प्लाट हो, या कार,
या टाटा-बिड़ला भी कोई चीज़ हैं?
बे-मोल हम, और हमारे जैसे,
कृपा करो, हमें ही ख़रीद लो।

डॉक्टर प्रमोद:
तुम्हें कोई क्या ख़रीद पाएगा,
तुम तो अनमोल हो,
हमने तुम्हें
बे-मोल पाया है।

पीयूष:
प्यार की चाहत तो है हमें,
पर कभी इतना भी न चाहें।
कि हम ही आपे में नहीं रहें,
ना-चीज़ थे, और वही रहने दें।

शातिर दोस्तों की क्या कहें,
सफ़ाई से चुराया मेरा दिल,
किसी को पता भी न चला।
पर हम तो गए इस जान से।

स्वरचित मूल लेख (गुफ्तगू) हिन्दी, उर्दू
"वाचाल चिकित्सक" पीयूष — डॉक्टर पी. एन. शर्मा 7 मई 2021

3. Taming The Words

Peeyush:

If you can decipher it, then please do,
but forgive me for today.
I don't know whether I said right or wrong,
or even what I said at all.

I truly feel that
whatever I said, I said the truth.
I believe I am fully in my senses;
perhaps it was my words that went astray.

The words kept wandering;
retakes kept happening, again and again.
Don't put the blame on me—
taming the words is not so easy.

Dr. Pramod:

It isn't easy for those who haven't tried taming words. You have done it, you instantly create a web of words, so why is it not easy?

Peeyush:

A plot on the highway, or a car,
or even the billionaires—what are they to me?
I am valueless, and so are others like me;
please be a sport, and just buy me.

Dr. Pramod:

Who could ever buy you?
You are priceless,
and yet, we have,
found you for free.

Peeyush:

I do want to be loved,
but never love me so much
that I lose my own sense of self.
I was a trivial thing; let me remain so.

What can I say about my cunning friends?
They stole my heart so cleanly, so cleverly,
that no one ever knew.
But in the process, I lost my very self.

Bantering in Hindi and translated into English by "Loquacious doctor"
PEEYUSH, Dr. P. N. Sharma, 7th May 2021

५. जिंदगी का एक फलसफा है

डा मधु :

दर्द की लहर आई थी, गुजर भी गई,
किया था बेचैन, फिर गुजर भी गई।

परेशानी का सबब बहुत था मगर,
हौसले के साये में, वो गुजर भी गई।

इक हिसाब सा था, अब खत्म हुआ,
बात थी, फिर ज़ेहन से उतर भी गई।

पीयूषः

"जिंदगी का एक फलसफा है"

जिंदगी का एक फलसफा है,
न वो रहता है, न ये रहता है।
वो भी गुजरा, ये भी गुजरेगा,
मन को समझाने की बात है।

आपने जज्बातों को हवा दी,
मन अचानक से कुछ बोला।
यूं कुरेदते रहेंगे आप,
तो सहर यूं ही बीतेगी।

चलिए अब बस करते हैं,
जिंदगी में और भी काम हैं।

स्वरचित मूल लेख (गुफ्तगू) हिन्दी, उर्दू
"वाचाल चिकित्सक" पीयूष — डॉक्टर पी. एन. शर्मा 5 जून 2021

4. "There is A Philosophy of life"

Dr. Madhu (Forwarded Lines):
Wave of pain forced its way, but then it passed,
it made me restless, but then it too settled down.

It was a cause of much anguish and concern,
but it passed under the shelter of my resolve.

It was like an appraisal, but now it is done,
it was a thought, now it is off my mind.

Peeyush:
"There is a philosophy of life"

There is a philosophy of life;
neither that persisted, nor will this.
That passed, and this too will pass—
it is a matter of convincing the mind.

You gave vent to emotions,
my mind suddenly uttered something.
If you keep probing like this,
the morning will pass just like this.

Let's take a break now;
there are other things to do in life.

Bantering in Hindi and translated into English by "Loquacious doctor"
PEEYUSH, Dr. P. N. Sharma, 5th June 2021

5. बेदर्द लोग

डॉक्टर वसंतः

दर्द सहन करने की यूँ आदत-सी हो गयी है,
कि अब दर्द न मिले, तो दर्द-सा होता है।

पीयूषः

"बेदर्द लोग"

बेदर्द लोगों से तआरुफ़ क्या हुआ,
दर्द ज़िंदगी का हिस्सा हो गया।
क्या आए वे ज़िंदगी में पल-भर,
तमाम दिनों का फ़साना हो गया।

कहना तो बहुत कुछ था हमें,
न जाने क्यों, कहने से रह गए।
शायद उन्हें कुछ तो सुनना था,
नहीं कहा, तो ख़फ़ा-से हो गए।

ख़याल न किया दीवानगी का,
मुँह मोड़ कर वो तो चल दिए।
भौंचक्के, मुँह बाए, उन्हें ताकते,
हम वहीं, खड़े-के-खड़े रह गए।

स्वरचित मूल लेख (गुफ्तगू) हिन्दी

"वाचाल चिकित्सक" पीयूष — डॉक्टर पी. एन. शर्मा 16 जून 2021

5. Heartless People

Dr. Vasant:
I have become so accustomed to bearing pain,
that now, if I do not feel pain, it hurts.

Peeyush:
"Heartless People"

When I came across heartless people,
pain became a part of my life.
They came into my life for but a moment,
and it became a story for a lifetime.

I had so much to say,
but I don't know why, I could not say it.
Perhaps they expected to hear certain words;
I did not say them, and so they became upset.

They did not care for my passion;
They just turned their face and walked away.
I stood there, staring at their back,
with my mouth wide open, in a daze.

Bantering in Hindi and translated into English by "Loquacious doctor"
PEEYUSH, Dr. P. N. Sharma, 16th June 2021

6. दिल मेरा, हैं आपका

डॉ. दीपक:

जब भी यारों के गिरेबान में झाँका मैंने,
हर वक़्त ख़ुदी की तस्वीर नज़र आई।

पीयूष:

"दिल मेरा, है आपका"

कहा तो था, "दिल मेरा, है आपका,"
यूँ ही मान लेते इस बात को।
क्यों कर झाँका था मेरे दिल में?
ऐतबार नहीं मुझ पर आपको?

डॉ. दीपक:

दोस्ती के लिए हमदम, हमदर्द और हमदिली ज़रूरी है।
दोनों ने ही एक-दूजे के दिल में अकेले झाँका ही नहीं है,
रहने की जगह भी बना ली है
और रहते भी हैं।

पीयूष:

यूँ तो बजा फ़रमाया आपने,
दर-असल, सवाल सिर्फ़ ये है:
ताका-झाँकी का सबब क्या था?
ऐतबार भी तो लाए होते हम पर!

स्वरचित मूल लेख (गुफ्तगू) हिन्दी
"वाचाल चिकित्सक" पीयूष — डॉक्टर पी. एन. शर्मा 16 जून 2021

6. My Heart is Yours

Dr. Deepak:

Whenever I looked into the hearts of my friends,
I always saw a portrait of myself.

Peeyush:

"My Heart is Yours"

I had told you, "My heart is yours";
you should have taken me at my word.
Why did you have to peep into my heart?
Do you not have any trust in me?

Dr. Deepak:

Friendship requires a partner, empathy,
and fellow-feeling.
Both of us have not only peeped into each other's hearts,
but we have even found a place to occupy and live there.

Peeyush:

You said it, and said it right,
but in truth, the only question is this:
What was the reason for all the peeping?
You should have brought some trust in me, as well!

Bantering in Hindi and translated into English by "Loquacious doctor"
PEEYUSH, Dr. P. N. Sharma, 16th June 2021

7. हम ही उन्हें मुरीद मान लेते हैं

डॉ. दीपकः
यारी में गुस्ताख़ी नहीं,
तो क्या यारी!
अजनबी को,
आवाज़ नहीं दी जाती।

पीयूषः
"हम ही उन्हें मुरीद मान लेते हैं"

आप ही हैं जो चूकते नहीं,
हर बार हौसला-अफ़ज़ाई से।
वरना कई दिल पसीजते नहीं,
"हम ही उन्हें मुरीद मान लेते हैं।"

स्वरचित मूल लेख (गुफ्तगू) हिन्दी
"वाचाल चिकित्सक" पीयूष — डॉक्टर पी. एन. शर्मा 18 जून 2021

7. I Just Assume They Are My Fans

Dr. Deepak:
If there is no frankness and insolence in friendship,
then what is the fun in friendship!
You do not call out,
to a stranger

Peeyush:
"I Just Assume They Are My Fans"

You are the only one who never fails
to encourage me, every single time.
Otherwise, many hearts do not melt,
and so, "I just assume they are my fans."

Bantering in Hindi and translated into English by "Loquacious doctor"
PEEYUSH, Dr. P. N. Sharma, 18th June 2021

४. मुझे मेरा मोम-दिल मुबारक

पीयूषः

पाँवों के छाले यक़ीनन दर्द देते हैं,
राह मुश्किल, चाल सुस्त होती है।
उसूल पे चलना सुकून-ए-दिल भी है,
ये आप पे है, ध्यान किस पे देते हैं।

डॉक्टर वसंतः

मोम-जैसा दिल लेकर फिरोगे तो लोग जलाते ही रहेंगे।

पीयूषः

जो भी चाहे, अकड़ के चले,
मुझे किसी पे ऐतराज़ नहीं।
मुझे मेरा मोम-दिल मुबारक,
आपको शिकवा हो, तो हो।

अकड़े दिल में इंसानियत
बसेरा कर ही नहीं सकती।
वो मोम-दिलों को ढूँढ़ती है,
अपना डेरा ज़माने के लिए।

मैं तो जो हूँ, सो सामने हूँ,
पर आपके दिल का मोम?
इतना मुलायम, कहाँ पाया?
ये बाज़ार में बिकता कहाँ है?

स्वरचित मूल लेख (गुफ्तगू) हिन्दी, उर्दू

"वाचाल चिकित्सक" पीयूष — डॉक्टर पी. एन. शर्मा 22 जून 2021

8. I am Happy with my Wax-Soft Heart

Peeyush:
Blistered feet surely give you pain;
the walking is difficult, and your gait is slow.
But to abide by one's principles is also the peace of one's heart;
it is up to you, what you choose to pay attention to.

Dr. Vasant:
If you roam around with a heart as soft as wax,
people will keep on burning you.

Peeyush:
Whoever wants to walk with arrogance,
I have no objection to that.
I am happy with my wax-soft heart;
if you have a complaint about it, then so be it.

Humanity can never reside
in an arrogant heart.
It searches for wax-soft hearts,
in which to set up its camp.

I am what I am, right here in the open;
but the wax-like softness of your heart?
So soft—where did you get it from?
Where is it sold in the market?

Bantering in Hindi and translated into English by "Loquacious doctor"
PEEYUSH, Dr. P. N. Sharma, 22nd June 2021

९. दर्द सैलाब बन, बह निकला

डॉक्टर तिवारी:

हसरतें पूरी हो न सकीं, अब इल्ज़ाम किसे दें?
हम ख़ुद ही बे-ख़बर थे, अब नाम किसका लें?
अरमान पाले बेशुमार, परवाज़ न ले सके;
पंख निकले देर से, करते तो क्या करते?
अब आया तीर चलाने का फ़न तो क्या आया?
अब तो इन हाथों में ख़ाली कमान बाक़ी है।

पीयूषः

"दर्द सैलाब बन, बह निकला"

ज़िंदगी ऐसे ही गुज़रा करती है,
कम तो कभी, बे-पनाह मिलता है।
इसमें गुलों की ख़ुशबुएँ होती हैं,
बाज़-वक़्त, वक़्त नासूर भी देता है।

ख़ुशबुएँ यक़ीनन सबब-ए-सुकूँ हैं,
ज़िंदगी बा-सबब हसीन बने है।
ज़ख़्मों के भी बड़े फ़ायदे होते हैं,
शायरी को यही तो ज़ुबान देते हैं।

अच्छा किया, दिल खोल दिया,
दर्द सैलाब बन कर बह निकला।
अब तो काफ़ी जगह बन गई है,
शायद सुकूँ वहाँ मुक़ाम बना ले।

अपने-आपको अदना-सा पाता हूँ।
कितना ही, और कुछ भी कह लूँ,
आपकी अज़ीम शायरी की शान में,
इंसाफ़ कर पाऊँ, दम नहीं मुझ में।

स्वरचित मूल लेख (गुफ्तगू) हिन्दी, उर्दू
"वाचाल चिकित्सक" पीयूष — डॉक्टर पी. एन. शर्मा 22 जून 2021

9. Pain Became a Flood & Gushed Out

Dr. Tiwari:
Desires could not be fulfilled, so whom do I blame?
I myself was unaware, so whom should I name?
I had countless desires, but they could not take flight;
my wings grew late, so what could I do?
Now that I have learned the art of shooting arrows, so what?
All that is left in my hands now is an arrowless bow.

Peeyush:
"Pain Became a Flood & Gushed Out"

Life passes by just like this;
at times you get little, and at others, your hands are full.
It has the fragrance of flowers,
but sometimes, time also gives you wounds that never heal.

Fragrances are definitely a source of comfort;
they are the reason that life becomes beautiful and meaningful.
But wounds, too, have their great benefits;
it is these that give a voice to poetry.

You did well to open up your heart;
the pain came out like a great flood.
Now there is ample vacant space;
perhaps peace can bestow it, its grace

I feel so insignificant.
No matter how much or how well I may try to speak,
in honor of your great verses,
I do not have the class to do them justice.

Bantering in Hindi and translated into English by "Loquacious doctor"
PEEYUSH, Dr. P. N. Sharma, 22nd June 2021

10. वफ़ा

डॉ. दीपकः

फ़क़त एक चाँद गवाह था मेरी बे-गुनाही का;
मुंसिफ़ ने पेशी अमावस की रात मुक़र्रर कर दी।

पीयूषः

"वफ़ाआशु-शायरी — "

ऐसी क्या बात थी हमारे नसीब में,
क्यों ऐसा होता आया हर दफ़ा?
कम न थी कभी भी मेरी वफ़ा,
जो हाथ आया, ख़ाली लिफ़ाफ़ा।

क़ुसूर हमारा कुछ भी तो न था,
हुज़ूर ख़ामख़ाह रहे हमसे ख़फ़ा।
क्या करते, कोई चारा भी न था,
सहते रहे ज़माने-भर की ज़फ़ा।

अहमियत-ए-शायरी का अंदाज़ा न था,
दिल जो टूटा, इसी ने मरहम लगाया।
जो छिपा था मुद्दतों, लबों पे आया,
बे-पर्दा हुए जज़्बात, छिपा न पाया।

आज इस पे यक़ीं हो गया,
कि चराग़-तले अँधेरा होता है।
जो होता है यहीं आस-पास,
उसे हम दूर तलक ढूँढ़ते हैं।

स्वरचित मूल लेख (गुफ्तगू) हिन्दी, उर्दू
"वाचाल चिकित्सक" पीयूष — डॉक्टर पी. एन. शर्मा 26 जून 2021

10. Loyalty

Dr. Deepak:
Only the moon was a witness to my innocence;
the judge fixed the night of the new moon for the hearing.

Peeyush:
"Loyalty" — An Extempore Poem

What was it that was written in my fate?
Why did this have to happen to me, every single time?
My loyalty was never in any doubt,
but all I ever received was an empty envelope.

It was no fault of mine at all,
and yet, for no reason, you remained upset with me.
What could I do? There was no other option,
but to bear the atrocities of the world.

I had no inkling of the power of poetry;
when my heart was shattered,
it was this that applied the healing balm.
What had been under wraps for so long,
finally came to my lips;
my emotions were bared in the open,
and I could not hide them.

Today, I have become convinced of this:
that it is always darkest beneath the lamp.
The one for whom we are searching is always nearby,
but we keep searching for them far and wide.

Bantering in Hindi and translated into English by "Loquacious doctor"
PEEYUSH, Dr. P. N. Sharma, 26th June 2021

11. ज़माने का इम्तिहाँ

डॉ. दीपक:

मैं मानता हूँ, ज़माने ने मुझे ठोकर दी है;
मेरा तो हो चुका, ज़माने का इम्तिहाँ बाक़ी है।

पीयूष:

"ज़माने का इम्तिहाँ"

"ज़माने का इम्तिहाँ" लेने से क्या हासिल?
पहले से ही दौर-ए-ज़माना रहा है बदनाम।
इसने कई हीर-राँझों का ख़ून तो पिया,
कमाल ये है, न इसके लबों पे रंग चढ़ा।
न किसी ने ख़ूँ-रेज़ी का इल्ज़ाम ही मढ़ा;
तुम ख़ुद से ही अपने ज़ख़्म सहला लो।
न पहले किसी ने किसी का इलाज करा,
न अब भी कोई खुले-आम साथ आएगा।

डॉ. दीपक:

तुस्सी छा गए, यारा!

डॉक्टर मुखर्जी:

पीयूष, आपकी क़लम न केवल बोलती है,
बल्कि कैनवस पर बेहतरीन चित्र बनाती है,
जिसे हृदय की गहराई से महसूस कर सकते हैं।

पीयूष:

ये सब आप लोगों का ही किया-धरा है,
और तो और, मैं भी शिकार हो जाता हूँ!

डॉ. दीपक:

कमबख़्त दोस्त ऐसे ही होते हैं।
तेरी बीबी तेरे से रोज़ कहती होगी,
"एक तो ये पहले ही बिगड़ा था,
अब कौन-से दीपक का असर पड़ गया है?"

स्वरचित मूल लेख (गुफ्तगू) हिन्दी, उर्दू
"वाचाल चिकित्सक" पीयूष — डॉक्टर पी. एन. शर्मा 25 अगस्त 2021

11. Judging the World

Dr. Deepak:
I accept that the world has kicked me;
I am done, but the test of the world is yet to be.

Peeyush:
"Judging the World"

What will be gained by "judging the world"?
The world has always been notorious.
It has quenched its thirst with the blood of lovers,
but what is amazing is that its lips were never stained.
No one has ever accused it of bloodshed;
you must soothe your own wounds, yourself.
No one has ever cared for anyone, in times gone by,
and no one will openly side with you now, either.

Dr. Deepak:
You are awesome, my friend!

Dr. Mukherjee:
Peeyush, your pen not only speaks,
but it also draws excellent pictures on the canvas,
which one can feel from the inner core of one's heart.

Peeyush:
All of this has been crafted by you people;
and what's worse, I, too become a victim!

Dr. Deepak:
Damn friends are like this!
Your wife must be scolding you every day:
"He was already spoiled,
and now, which Deepak's[40] influence has fallen upon him?"

Bantering in Hindi and translated into English by "Loquacious doctor"
PEEYUSH, Dr. P. N. Sharma, 25th August 2021

---

[40] A pun on the name 'Deepak,' which also means 'lamp.'

SECTION III
"PASSING THE BATON"

"वो माँ हैं मेरी"

स्वरचित मूल लेख (हिन्दी) — प्रत्यूष (10th March 2006)

वो माँ हैं मेरी।

हम मिल बैठते बातें करते,
मैं करता तारों की बात, झिलमिल सफेद।
सोचता कि उड़ जाऊं, किसी तरह उन्हें छू जाऊं,
पर उसकी उड़ान, घोंसले के परे ही न थी।
क्या पता था, कि उसके तारे घोंसले में ही बसते थे।

वो माँ हैं मेरी।
वो तारे जो मनुष्य की चाह हैं,
कुछ दूर, बहुत दूर, मेरे तारे।
और कुछ वहीं, ह्रदय के पास,
माँ तो हमेशा उन्हें ही चुनती थी।

वो माँ हैं मेरी।
उसकी अपनी ही, एक छोटी सी दुनिया,
शायद बड़ी दुनिया उसकी समझ के परे थी।
तभी तो सोते जागते,
एक ही ख्वाब देखती।

वो माँ हैं मेरी।
वो घोंसला तो उसी का था,
उसी में कभी रोती, कभी हंसती,
घबराती, डर जाती,
पर फिर चाह लिए उसे ही बुनती जाती।

वो माँ हैं मेरी।

कोई पूछे, ऐसी ही क्यों है,
क्या कहूं, शायद प्रकृति का घमंड है।
क्योंकि सुंदर तो इतनी है,
उसकी सुंदरता अपनी ही थी।

वो माँ हैं मेरी।

छोटी सी, गोल मटोल,
यूं ही लुढ़कती-फुढ़कती, ठोकरें खाती।
पर सच वही है, जो उसे दिख जाए,
होगा वही, जो उसे भा जाए।

वो माँ हैं मेरी।

"She is My Mother"

Translated into English by "Loquacious doctor" Dr. P. N. Sharma

---

She is my mother.
We used to sit together and talk;
I would speak of stars, twinkling white,
dreaming of flying up, to somehow touch them—
but her flight never went beyond her nest.
Who knew, her stars always stayed nestled in her nest.

She is my mother.
The stars that are the desires of mankind—
some were distant, so far, those were my stars.
But some were right near her heart;
Mother always chose those, leaving the rest apart.

She is my mother.
She had a small world of her own,
the bigger world was perhaps beyond her reckoning.
Maybe that's why, asleep or awake,
she always saw the same single dream.

She is my mother.
That nest belonged to her—
in it she sometimes wept, sometimes laughed,
at times became frightened, sometimes panicked,
yet every time, she gathered herself and
kept weaving it with passion.

She is my mother.
If someone asks, "Why is she like this?"
I'd say, perhaps it's nature's pride—
for she is so beautiful,
with a beauty uniquely her own.

She is my mother.
Short and chubby,
rolling and stumbling, taking many knocks.
But the truth is only what she sees;
only what pleases her will happen.

She is My Mother

www.ingramcontent.com/pod-product-compliance
Lightning Source LLC
Chambersburg PA
CBHW050521240926
51846CB00003B/640
9789348945280